Noisy Memory

Noisy Memory
Recording Sound, Performing Archives

Brian Harnetty

The University of North Carolina Press CHAPEL HILL

© 2025 Brian Harnetty
All rights reserved
Set in Merope Basic by Westchester Publishing Services
Manufactured in the United States of America

Library of Congress Cataloging-in-Publication Data
Names: Harnetty, Brian, author.
Title: Noisy memory : recording sound, performing archives / Brian Harnetty.
Description: Chapel Hill : University of North Carolina Press, [2025] |
  Includes bibliographical references and index.
Identifiers: LCCN 2025013866 | ISBN 9781469691336 (cloth ; alk. paper) |
  ISBN 9781469691343 (paperback ; alk. paper) | ISBN 9781469688053 (epub) |
  ISBN 9781469691350 (pdf)
Subjects: LCSH: Harnetty, Brian—Sources. | Composition (Music)—Social
  aspects. | Sound archives—United States. | Sound archives—Moral and
  ethical aspects. | Listening. | United States—History—Sources. |
  BISAC: MUSIC / Ethnomusicology | SOCIAL SCIENCE / Folklore &
  Mythology | LCGFT: Autobiographies.
Classification: LCC ML410.H2035 A3 2025 | DDC 781.49—dc23/eng/20250606
LC record available at https://lccn.loc.gov/2025013866

Cover photograph by Jonathan Johnson.

For product safety concerns under the European Union's General Product
Safety Regulation (EU GPSR), please contact gpsr@mare-nostrum.co.uk
or write to the University of North Carolina Press and Mare Nostrum Group
B.V., Mauritskade 21D, 1091 GC Amsterdam, The Netherlands.

publication supported by a grant from
The Community Foundation for Greater New Haven
as part of the *Urban Haven Project*

*For my parents, Paul Harnetty (1930–2021)
and Marilyn Harnetty (1937–2024),
and my sister, Jane Boback (1963–2018)*

Contents

Illustrations xi

INTRODUCTION
Noisy Memory and Family Gifts 1

CHAPTER ONE
Berea, Kentucky: Learning to Listen 8

CHAPTER TWO
Berea Projects: *American Winter, Rawhead and Bloodybones* 30

CHAPTER THREE
Junction City, Ohio: *Silent City* 48

CHAPTER FOUR
Chicago, Illinois: *The Star-Faced One* 68

CHAPTER FIVE
Shawnee, Ohio: Listening to Community 89

CHAPTER SIX
Performing *Shawnee, Ohio* 112

CHAPTER SEVEN
Trappist, Kentucky: *Words and Silences* 136

CHAPTER EIGHT
Home: *The Workbench* 157

Afterword 167
Acknowledgments 169
Notes 171

Discography and Filmography 179
Bibliography 181
Index 185

Illustrations

Inside the Berea Appalachian Sound Archives 13
Musicians in a covered wagon 14
Addie Graham and Rich Kirby 29
Leonard Roberts's tape recorder 43
Harnetty home and orchard 50
Harnetty's grandparents' backyard 59
Paul Harnetty in a graveyard 60
Harnetty family portrait 62
Postcard of Sun Ra 69
Still from a video for *The Star-Faced One* 76
Album cover for *The Star-Faced One* 80
Harnetty's hand-drawn project maps 81
Main Street, Shawnee, Ohio 91
Tecumseh Theater, Shawnee, Ohio 95
A piano in the Tecumseh Theater 97
A box of cassette tapes from the Little Cities of Black Diamonds 100
A Hungarian band 106
Memorial Day parade in Shawnee 107
Shawnee High School orchestra 115
Jim Bath cassette tape 117
Harnetty and ensemble performing "Boy" 134
Portrait of Thomas Merton 138

Words and Silences band with Brother Paul Quenon 155

Album cover for *The Workbench* 159

Video still from *The Workbench* 165

Noisy Memory

INTRODUCTION
Noisy Memory and Family Gifts

My father was a typewriter repairman, and in his spare time he fixed old radios, clocks, and record players. My mother was a contemplative, immersed in traditions that advocate quietly turning inward and a deep connection to the world. And both of my parents' ancestors are rooted in the hills and small towns of Appalachian Ohio.

I see these traits—material and spiritual, noisy and quiet, and imbued with rural sensibilities—as gifts. My mother helped me to appreciate silence, to carefully read books on spiritual practices, and to pay attention to everything around me. She was not a musician; and in retrospect it seems odd that I would go on to become a composer and sound artist. But it was her qualities of insight, empathy, and a creative impulse that found their way into my interests in listening and sound.

As for my father, he was not a musician either but a bit of an inventor, and the hum, scratch, clack, and glow of his workshop were a part of my daily life. The constant search for a radio signal amid the din of static or the pleasure of a record needle contacting vinyl and exploding with sound—these moments were just as integral to my education as piano lessons or learning how to read. And although I do not personally identify as Appalachian (I grew up near Columbus, an hour north of the region), all the childhood day trips to visit his family in Appalachian Ohio made an indelible mark, leaving a strong sense of place that I still carry with me today.

As an adult, it took me a long time to appreciate these qualities and to see how they fit into my work. It was only recently when I realized the objects my father cared for and repaired represented a curious mix of words, sound, and time. The typewriters, for example, use the symbols of the alphabet to inscribe language; likewise, the clocks offer a mechanical depiction of time passing. Sound recordings, however, skip the symbols altogether and go directly to the sounds as they are: full of music and voices, background noises, and even the sounds of the record or player itself. These recordings, according to the media theorist Wolfgang Ernst, are "nonsymbolic," and they also have a "noisy memory": That is, they contain all the extra sonic information an alphabet cannot capture alone.[1]

If I listen back to the first sound recording ever made, of Édouard-Léon Scott de Martinville singing the French folk song "Au Clair de la Lune" in 1860, I hear many things at once.[2] His singing voice is the most obvious sound, slowly making its way through the first line of the melody. All manner of noise accompanies his voice, however, including the scratch of the paper it was etched onto and the distorted rumblings of each note. From the beginning, recorded sound was capturing both signal and noise, so that the medium, the history, and the voice's grain and texture were rolled into one.

In the late 1990s, I was a student in London, England, studying music with the composer Michael Finnissy. I was enamored with his ability to collage fragments of notated music and transcriptions from the past. In doing so, he was critically exploring and commenting on history, as heard through music. In the following years, I made piece after piece of music that emulated Finnissy's approach, in vain. These pieces failed to capture the mood and textures that I loved in old recordings, and I could not figure out a way to bridge the gap between the two.

It was only when I gave up on notation altogether and began to improvise with, sample, and collage sound recordings by themselves that everything clicked into place. Much like the alphabet, I realized that music notation is also a symbolic language, and it can only go so far in representing the sounds around us. In a sound recording, however, the complexity and layers of sound and noise I desired were already there; they were built in. I also had the feeling that I was witnessing, sharing, and presenting the material, instead of describing, imitating, or giving an approximation of it.

In making this shift from notated to recorded sound, I changed, too: Listening became the most important part of my practice, more so than virtuosity or a complex written score.[3] There is nothing new in this discovery, and a long line of composers, musicians, and artists have already figured this out for themselves. I am making a note of it here because it was personal, something I immediately felt in my body and heart when I finally put everything together. This was the first time in my life that composing music truly made sense to me and sounded like what I had been imagining.

Later still, I would find ways to make hybrids between notated and sampled music, which I continue to make today. I also learned how to spend more time outside of the studio, developing relationships and connections with people and places that I cared for. I began to incorporate community-based ethnographic methods borrowed from anthropology and folklore into my practice, of observing, participating, interviewing, socially engaging, and of course, listening. The resulting albums and performances that I made are between the symbolic and something beyond it, something closer to what feels, to me, intimate and tangible. I have shared these projects here—which go back nearly two decades—of time spent in archives or with communities across Appalachia and the Midwest or rediscovering the stories of my family and ancestors.

Over the years, I have come to know these projects as *archival performances*, which is a fancy way of saying that I use archival recordings to make new music from them. A more formal definition of an archival performance is any embodied interpretation of an archive.[4] My idea of "interpretation" is simple: It is to make something new from something old. It can include many different reimaginings of the archival materials: An arrangement, a cover of an old song, or a reworking of lyrics would all be interpretations. Or it can extend to working with the archival materials more directly: Sampling (cutting out digital fragments of a recording), collaging, and remixing archival recordings are new interpretations of older sounds. My definition of "performance" is broad, too: Not only does it include playing music or giving a speech or acting in a play, but it can also encompass all manner of everyday and otherwise routine activities, from a conversation to washing the dishes to the simple act of listening. Putting archives and performance together opens the possibility for a new music that stays close to the material, much like a documentary. At the same time, the sounds are heard independently, in new contexts, and in relationship with each other, moving in and out of tension and harmony and alongside my own voice. To borrow a musical term, they are in *counterpoint* with each other.

There is a long history of musicians and artists who work with sampled and preexisting material, from hip-hop artists today to the tape pieces of Steve Reich to the early twentieth-century visual collages of Kurt Schwitters and sound collages of Charles Ives, all the way back to medieval masses.[5] The difference here is that I am working with more formal sound archives, and the recordings they contain are often of people who have been historically disadvantaged. This means I need to contend with many ethical, historical, and social issues. In doing so, I have learned that an archival performance is not an invitation to take and use whatever you might like. Instead, there must be what I am calling an archival stewardship, which is a practice of caring for archives that is collaborative and rooted in a community and in which power, permission, history, and authorship are all considered.

This book, then, is about creatively and ethically listening to and interpreting sound archives. It is not necessarily a practical "how-to" book, however, although I hope it might encourage you to work with archival materials to make something new. Instead, it shares a two-decade journey of self-discovery and tells a personal story of my deepening understanding of people and places through sound. I move through towns and cities and up and out from the archival basement into the open air. In each new place—Berea, Junction City, Chicago, Shawnee, Trappist, and home—I learn something about the people there. I learn something about myself, too, and every new experience is an opportunity to discover my own place in the world.

All along, I learn about the magic of recordings and how each tape, record, or field recording tells a story. Here, it is important to note that I am not only listening to the recordings; I am also listening *with* the people on them. My friend and mentor Marina Peterson shared this way of listening with me and helped me to shift my understanding from my perspective alone to something that is built on relationships. And even though microphones and sound recordings are not the same as our ears and lived experiences, as Peterson points out, they nevertheless provide an opportunity to listen "along with those who are there."[6] I listen carefully and critically to these recordings; and in recounting their noisy memory, I feel connected with the people and places they reflect.

This leads to several overarching questions: How are archival performances relevant? What purpose do they have? What can they offer beyond nostalgia and sentimentality? For me, an answer begins with turning history into a creative act for the present moment, for right now. I do not have a desire to go back in time or to make things as they were or to get caught in a mindset that says the past is always somehow better. Instead, the past becomes material, a lens, a cautionary tale, a teacher.

Performing the past also becomes a way to break us from our current thoughts and patterns, to see things in a new way. Paying attention to overlooked and in-between sounds (in both archival recordings and in everyday life) can also shift our perspective away from nostalgia; in those spontaneous and vulnerable moments just before a song or after a conversation, a new space is opened, one that is human, imperfect, uncertain, and rich with significance. Archival performances present opportunities to understand this reframed past, which are fascinated with its history, yes, but are also informed, critical, and often challenging. I am not only sifting through seemingly endless documents and recordings to find compelling stories; I am also seeking out clues to move forward into the future.

And finally, because these performances are always built on relationships, they are doing the work of reaching out and connecting with others. When you approach archival materials earnestly and in conjunction with a community, something unexpected happens; cynicism and detachment fall away and meaning and interdependence become central. Bringing archives and relationships together is an opportunity to consider contexts and viewpoints both within and beyond an archive. An archival recording can point to many things, but it alone cannot fully capture the nuances of a friendship or the bonds of family or the interrelation of people working together toward a common goal. Archival performances, then, are both subjective experiences and a larger practice that might help us relate to others with empathy and curiosity.

I begin the stories of this book in Berea, Kentucky, where I first worked with archival materials situated within a community. Chapter 1 shares how I learned to listen to sound archives while there and how this process involves much more than the recordings themselves. It also tells of my first steps toward archival stewardship, in which working alongside the families and communities related to the recordings becomes an integral part of my practice. The result is something between archival ethnography and an account of my emerging creative process. Chapter 2 is focused on *American Winter* (2007) and *Rawhead and Bloodybones* (2015), two composed recording projects that came out of my time at Berea. Here, I recount stories of listening and composing, alongside detailed explanations of each project. I also offer insights into both the contexts of the archival recordings and my responses to them.

Chapter 3 is an exploration of silence through the lenses of family and place. I talk about my father's hometown, Junction City, Ohio, and share my earliest memories from there. I also write about death and birth, listening to photographs, the loss of memory, and how family can connect us to the land. Finally, I provide insights into the album *Silent City* (2009), which brings together samples from Berea and my memories of Junction City to create a mythological town.

Chapter 4's archival material—of the experimental musician and bandleader Sun Ra (1914–93) in Chicago—may at first feel like an outlier in this book. And yet, I share the same curiosity and respectful approach to the recordings as I do with the other archives. Here, I dive into the fascinating sonic world of Sun Ra's music and provide insights from making the project *The Star-Faced One* (2013). I also continue to build a steadily growing tool kit of archival listening and performing techniques. Finally, I explore the issues of authorship and power, archival homophones, and ways to ethically interpret and reuse archival materials.

Chapters 5 and 6 illustrate a decade and a half of discovery, friendships, and creative growth in Appalachian Ohio. These chapters begin with my story of visiting the village of Shawnee and its people. I also uncover the early life of my grandfather, who grew up there. Along the way, we meet many of the archival characters and current residents who became integral to the sound recording project *Shawnee, Ohio* (2019). I write about my process of making the album, how residents became cocreators of the project, and how a special performance in Shawnee affected me.

In chapter 7, I travel back to Kentucky to listen to the archival recordings of the monk, writer, and activist Thomas Merton (1915–68). I recount my years-long process of research and how I gathered and assembled material for the album *Words and Silences* (2022). I also talk of my own journey: alone and with family, across the nation and at home, and before, during, and after the pandemic. Throughout, I detail how this journey deepened my understanding of the archival material and the contemplative silence of Merton's words.

And finally, in chapter 8, I return to my parents' home in Westerville, Ohio, to create a sound and video project called *The Workbench* (2024). Here, I explore the power of inherited objects from my father, Paul. This archive is not public but personal: a lifetime's accumulation of things my father repaired and cared for. I became curious about the objects' sonic traces and whether they had an agency that we might activate and listen to. This final chapter brings me full circle; I return to where I began my life, to relisten to the sounds I was born into and grew up with. And yet, as with all my projects, this was not a purely nostalgic or sentimental endeavor. Instead, I learned that attentive listening to the past—of seemingly trivial details from my father recounting everyday moments—might reveal something to us right now: a way to feel and think deeply about ourselves and others and to work toward making our relationships and the places where we live more meaningful.

As I write this, it has become clear that the projects in this book are a product of the gifts my family, teachers, friends, and students have given to me, so much so that I am sometimes not sure what I have contributed or where I fit within them. For example, all the women in my family have been (or are) quilters. As a child, I remember playing in the fabric store, hiding among bolts of cloth and sorting through spools of colored thread. Or at home, I would open a century-old yellow cabinet with pullout drawers and run my hands over the soft swatches and fragments of fabric patiently waiting to find their place in a quilt. Everyone had their own distinct style, too: My grandmother's hand-stitched embroidery, my mother's impressionist collages, and my sisters' precise geometric patterns reveal and record their interests and aesthetic tastes.

Watching my family make these objects left a mark on me; I loved witnessing the creative process, and I felt comfortable among the quilts' humble, practical uses, without any pressure to be masterpieces or great works of art. I am certain this process of making found its way into my own. Gathering and taking pleasure in material felt natural to me; and in hindsight, making the leap to understanding archival recordings as found sounds to then listen to, organize, pattern, combine, and thoughtfully arrange together now seems obvious. The sampled recordings are like those small pieces of cloth, and I add my own music as I go along, to sew and join them together.

I hope that you can take delight in the depths of beauty and connectedness that can be found in these archival recordings. I hope you find gifts here, too, and that you make use of them and pass them to others so that they continue to grow and thrive in their exchange.

CHAPTER ONE

Berea, Kentucky: Learning to Listen

The Past Is Present

In the early spring of 2006, I packed up my car and drove to Kentucky. I had been invited to Berea College on a fellowship to listen to its Appalachian Sound Archives and make something new from them. Even though Berea was only a few hours from my home in Columbus, Ohio, it felt like a distant and uncertain world away.

I was surprised to be going. I was not an expert in folklore or Appalachian studies, nor did I have a fully thought-out plan of research. Instead, I proposed to be there as a composer and artist, simply offering to listen to Berea's collections and to create a sound collage of historic recordings alongside newly written music. I was certain a project like this would be controversial in a formal archive. And yet, when I heard that my proposal had been accepted, I was grateful and excited. In my work as a composer, I had been using samples, field recordings, and found sounds for years. But this was a new opportunity to do so with permission and in collaboration with historians, archivists, musicians, and community members.

When I pulled off the highway and onto a small country road north of Berea, I remember feeling a sense of relief. The landscape was welcoming, and the trees and plants were coming alive weeks earlier than in Ohio. I drove past the Boone Tavern and turned left on Prospect Street. I found the apartment I would be staying in and met the caretaker there. When she handed me the keys, she said, "You know, the writer James Still once stayed here." An author I greatly admired, Still wrote many books focused on Appalachia and lived in Kentucky. I was impressed that the caretaker shared this knowledge. It was the first of many signs of the history and culture present in Berea, which I continued to feel as I walked, listened, and became familiar with the town.

The apartment was quiet, spare. It had a table, chair, lamp, bed, and couch and not much else. Trees surrounded the building, and at the corner of the property, there was a gate; beyond that was a path that led to student-run gardens in an adjacent field. I remember thinking that it felt like the first day of summer camp: nervous, fidgety, lonely. That night, it rained. I ate veggie burgers and chips and drank beer from small half bottles. I slept restlessly, listening to the quiet patterns of water hitting the roof. In the middle of the night, I awoke and scribbled on a piece of paper: "Only this, only all." I can't say exactly what the note meant. But I suspect it was a feeling of anticipation, of appreciation, of calming myself, and of a deep knowledge that connection and meaning can be found anywhere if I only opened myself to it.

This was an entirely new experience, one outside of my comfort zone. In many ways it felt like the opposite of what one should do to be a composer. I had been told again and again that the only way to succeed was to move to a big city and join its cultural scene. But something felt subversively pleasurable in coming to this rural and quiet place. I already felt it affecting me, offering a space to be curious and receptive to the town and its people.

Berea College is situated about forty miles south of Lexington, Kentucky. It has a long history of racial integration and free tuition for its students. My work was to take place at Hutchins Library, where the Berea Sound Archives were held. One of the archives' strengths is the variety of their collections and styles of music, which span a century. Many of the thirty or so collections refer to the people who sought out and recorded musicians across Appalachia, such as John Harrod, Leonard Roberts, Bruce Greene, and Barbara Kunkle. Other collections focus on self-made recordings and documentation of professional or amateur musicians, such as Nora Carpenter or Asa Martin. Still others focus on radio, public events, or festivals like the Celebration of Traditional Music that takes place every year in Berea. Within these collections, different genres are represented: ballads and banjo music, fiddle tunes and folk tales, radio gospel programs and lined-out hymns.

Most importantly, however, is the way these collections have been gathered and whom they represent. There is no single, authoritative voice, no top-down structure. Instead, the recordings are assembled "from below," featuring everyday people—across race, age, class, and gender—who might otherwise be marginalized or overlooked. The result is an intricate gathering of individual voices, each with a story to tell. The stories begin with the performers yet are ever expanding to include collectors, archivists, historians, and even listeners hearing these accounts for the first time.

The number of recordings is overwhelming. Their variety and depth present a challenge to those who wish to access them: it becomes increasingly difficult to navigate the archives with respect for the many historical contexts they contain. At the time, I found myself earnestly—but blindly—working to understand these contexts. I also struggled to reconcile a creative impulse on the one hand and the need for an archival stewardship on the other.

In those first days at Berea, I felt paralyzed. It took me a while to acclimate to the collections. I knew that my interests were too broad, so I began with reading—about the collections and Appalachia—and tried to grasp the complexity of so many recordings. I was searching, paying attention to things and people around me, looking for a glimmer or clue to show me where to go next. While the other fellows were able to immediately begin working with their chosen material, I languished. I knew that I was interested in sounds and music that were often overlooked—in-between sounds of people talking and laughing, ambient noises, and mistakes—sounds that are nearly always discarded when making commercial recordings. But at first, I did not know how to articulate this interest to others. In hindsight, I am sure the archivists were concerned about my approach. Finally, after a couple of days, the archivist Harry Rice came up to me and kindly said, "Aren't you going to actually listen to anything?"

So, I gave up and dove in.

1973. Lexie Baker and J. P. Fraley, Wise County, Virginia. A tape begins. Just as Fraley says, "Bring some more chairs in here," a cuckoo clock strikes, and all at once the room erupts with cackles. "That's going to be the best beginning of a tape I've ever had!" says Barbara Kunkle, the folklorist making the recording. Conversation takes over, splits into twos and threes, and is passed around the room. I hear Fraley say, "I can't . . . I just . . . I just can't . . ." as if he is unaware of the tape recorder and is searching to remember one of the many tunes in his mind. Amid this banter, he begins to play his fiddle. A melody soon emerges. A guitarist joins in. Slowly the din of voices dies down, and the room listens. When the musicians finish playing, the conversation picks up right where it left off, and Fraley is already sounding out the key notes to another tune. Songs come and go and are comfortable against the backdrop of noises and events of home. There are no exact beginnings or endings. Everything blurs together: the conversation becomes music, the music conversation.[1]

I thought, *This is what I have been searching for*. I listened to another recording.

1958. WBVL Radio, Barbourville, Kentucky. A young girl rattles off a long list of names, presumably listeners to the program. She states as fast as she can, "We'd like to sing our next number for Mr. and Mrs. Kedger Warfield and family in Rockhold, Route 2; Mr. and Mrs. Ed Powers and family in Corbin; Mr. and Mrs. John R. Parton and granddaughter Gina Mackiabend . . ." She continues, reading quickly, and I imagine each family has called in to make a request to be heard, to sit at home and listen to their own names sent back to them through the radio. As the young girl continues to read, the piano warms up, playing an arpeggiated chord. It is out of tune. A telephone rings in the background. The Prichard Quartet begins a gospel hymn titled "He Is Knocking." Individual voices can be discerned within the group, and the singing is informal, imperfect, earnest, and amateur—in the sense that it is done out of a love for the act of singing and not necessarily for professional or monetary ends.[2]

This is remarkable, I thought. I couldn't help but keep listening.

1977. Hiram Stamper, Knott County, Kentucky. The tape whooshes as it is turned on. Stamper plays a short riff on his banjo and asks in a crackly old voice, "Can you hear it? Okay." And he is away—his foot pounds to keep rhythm as he plays "Young Edward." Sometimes he misses notes, or they are out of tune; but I do not mind. Stamper may not possess the technical ability he once did as a younger man, but his rendition is no less musical. He is present and active in the music, and any distinctions between right or wrong notes fall away. The recording is both a reflection and a celebration—mistakes and triumphs together—of a person and who he is at that time in his life. The playing only stops after Stamper's wife interjects, letting him know she is going up the hill. To my ears, even this exchange is part of the music.[3]

As each recording unfolded, I marveled at the vitality of the voices and music. Slowly, I learned to use listening as my guide. I listened with a composer's ear, reflective of my background and training as a musician. I paid attention to other forms of listening, too. I listened in solidarity with the voices of those who were recorded, and I listened ethnographically; that is, I sought out the social and historical contexts of each recording, as well as the sonic information and noise of each medium.

Every morning, I would arrive at the archives and set up a small recording station at a table. It was often a solitary experience, and I would listen for eight or more hours a day. Invariably, fatigue would settle in, and my concentration suffered. I sometimes became uncertain if the sounds I heard were coming through my headphones, were occurring in the room, or were auditory hallucinations. Sleeping at night was no different; it felt like another shift at the library, and in my dreams, I would fall asleep at my listening desk only to wake up in my bed sweating, lost. I continued to listen and gather material, but often I was hearing without fully listening. As a result, my process felt akin to groping in the dark, and whatever initial plans I had quickly became improbable and obsolete. The number of archival materials engulfed my enthusiasm. Any attempt at a systematic exploration of them was met with the realization that it would be too difficult and might take years or a lifetime.

The author Shannon Jackson also felt this sense of being overwhelmed while working at the Hull-House Settlement Archives in Chicago. It was an uneasy, disruptive process for her, often with the feeling of being in two places at once. She wrote, "I find myself caught red-handed in a dialectical history whose presence I never imagined, stunned to find myself holding onto a body without ever having reached for it."[4] During my day-to-day listening, this embodied way of understanding history became more and more dominant. The past—through sound—seeped into the present. It did not feel nostalgic, and I did not desire to be in the past or to relive it. Instead, I heard my own voice and those of the people around me in conversation. A fiddle tune listened to in the basement of the archives leapt into my car radio as I drove to the grocery store. A discussion overheard in a café was echoed and confused with a field recording listened to later in the archives. Each time, the gap between an inaccessible past and the ever-changing present abruptly and momentarily disappeared.

This immediacy could be felt in those first recordings I listened to. When I heard that WBVL Radio program, for example, I noticed the individuals, the group, and the play of sounds and music between them. I thought about how radio, at that time, would have been a religious and community connector, especially in such a rural place. And even though the broadcast was only intended to be heard once, in 1958, it acted as a bridge between the time of the recording and my listening to it half a century later. The past is present and embodied.

Listening Strategies

The archives looked as you might expect them to be. They felt out of time: windowless rooms with neat wooden tables; metal shelves full of color-coded books; old industrial turntables and reel-to-reel tape machines meticulously cleaned and maintained for decades. Among the recordings, there were large vinyl and shellacked disks with transcriptions of radio broadcasts and concerts or racks of cassette tapes, each with a handwritten label. The sound recordists' desks were full of pins and processing labels, archival document repair tape, and piles of unsorted papers and sticky notes ("can barely hear voices at full volume," one read). I loved taking breaks and chatting with the technicians, learning about what they were listening to and cataloging each day.

Inside the Berea Appalachian Sound Archives. Photo courtesy of the author.

I developed strategies for moving through the archives' materials. I pored over song lists looking for themes and word associations, such as "winter," "night," or "traveler." I also listened for aural gestures—tuning instruments, coughing, laughing, clocks chiming—that led to a series of encounters with the recordings that I could not have planned. I was no longer listening solely for harmony, rhythm, and melody; now, I was searching for subtle stories and everyday sounds embedded on the tapes and the contexts that spun out from them.

Often, I would wander through the stacks and make choices of what to listen to based on visual cues: a torn piece of paper, an inviting record sleeve, a half-open drawer. Or sometimes I would come across a provocative, almost surreal photograph, such as one titled *From Hazard to California*, depicting two oxen leading a covered wagon on its westward journey. In the photo, there are six men posing for the camera, Black and white. Three are holding guitars; one holds a fiddle in one hand and a shotgun in the other; one is carrying an oxen whip, and a dog sits at his side; and finally, a man is sitting on a stool with a typewriter in his lap, facing away from the camera and dutifully recording the moment in words. I became curious about the men and their unknown stories, which then sparked my imagination. These random signs—that did not necessarily have anything to do with sound—opened

From Hazard to California. Photo courtesy of the Berea College Special Collections and Archives.

new associations and connections between archival materials. This process reminded me of how, as a teenager, I would check out neglected books, scores, and music from my hometown library to keep them moving, in circulation. I was afraid these overlooked items might otherwise end up in the trash.

My strategies in the archives would sometimes yield fantastic results; mostly they were dead ends. But I did not mind. There was something beautiful about each new search that was filled with an anticipation of the unknown and the resulting objects or experiences that were full of surprise and meaning. This process was a reminder to remain open to chance connections. It also served as a way to become familiar with lesser-known recordings and to better understand the archives overall.

Most importantly, I came to appreciate recommendations from those who were most familiar with the collections: the archivists, librarians, scholars, and sound preservationists working at the library. I took advantage of each coffee break, gleaning hints and traces of stories and opinions that floated across the cafeteria table. Every day, someone would walk up to me, excitedly offering a recording. Or, when I arrived in the mornings, dozens of meticulously stacked tapes would already be waiting for me, based on the previous day's conversations. The generosity and exchange that took place within these interactions became central to my understanding of the Berea

Sound Archives. They were a reminder that despite the many riches of archives, the missing element is an exchange between people to bring the materials alive. I was grateful to learn from the kind people there, to pay attention not only to their expertise but also to their experiences and humanity. Here is one recording an archivist shared with me of Jackie Helton and his family.

Immediately, fiddle and voices are heard together. After the first phrase, the recordist Bruce Greene asks, "What is this?" Jackie answers, "I Know It Was the Blood," while continuing to play. When the family finishes the tune, there is no silence, no pause or reflection. There is not even a single beat of rest. Instead, the room immediately transforms into several sonic events at once: A man in the background begins a conversation; a young girl continues with the hymn, singing quietly into the next verse; and Jackie immediately continues his conversation with Greene, then clears his throat. He describes the song: "Now that's a popular old . . . 'I Know It Was the Blood,' that's an old one!" He continues:

> I know it was the blood
> I know it was the blood for me
> One day when I was lost
> He died upon the cross
> I know it was the blood for me

The fiddle picks up once more, enthusiastically switching to a new tune (again, not missing a beat). Greene asks, "Is that in the . . . Do they have that in a hymn book somewhere?" Jackie answers and then comments on the new tune already underway, "I don't know. It's over the hills! Now there's a good one! I bet you can play that one."[5]

In this recording, there is no difference between singing and talking, between music and life. The only way I can describe how this tape unfolds is that it feels natural; it is not forced or contrived. It is also complex: There are so many things happening at once that it would be impossible to re-create them. Here, my training as a composer betrays the way that I listen to this tape. Conversations, stories, and voices come together in a form of counterpoint. Many individual voices, each with their own story to tell, are heard at the same time. Sometimes they are together; other times they are in tension with one another. My ears move back and forth from the individual to the whole, and I listen with pleasure to the improbable combinations of documentary-style tape and contrapuntal sounds.

Many years later, I called Jackie Helton. When he picked up the phone, I couldn't believe that his voice sounded the same as it did on those tapes from decades before. Helton was friendly, and I appreciated his willingness to talk with a stranger. I was calling to ask him for permission to use a recording he had made with his family. He laughed and said, "Will it make me rich?" "Sadly, no," I said, embarrassed to tell him that I did not think the recording would make any royalties. He laughed again and said, "Aw, it doesn't matter! Go ahead!"

Over the years, I listened to the Helton tapes many times and memorized every word, tune, and sound. As a result, I felt an intimate connection to the people on the recording. But this is a lopsided relationship, a one-way letter that I as a listener cannot respond to. My phone call with Jackie briefly opened that connection, but it was also a reminder that familiarity with a recording is not the same as an exchange with a living person, even though sometimes they get confused and blend together.

Memory and Song

This blurring between song and everyday life is present in the recordings of Addie Graham. In them, we catch glimpses of her character not only in the songs she sings but also in the dialogue that takes place before, during, and after. At the time Barbara Kunkle made the recordings in the 1970s (along with Addie's daughter, Opsa Guthrie), Addie was in her late eighties. She was still full of personality, humor, and the ability to recall dozens of songs from memory. This included ballads, folk songs, and religious music that she learned prior to 1920 and held in her memory for the next fifty years.

As I began to listen to Kunkle's recordings, I first noticed that Addie was aware and unsure of the microphone. Kunkle asked her many questions and reassured her, but Addie's initial response was, "Oh, I was afraid to talk." Later, she revealed both her sense of humor and a self-awareness of being recorded, saying, "I'm going to get my voice cleared by goin' to Florida. I have to get right here, now. Do I have to get right in front of these things [the microphones]? Well, I can't look at nobody and sing. Now, let's see . . . I look so bad. Let's see now. I tie that up to bronchitis hurting my neck. I hope I haven't forgotten [the song]."[6]

On the tapes, Addie recites poems, tells of her family history, and remembers local and religious events. She often coughs and clears her throat. She quips, "I've got bronchitis; ain't worth a dern," and even these offhanded gestures feel melodic and musical to me. Throughout, Addie shares her spry humor, and the banter and room noises of the field recordings take me back in time: I hear her home and the rhythms of age and health, conversations, laughter, and memory. Often, she delivers quick-witted remarks, stating, "Barbara, let's me and you go into business on some of my songs." At other times, Addie searches through her mind, fumbling to remember: "My goodness, since I've been sick, I haven't got my memory." At one point, she must take a break from recording, saying, "I've . . . I've lost track of some of 'em. See if I can remember. I can't help it; can you turn it off?" The recording stops, and I am left with the lonely hiss of the cassette tape as it continues to turn.

At the beginning of songs, Addie's voice moves up and down, searching for the correct pitch that will set her off singing. During these small, seemingly trivial moments, she reveals her personality. Over the length of the tapes, I hear her shift from unsure to comfortable in front of the microphone. I hear moments of recollection and reflection, as the physical act of singing triggers Addie to become lost in thought. And I hear the frustration that comes from not fully remembering or from not getting a song exactly right.

As I listened, I began to feel as if I were in the room with Addie, her daughter Opsa, and Kunkle. I was aware of my own presence as a listener, too. I heard subtle changes in voices and observed the ebb and flow of conversation. I was receptive to the fleeting emotions and inflections that are transcribed onto the magnetic tape.

Before singing a ballad called "Young People Who Delight in Sin," Addie speaks of the fear she had when she first heard the song as a young girl.[7] She states, "Now let me see if I can remember it. It's coming to my mind, one that I heard sung when I was a baby and I *never* liked it myself since. And I never did get over it. Scared me to death." The lyrics reveal a particularly gruesome story:

> Oh, mother fare you well
> Your only daughter screams in hell
> . . . .
> Am I to burn forevermore?
> Till a thousand, thousand years are o'er

Immediately after finishing the song—and without waiting for it to settle in the room—Addie states, "Now would you want to hear a thing like that?" Opsa, astonished, notes that she has never heard Addie sing the song before: Addie has waited until her eighties to reveal that it has haunted her since learning it as a young child. Impressively, she does so without forgetting the words or melody. Opsa comments on the song, saying, "It did *something* to you." Addie agrees: "That did something to me, it did so. Never would

Berea, Kentucky 17

sing it. It scared me till I never got over it in my life. . . . I guess I was just three or four years old. I was right little. I'll tell you that scared me till I'd like to have died." Addie continues, chiding the man who taught her the song: "And I remember that . . . And of course, you know I have a memory. I suffered and I suffered, and I couldn't get to sleep at night. It scared me to death. And did you know that old turd hole had his ass kicked for singing that [to me]?" Peals of laughter erupt in the room. There is a collective sigh of relief, breaking the song's tension and the spellbound listeners. Kunkle, laughing, asks, "May I quote you on that?" After the laughter dies down, Addie again makes known her dislike of the song and how it affected her entire life. "That stayed with me . . . but I tell you right now I don't like those songs, I don't like that one."

For Graham, the act of singing "Young People Who Delight in Sin" triggered both reminiscence and a visceral reaction. The sound scholars Jean-François Augoyard and Henry Torgue call this sonic effect "anamnesis," where a sound or song can bring back the past in the listener; in this case, the past travels the entire span of Graham's lifetime.[8] Listening to this recording reminded me that archives need someone in the present moment—a listener—to make them come alive. At the same time, archives reflect my subjective listening as much as they disclose the past. Heard together, subject, listener, past, and present conspire to make a complex time machine moving backward and forward at the same time. There are as many "presents" as there are listeners: the present of when the recording was made in the 1970s; my own present moment in 2006 when I first listened in; even the present moment of my writing about this recording right now. And in the content of the recording, I hear Graham leaping back into the past through her memory of a song. She remembers the time as a three-year-old child when the power of a ballad transfixed and terrified her. All these moments, occurring nonlinearly, are brought together through a single tape. I listen back to be in the room with Graham, and she moves forward to greet me.

That night, I returned to my apartment, tired. I went to bed early, dreaming of Addie's songs and voice. I slept restlessly yet awoke excited, happy.

Close-Ups and Up-Close Listening

Working in the archives began to feel like a regular job. I would show up at 9:00 a.m., have lunch at noon, and finish at 5:00 p.m. during the week. In the early evenings, I found myself taking walks, enjoying the longer days. Outside my apartment, I would walk through the old gate that led to the

Berea College Farms. I first moved through tall grass and then among neat rows of fruit trees and hoop greenhouses filled with vegetables and herbs. An apiary's murmur was nearby, with bees coming and going, doing their last bit of work before dusk. As I walked, I noticed my attention focus; I was listening to the natural environment with the same intensity I had with field recordings all day.

I would then walk alongside an overgrown field, where old goalposts stood like forgotten monuments. From there, I slipped between buildings to reach campus. I could hear students practicing their instruments in the music building, with scales and arpeggios crowding into the night air. I would arrive at a stoplight on Chestnut Street, and a crosswalk recording beckoned me across with a kindly vernacular accent. On the campus green, the dogwood trees were in full bloom. I moved among them, following crisscrossing paths through the grass. Students passed me in pairs and groups, heading to dinner or to the residence halls. Finally, I would finish this loop of a walk and return to my apartment, ears still buzzing from so many sounds.

This careful, up-close listening of natural and human sounds in Berea became a daily practice. I was beginning to understand it better as a place, through sound. I also found myself walking the same routes every day, noting the subtle differences I would hear. When I would return to the archives in the mornings, my experiences of listening to the town affected how I approached the recordings. Inspired by my walks, I began to listen to the same recordings again and again. Each time, this repetition yielded new insights, ones that were not apparent at first. Slowly, I could identify minute, up-close details that only showed themselves after many hearings. Chance occurrences and everyday sounds—a door creak, a cough, a mistake—all came to the fore.

This may seem obvious now, but the ability to listen repeatedly to the same exact recording is relatively new, only possible after the invention of sound recording in the late nineteenth century. Even more novel is the fact that I can listen to a digital recording many times over without the fear of losing fidelity.

This up-close and repeated listening is not limited to sound, obviously. There is a long history of cultural and critical theorists who have considered how we perceive the world around us through the media we use. In thinking about film, for example, the author Walter Benjamin notes how close-ups can change the way we see. "With the close-up, space expands," he writes. "It reveals entirely new structural formations of the subject."[9] For

Benjamin, everyday objects take on new meaning and divulge new details because we can see them in a new way.

In a sound recording, placing a microphone close to the subject—or, in the listening process, simply turning up the volume—can achieve a similar close-up effect. And any meaning we find in a recording is not limited solely to narrative, language, or music. When listening, I can shift my attention to many different aspects, like jumping from conversation to conversation in a crowded room. In music, this method of listening would be akin to focusing on an inner melodic line or a harmonic progression of chords.

Field recordings—with their spontaneous sounds, informal conversations, and locations outside of a studio—are especially compelling for repeated listening. As I listened again and again to the Berea recordings, even the smallest details became captivating, so much so that I started to feel that the recordings themselves were changing. I realized that through listening (and despite the fact I was not altering anything), my perception was shifting. The musician and composer David Grubbs has also noticed this process, saying that "repeated listens . . . can make manifest otherwise impossible-to-perceive details," and "each listen increasingly resolves into something closer to a musical composition."[10] In the randomness of field recordings, our ears recognize patterns and transform them into music motifs, melodies, or rhythms. For example, here is one tape I listened to many times:

At the Maggard Mines in Kentucky, a mining manager named Ralph Maynard speaks of illegal coal mining taking place throughout the region. He begins, stating, "Coal is supposed to be marked on a map. 'Cause, you see, the people that own the coal get a royalty payment from the coal. They don't mine it themselves, but they lease it out to Maggard." As he speaks, the machinery of coal mining can be heard in the background: metal clanking, trucks driving, the low drone of motors, whirring belts, and men shouting. The manager continues, stating, "But many, many times in the past there have been coal operations that have gone in, and they paid no attention to the boundary lines; they just take coal. And somebody else leases that boundary of coal and wants to operate it, and they go in, and it's already worked out, see." Here, the man takes a pause, lasting seconds as the machines continue to spin. Then, he dryly quips, "It's called 'theft' in unglamorous terms." The interviewer laughs, and the recording ends.[11]

When I first listened to this recording, I heard a man explaining coal operations at Maggard Mines. After repeated listens, however, I noticed the storytelling, the cadence of the language, and the man's sense of timing. He allows the narrative to develop and build, even adding a pregnant pause at the end to strengthen his story. Then, listening again, I started to hear the conversation and the industrial noises as musical gestures: foreground and background moving with and against each other, in counterpoint. And finally, another listen yielded subtle patterns and rhythms of class, industry, land use, ownership, extraction, and culture, as well as the tensions present between them. This brief story, humorous at first listen, later begins to point to the inner structural workings of coal mining. There is confusion between ownership and stewardship, and I was left considering what "theft" is. It became unclear in my mind as to who exactly is stealing in a culture of extraction: those who do not obey the laws or those who receive royalties because of their possession of the land.

Repeated and up-close listening not only can reveal cultural and historical contexts but can also point to more personal traits: voice, memory, humanity. One day, an archivist came up to me and slid a couple of the collector Bruce Greene's tapes across the table, saying, "You should listen to these! I think they are right up your alley." I placed a tape in the machine and pressed play.

In Walter McNew's performance of "Girl I Left Behind Me," the recording begins with a solo violin. The tempo is languid and slow. A banjo begins to play along, picking up occasional notes from the fiddle as if its performer is learning the tune while listening. The melody is mournful, and Walter's playing is nuanced. He includes strong phrasing, bended notes, and harmonics that bring a welcome variation to the melody. After he finishes, the sound recordist Bruce Greene states, "It's beautiful," and another man agrees, saying, "It's lonesome." "Yeah," says Walter, "that's an old . . . Ah, let's see, I knew *some* of the words on it." Walter sings through a verse of the song:

> I quit my work one evening, walked into the public square
> The mail was just arriving; I met the driver there
> He handed me a letter, that I might understand
> That the girl I left behind me had gone with another man[12]

He ends his singing, immediately breaking into laughter, and the two other men laugh along, saying, "Whoo!" However, Walter is not finished. Despite saying, "That's all I know of that," he begins to sing again, in fits and starts: "For I have money a-plenty, to serve both you and I." He stops once more only to begin once again, saying, "And right there, see, is where I can't remember to save my life what them words are. But anyway . . ."

Walter then remembers, singing, "And we'll ramble around, from town to town / With the girl I left behind." Everyone breaks into laughter once more. There is a palpable sense of relief in the room, and the recording moves on.

In this recording, I witnessed memory and music colliding, and I was only able to do so through up-close and repeated listening. Walter struggled to remember the lyrics (no easy feat in front of a rolling tape recorder), and then as he relaxed, they surprisingly spilled out. Or perhaps it was Walter's modesty revealing itself on the recording, a characteristic I have noticed again and again across the Berea Archives. Perhaps Walter did not want to seem boastful of his knowledge, as if he were showing off, and instead he allowed the lyrics to come out slowly, organically, within the context of an artfully performed conversation.

Both Message and Noise

On weekends, I would take long drives into the country surrounding Berea. Often getting lost (this was still a time before I had GPS or a smartphone), I relied on a travel map and the kindness of strangers to find my way back. This, too, mirrored my experiences with the archives, where uncertainty and confusion (followed by gentle guidance from residents) invariably led to new ways of seeing and understanding.

On these drives, I got to know the region's landscape. It was spring, and the roads were frequently lined with bright yellow Forsythia bushes. I would stop and take photos of them alongside waking trees as they leaned against the sides of buildings, their new and vibrant colors contrasting with worn wood and metal hinges and leftover political signs, faded and torn. Occasionally, I would see farmers working in their fields or along shorn hillsides dotted with trees, resting cattle, and old cars. There were neat black tobacco barns, too, with red painted doors and nestled in green fields of high grass, away from the road. Power lines cut across the sky above them, then, further up, a thin slick of clouds, then nothing but blue.

Sometimes, I visited country churches, white-roofed and straight, sitting on hills next to old oak trees barely in bloom. Village cemeteries were often at the back, with plastic flowers sitting agelessly on stones. One time, I saw a newly dug grave with a neat mound of dirt sitting beside it, patiently waiting to be tenderly placed back. I would often stop at antique stores with makeshift wares, faded Pepsi signs, and strewn Christmas lights. Or I would pause to admire run-down but cared-for houses with rust-streaked tin roofs, their walls repaired with a scrap-wood bricolage and their windows adorned with handmade curtains, half closed.

I was not driving with purpose; if you would have asked me where I was going, I could not give you an answer. And yet, the more I drove, the more I changed. I felt connected to the places I went and curious about what might be next. Each turn or hill offered something new, always beyond reach.

My perception on these drives changed over time. In the archives, the drives helped me to see how recordings change over time, too. Wax, wire, vinyl, shellac, tape, disk, file: Each medium leaves its own signature. So, too, do digital transfers and new formats, fragmentation, editing, and age. And from the beginning, noise is always present; it is built in and evolving alongside the music. The media scholar Wolfgang Ernst encourages us to listen to all the sounds on recordings and not just the music or words. He states, "What we hear is both the message . . . and the noise."[13] The scratches, crackles, tape warbles, and digital skips contribute to the information contained within each recording and have their own stories to tell. I, too, listen for both, allowing them to coexist, each with layers of meaning and beauty.

I began to pay attention to these extra sounds in the archival recordings. In June 1968, the sound recordist William Tallmadge traveled to Decoy, in Knott County, Kentucky. There, he recorded and interviewed Frankie and Lionel Duff. Frankie sang hymns and ballads in a clear and unwavering voice. I listened in: The recording begins with feet shuffling and something sounding like a coin being placed on a table. The room reverberates slightly, betraying its small size and lack of carpet; perhaps it is the kitchen, with linoleum floors and Formica-topped table, much like my own grandparents' home. Sometimes, the tape's recording level is too high, and it distorts. I can also hear the spinning reels of the tape as the recorder records itself. There is tape hiss, too, a perpetual accompaniment, different from the digital silence of today (which has its own distinct sound). As ice cubes are dropped into glasses, Frankie states, "And then I had an older brother. [He] got killed when I was about eight years old. I remember how . . . I can remember how he used to sit on the front porch and sing. I remember two verses of the song he sang. But I can't find anybody who knows the song." This gets Tallmadge's attention (for an unknown song is like gold to a song collector). He encourages Frankie, excitedly saying, "Sing it!" Perhaps realizing he is sounding too forceful, he gently adds, "A song that nobody knows is a pretty . . ." But she has already decided to sing:

Do you remember what you promised me
Down by the riverside?

> You promised you would marry me
> And make me a lovely bride
>
> If ever I promised to marry you
> It's more than I will do
> I never intend to marry an old boy
> So easy fool'd as you

After she finishes, they laugh. Frankie recalls when she first heard the song from her brother: "I remember sitting on the front porch one evening, after dark, and he's sitting there in a chair, singing this song. Playing the banjo. And I was just sitting on the floor, and I thought it was the most beautiful sound I ever heard. I thought the tunes they played on the banjo . . . there'll never be anything as pretty in all the world."[14]

The song, "Down by the Riverside," tells of unrequited love. It is haunting, and we never do learn how it ends. If this was a commercial recording, Frankie's words and the song—along with the sounds of the room and tape— might be dismissed as a noisy fragment. But for me, as I listened to the recording many years later, it was exactly these contexts that became entwined and inseparable. Frankie had held onto this song in her memory. The song and the recording transported her back to her childhood, to her front porch at night, listening to her brother. Frankie, the music, the story, and the media signature of the recording—they all came to me and touched me as I listened, only to continue moving outward once more.

Heterophonic Archives

To "tarry" is to remain in a place longer than intended. In the archives, I lingered with the recordings that touched me, and the recordings lingered, too. The longer I listened, the more detail I could perceive, and insignificant moments became music. I enjoyed feeling like a fly on the wall and appreciated how the field recordings often continued to record longer than a given song, accidentally and silently capturing spontaneous moments when there was no intention to perform, no self-conscious dialogue.

One day, I came across another William Tallmadge recording, called "Tarry with Me O My Savior." On this tape, Chalmer Howard leads a group of men and women in "lining out" the old hymn. A lined-out hymn is often sung during a religious service in small, rural "Old Regular Baptist" churches. A lead singer guides the others, beginning a melody for each line, and the group follows with a melodic variation.

When I turned on the tape, this is what I heard: There is a group discussing what music Tallmadge might be interested in recording. "Why don't you take turns," a woman states. "Both of you do some lining. He wants to see . . ." Howard, aware of the recording device, interrupts, and an awkward and beautiful exchange takes place. Howard states, "You can, uh, I mean, uh, leave your recorder off, now. I'll start one line, see if I got the right key, and then I can drop back, and you can turn your recorder on, and I'll tell you when we're ready to start." Tallmadge acquiesces and begins to say, "All right. This is not a, uh, this is just to see how it really works," but Howard has already started, not waiting for the others to finish speaking. He decides to begin despite the tape recorder's presence. The first sung words are inaudible, but his voice dovetails with the conversation and then rises above it, strong and clear, as he becomes more comfortable:

HOWARD: Tarry with me, O my savior, for the day is passing by
GROUP: For the day is passing by
HOWARD: See the shades of evening gathering
GROUP: See the shades of evening gathering
HOWARD: And the night is drawing nigh
GROUP: And the night is drawing nigh

The hymn continues, with Howard and the group exchanging lines:

Many friends are gathered round me
In the bright days of the past
But the graves have closed above them
And I linger here at last[15]

As the group joins in, they are singing a single line. Yet each voice is distinct and makes subtle changes, turns, and inflections that serve not only as embellishments but also as marks of individuality. In other words, they are singing *heterophonically*, like a group of people walking together—some faster or slower, some shuffling or pausing—and all moving toward a shared goal.

I notice that the lyrics are altered, too. Occasionally, two or more of the singers are simultaneously using different words, adding to the meanings of the text. At one point, some sing "are" while others sing "were." At another point, Howard clearly sings "night," but in the recording, I hear "knife." More sounds become part of the musical fabric of the recording: I hear children playing in the background. A bell rings, and later a distant train whistle blows, both coinciding in pitch with the singing. The tape warbles, too, indicating its age and how it has changed while sitting on a shelf waiting to be listened to. In Tallmadge's own notes from that day, he wrote, "The door was open and children on bicycles stopped occasionally to hear what to them was the strange music."[16] These sounds come together to offer a trace of the time and place in which the recording was made, as well as the changes that have occurred to the tape during its lifetime.

As the group completes lining out the hymn, they finish slightly higher in pitch than when they started. Their singing, without accompaniment, is unmoored; and as a result, the intensity pushes everyone up, yet all remain together. As I listen, my body moves sympathetically, tensing up and relaxing, my spine imperceptibly straightening and raising me in my chair along with the sound. After a few moments of silence, a member of the group says, "Well, I'd say brother Chalmer has done about as good a-lining as you could find."

In this recording, the lingering occurs both in the sung hymn and in the room, opening a space of vulnerability and expression. I remember sitting in the archives and turning the tape on, not knowing what to expect. When the singing began, I was immediately brought to tears. I am sure it was quite a sight to see me, a large grown man with headphones on, weeping uncontrollably in a silent room. When I returned the tape, with red eyes and flushed cheeks, the archivist said, "Don't worry. It happens more often than you think."

It is this image of several individuals and everyday sounds coming together to sing in a beautifully imperfect unison that I carry with me throughout the Berea Archives. The archives are held together through their connection to Appalachia and its many cultures, but they also allow for hundreds and thousands of distinct voices to exist alongside each other with no single dominating style, performer, or collector. They remain independent and interdependent, singular and connected, and powerfully express the history of the region as it continues to unfold in the present.

Moving Outside

There is a divide between inside and outside an archive. This divide is both in the archive's physical space and with its materials. When I walked from my apartment, across the green and down into the library basement where the archives are housed, I was outside, walking in. But I am outside the recordings, too. There will always be a gap between myself and the people on the recordings: of time, place, culture, knowledge, experience, and more. I am always on the outside, listening in.

And yet, this "outside" is needed to help define and understand the archival recordings. It activates them, giving them shape and meaning. The philosopher Jacques Derrida used the term "exergue" to describe this push and pull between inside and outside an archive.[17] An exergue is a space outside the materials to give them order; it is an archive becoming. For Derrida, the tension between the two is violent, between a desire to preserve and a desire to destroy.

This tension points to a paradox: an archive cannot remain a perfect, closed system. It needs human interaction to add to and change the archival materials, to disrupt them, and to keep them in circulation. Here is another paradox: This movement flows both ways. The theorist and semiotician Roland Barthes recognized this when looking at a photograph, stating, "it animates me, and I animate it."[18] The same is true for a recording. When I listen, I animate it, and it animates me in return. So, the process of listening to and working within an archive must be opened outward and set in motion. And the only way to do this is through the one thing an archive cannot contain: human connection.

A few days after first listening to the recordings of Addie Graham, I traveled to Whitesburg, Kentucky. I was visiting friends at Appalshop, a nonprofit arts center focused on Appalachian communities and culture. While at a party, I found myself enthusiastically talking with a group of strangers about Addie's recordings and how much they touched me. A woman who had been listening gave a knowing smile and said that Addie was her great-grandmother. Humbled and taken aback, it was at this moment I realized I could not focus on archival materials alone. Each recording neither is static nor possesses a single meaning. Instead, it is at the center of a network of people, alive and dead, that stretches back in time well before the recording's creation and extends to the present and beyond. What began for me as the solitary act of listening to a recording on headphones was merely a single join in a complex web of family, relationships, traditions, culture, and time. This was the first human-archival encounter I had that deeply affected me.

After I returned to Berea, I was asked to present my work to the public. I remember feeling nervous when I stood up to give my talk. In the audience, I could see many prominent community members, including the much-loved folklorist Loyal Jones, who contributed many recordings to the collections. Family members of the people in the recordings were also there. I was worried that they might disapprove of my using the recordings, that I had gone too far into the realm of appropriation, stealing, or destroying.

I shared several pieces I made and talked about my working process. To my relief, the opposite reaction happened. "It was like hearing the ghosts of my relatives," one woman remarked to me.

There is a video documenting my talk that day, which I only found recently.[19] It is such a strange experience watching a younger version of yourself, awkward and excited, fumbling with words but also doing so with heart and a genuine love for the recordings. There isn't much I remember about that day, except for being anxious, especially about Jones and his reaction. To my astonishment, I watched him in the video get up after the talk and enthusiastically shake my hand. We then chatted for several minutes more. I can catch glimpses of us in the background as the camera documents other conversations. I wish I could remember what he said to me. But I am thankful for this video, which shows an interaction I thought had been forgotten, now returned. It is not lost on me that I too have become part of the archives and that the act of seeing oneself many years later is at once astonishing and unnerving. This was the second human-archival encounter.

Two years later, I came back to Whitesburg. This time, I was to share the music I had made from Addie Graham's recordings with her grandson, Rich Kirby. Kirby was a well-known musician in his own right and had been instrumental in releasing an album of Addie's singing in the 1970s. I felt reluctant and nervous, aware that I was an outsider to this tight-knit community. During a public workshop, I played a recording called "The Night Is Quite Advancing," which brought together samples of Graham alongside newly composed music. After listening to it, Kirby commented that he thought he was sure he wouldn't like it at all but instead was mystified. He could see that I was trying to do something different and taking a more global approach to show how the different recorded stories were connected. He concluded that he didn't know exactly what Addie would have thought of the new music, but he thought she would be okay with it.[20] I was grateful for Kirby's insights, and I was encouraged to see how these musical experiments might connect with the communities where the sampled recordings came from. Bringing this recording out of the archive and back to Whitesburg felt like the music had come full circle.

This was my third archival encounter. Together, they showed me how archives are not only composed of documents, recordings, photographs, and letters; they are built of families, relationships, and communities. I also came to realize that the presence and commentary of these people changed me and changed the way I worked with the recordings. I had Kirby in mind, for example, when I assembled my own pieces, and I felt a responsibility to take

Addie Graham and Rich Kirby singing together. Photo courtesy of the Berea College Special Collections and Archives.

care of the recordings of Graham. It was my job to add another layer to the mix and then to pass it along once again, into the world.

A practice of sampling that draws from both inside and outside an archive lays the groundwork for an archival stewardship. If the technology of sampling allows us to copy and manipulate recordings and then detach them from their original contexts, then the process of returning those samples back to their places of origin opens a new space of engagement. This space does not exclude the relationships that were already there. Kirby's presence helped situate the recordings of Graham in their familial, physical, and historical contexts. This, in turn, directly influenced how I heard and used them. And finally, I did not have complete control; I willingly yielded some to stay connected to others. Bringing these relationships into the fold created a physical link between past and present and allowed the archives to be embodied and in motion.

These three encounters—along with my other experiences at Berea—offered a new way to create, one that was both experimental and connected to communities and tradition. I did not know it at the time, but this would alter my life as an artist in ways that still affect me today. I was learning how to perform an archive.

CHAPTER TWO

Berea Projects: *American Winter, Rawhead and Bloodybones*

American Winter

After the fellowship ended, I returned to my home in Ohio and went to work. I brought hundreds of newly digitized recordings with me. I gladly agreed not to share them without first seeking permission from the Berea Archives. I began to organize the recordings, and once again I felt overwhelmed. Slowly, I made large, hand-drawn maps of the collections to orient myself: of themes, tonal and modal centers, different singers, stories, concerts, radio programs, and titles. I relistened to the recordings, adding more and more notes—"might be good for background," "solo banjo + foot + interviews," "three-part harmony," "rain and snow," "as I went out walking," "Egypt land," "Stravinsky-like fiddle," "raised in Troublesome"—and my own personal system of stars, check marks, and colored charts.

It was during this time that I first understood how a collection of gathered recordings can be a community-created composition. In fact, I did not need to change or alter anything—except my perception—for this to happen. The combination of time, performers, collectors, archivists, and historians all contributed to the composition. Or, perhaps more accurately, the archives became a large instrument, and its listeners were the ones who were creating personal compositions with each selection they chose.

This was a revelation to me. I saw that there was no single, authoritative, top-down structure or approach to the recordings. Instead, I was acting as a subjective guide, sharing my personal experiences as I moved through the collections. This means that there are as many ways to understand the recordings as there are listeners, reflecting each person's taste, interest, and personality.

The first project to come out of these recordings was *American Winter*.[1] It is an album that uses samples from Berea and combines them with my own composed music. Many of the people I met, learned about, and listened to while at Berea were central to the project; their voices and stories came together to create a collage that was a survey of the archives and a reflection of my experiences there. Once organized, the puzzle pieces of the archival recordings came together quickly, over a few months. But the music has a longer story.

I had been working on *American Winter* long before I came to Berea. In 2003, I finished an album called *Pretty Bird*, which was made entirely out of samples.[2] The ways in which historic recordings could be combined to create rich, complex music encouraged me. But I also began to see growing ethical concerns of appropriation and misuse of the materials. It was becoming apparent that I could no longer make pieces in the way that I had been. It did not work anymore. Berea became a turning point, offering a new path to use archival recordings with permission, respect, and stewardship. I was determined to carry this knowledge into my work, even if it meant giving up some control.

At the same time, I was looking for ways to incorporate live instruments along with samples. Remarkably, in my small apartment, I had two pianos: an old, beat-up, blond-colored school upright and a pristine 1930s eight-foot Steinway grand (that my landlord had left for me to take care of). I also had an assortment of instruments: a banjo, toy piano, accordions, my sister's hammered dulcimer, old record and tape players, and a variety of noisemakers. I had recently won a local arts council grant, allowing me to purchase a computer (and a root canal); and my girlfriend at the time (now my wife), Jen, presented me with an inexpensive microphone to record with. You could say that this equipment and these instruments reflected the push and pull in my own mind, between different music and styles I loved equally and was trying to reconcile. I was letting go of traditional notions of being a composer—with its notated music, established ensembles, precision, virtuosic performing, and so on—and embracing DIY art culture and home recording, as well as the community-based music I later witnessed in Berea and Whitesburg.

The political and social landscapes of the early 2000s entered the music as well. *Bush v. Gore*, 9/11, the "war on terror," the Iraq War, US imperialism: these events and movements deeply disturbed me. They directly and indirectly influenced what I was working on and how I did so. As a quiet form of protest music, I turned to the past to shine a new light on the present. The music and sounds I chose to work with pointed not only toward the season of winter but also to broader ideas: the winter of war, power, emotion, politics, and history. My hope was to allow the myths, ambiguities, and struggles of the past to serve as a critical lens on current social and political issues.

In that apartment, I recorded myself over and over. I learned how to improvise based on found material—books of folk tunes, transcriptions of songs, fragments of classical pieces, the rhythms of machinery, the noise of recordings—and then use these improvisations to create new music. For the earliest iterations of *American Winter*, I was creating a mash-up of notated songs that revealed different parts of myself: a thrift store copy of Alan Lomax's *Folk Songs of North America* and a careworn score of Franz Schubert's song cycle *Winterreise* (Winter journey). Not only was the title *American Winter* a blending of the two book titles, but the music was as well: In my mind, they came together, and sometimes I could not tell them apart. Even the poetry and lyrics became tangled up, as I began to combine the first lines of several tunes and songs, based on alphabetical order. For example, here are a few lines that begin with the letter *I*:

> I rode out last winter's night (folk song)
> I arrived a stranger (*Winterreise*)
> I'm goin' away to Texas (folk song)
> I am used to losing my way (*Winterreise*)

The process of bringing the fragments together yielded new sounds and material, which I then used to compose some two dozen pieces. I remember working with a frenetic purpose, feeling like I was close to making what I was searching for. And yet, when I completed the initial drafts, the project could not hold together; it was lacking, unfocused, and often tedious. I was forced to let it go, unfinished. This was in 2004.

By the time I returned from Berea, some two years had passed. I became curious about those earlier *American Winter* recordings. I relistened to them, and enough time had gone by that I could edit them with detachment. I began to find affinities between the Berea recordings and the earlier pieces. I realized that I had *two* archives to work with—one from Berea and one of my own makings—and my job was to find the crossover spots where the materials complemented each other. Three elements came together that helped me organize the album: songs made from interviews and singing; brief interludes from radio programs, homemade recordings, and field recordings; and story pieces where extended interviews and broadcasts are featured. Then, the composed music served as a glue between these elements, sometimes residing in the background and sometimes on equal footing with the samples. I thought about many personal and cultural elements, too: documentary films, memory, forgetting, dreams, nighttime, journeys, war, contemplation, tension, counterpoint, places, and landscapes. I also thought about the work of the artists and composers Harry Smith, Steve Roden, Harry Partch, Pauline Oliveros, Robert Ashley, and my former teachers Michael Finnissy and Steve Martland. These themes and influences were latent, lying under the surface of the music, informing my decisions. Finally, after this long period of curious searching and experimenting, I began to collage and compose.

"Drunkard's Dream"

Many of the people I listened to in the archives became central to *American Winter*, as if they were characters in a play. Unsurprisingly, the most prominent person on the album is Addie Graham. In fact, she appears on it five times. Her voice and spirit affected me more than anyone else; they helped define the ethos of the project.

In "Drunkard's Dream," for example, the composed music begins with the steady clicking of an old electronic metronome that my father had given to me. Immediately, we hear Addie alongside her daughter Opsa. Addie prepares to sing, first humming four ascending notes, then three more, searching for melody and pitch. Then, she begins:

> Oh, [Willy] you look so healthy
> Your dress so neat and clean
> I never see you drink around
> Pray tell me where you've been[3]

In between the sung lines, and keeping in rhythm, Addie speaks to Barbara Kunkle as an aside, "This is 'Drunkard's Dream.'" At this moment, two short interlocking melodic patterns begin — both based on folk tunes — played on bells and toy piano. Over the next verses, additional instruments are added: hammered dulcimer, then low and high piano lines, and finally accordion. On the field recording, a door opens in the room, adding a mysterious, ominous sound. Addie continues:

> And are your wife and children well?
> You used to treat them strange
> And have you, too, been kindly been
> How came this sudden change?

> Last night I dreamt a warning dream
> That heaven sent to me
> To snatch me from a drunkard's grave
> Of woe and misery

After Addie finishes several more verses, she immediately begins to talk about when she learned the song. At this point in the music, the individual melodic patterns begin to fall apart; they are reflecting the "strangeness" of the dream.

Berea Projects

When making the recordings, I remember wanting to keep each melodic shape but also to gradually alter or change it. I became more and more reckless with the material, as a painter might smear color across canvas. Amid this commotion of music, Addie begins to talk about when she learned the song, stating, "Now that was—I learned that when I was a little girl . . . No, no, my brother-in-law, my sister's husband sang that. John Henry Coffee. Coffee, John Henry Coffee, a finer man [indecipherable] . . . Yeah, that's 'Drunkard's Dream,' nearly everybody knows it. Yeah."

As soon as Addie states, "Yeah, that's 'Drunkard's Dream,'" the instruments (and metronome) stop at once. This is the first time the listener can hear the unaltered field recording, and the quick shift from chaotic music to Addie's voice alone feels like the moment when one is hurled out of a dream and involuntarily sits straight up in bed. We then hear Kunkle stating, "Yeah, I've heard it a different . . . that's beautiful." Addie responds, "Yeah. That's about . . . I've always liked it right well. Drunkard's Dream. [humming] Yeah." With these last words, Addie sounds wistful, lost in thought. Her voice slows down, becoming quiet and contemplative. Each time I hear this moment, I imagine Addie thinking about what she has sung—its harrowing imagery and message—and how it still haunts her, even at the end of a lifetime.

"Briny Ocean"

Much like the singers and musicians, the song collectors also became part of *American Winter*. In "I'll Cross the Briny Ocean, I'll Cross the Deep Blue Sea," I once again visit William Tallmadge's recordings of Frankie and Lionel Duff. Immediately before the recording starts, however, I add a sampled excerpt from a local Kentucky radio program, *The Renfro Valley Barn Dance*. The crackle of the recording joins with the announcer's animated, singsong voice: "Well friends, come along with us as guests of the Keystone Steel and Wire Company of Peoria, Illinois, makers of Red Brand fence and barbed wire, and sole distributors of Red Top steel posts. It's wintry outside tonight, but inside the old barn all is cozy and warm and bright!"[4]

Then, we are disoriented as the piece shifts to Frankie and Lionel's house. The composed music is written for piano and is played with a crisp intensity. On the archival recording, Frankie sings her version of the song "Lonesome Scenes of Winter," and her clear and powerful voice soars. Lionel and Tallmadge are present on the recording, too, and they become part of the scene as it unfolds. Preparing to sing, Frankie states, "Oh, shoot . . . Let's see . . ." as Lionel offers Tallmadge a cup of coffee. Frankie begins:

> In lonesome scenes of winter
> In thunder, frost, and snow
> Dark clouds around me gather
> And stormy winds doth blow
>
> This night I went to see her
> She seemed quite soberly
> I asked her if she'd marry
> She would not answer me
>
> I sat there all the night long
> Until the break of day
> Awaiting for an answer
> Kind love, what do you say?

The music relaxes, and we shift back to more fragments of conversation between Tallmadge and the couple. Tallmadge states, "Right. I'll, uh, record that one again, on a fast speed," as Lionel asks, "Frankie, why don't you sing . . ." Finally, Tallmadge asks another question, "Who sings it?" before we are whisked back into the song, with Frankie singing,

> I chose the single life
> I never thought well-suited
> For me to be your wife
>
> Take this for an answer
> And for yourself goodbye
> I found another suitor
> And you may step aside
>
> I'll cross the briny ocean
> I'll cross the deep blue sea

Amid swirling piano lines, conversation once again interrupts the song, with Tallmadge declaring, "Sad songs!" and Lionel agreeing, "Sad, um, hum." "She learned them, I suppose," Tallmadge continues, "going to church," and then the music drowns the dialogue one last time, with Frankie singing, "I'll cross the briny ocean / You never will see me."[5]

The interaction between Frankie, Tallmadge, and Lionel becomes an integral part of the recording. Their conversations, fragmented and in between

Berea Projects 35

the singing, have their own cadence and variety. It is as if we are there in the room with them, learning about their lives through everyday words and a mythological song. The piano accompaniment mechanically repeats itself, closely, pulsing with a sense of urgency. Throughout, the recording is doubled, with the two piano tracks slightly apart from each other, one always a beat behind the other. Sometimes, the recording is played backward and full of tension around Frankie's voice. The piano ebbs and flows, allowing space for both singing and dialogue, and at the end, it strikes three high notes before receding.

"The Funeral"

Even the archivists, historians, and technicians at Berea found their way into *American Winter*. One day, I asked archivist Harry Rice if he had a favorite recording that touched him. He paused, thought for a moment, and told me of an interview he conducted with the musician A. L. Phipps. On this recording, Phipps recalls a memory that ingrained itself in his mind, sparked by a funeral he attended as a child. I included the entire conversation here because I find it rich with meaning and compassion.

Harry Rice begins the conversation, stating, "Go ahead," and Phipps responds, "Oh, it's already on!" "Oh yeah," Rice continues, "I was interested in the story you just told me about the funeral, and how, uh . . ." He trails off, but Phipps picks up the story again:

> Okay, I'll go ahead and repeat that. This was in the year of about nineteen and twenty-eight, to the best of my memory, uh, one Sunday. It wasn't in the summertime, naturally, more or less I'd say, maybe about this time of year. Anyway, that Sunday morning we went to this funeral. The funeral was around nine thirty or ten o'clock that morning. And, uh, the old-time preacher got up to preach and preached a funeral, and I mean, he preached, too. You could feel what he was saying. He was spiritual. And you didn't have to have a microphone to understand what he was saying. He didn't care to raise his voice. So, uh, a crowd of people, [there was] a good crowd of people there, because people loved one another back in those days, and they would come a long ways to help in time of trouble and time of need. Because we all needed help back in them days, and we helped one another, and we didn't have all the conventions we got now. So, uh, about middle ways of this preacher's message . . . [adjusting microphone] Uh, I'll go back in . . . About middle ways of this preacher's message, it started raining. The casket was out in the yard, and

people were gathered mostly in the yard. A good crowd of people there. And, uh, it started raining. So, the ladies grabbed the umbrellas and held over the casket, kept it dry while the preacher preached on.

Now this preacher never stopped preaching. It never fazed him. The rain didn't bother him at all, and it didn't bother the congregation. And I was just an ole boy, probably twelve or thirteen years old—twelve years old, I'd say. And I didn't get out of the rain. I could have gotten out of the rain. All of us could have got probably back in the house or got in the porch. But we stood right there and listened at the man preach. And we all got wet. Uh, but we respected the man a-preachin', and we respected the dead man that was in the casket. We were taught back in them days to do everything we could to respect, and that is exactly what we did. The man a-finished his sermon, the preacher did. They sung a song at the end of this message. The old hymn about "Rock of ages, cleft for me / Let me hide myself in Thee." And there was something about that song and it a-ringing that stands out in my memory today. I mean, it, uh, I get a-thinking. I hear the song sung, if I get a-thinking about it. Uh, there's something there that happened that day that's never happened since. Don't know what happened before that, but it's never happened since in my life. But, uh, it gave me a sense of respect that we need more of today. There's no question about that. We went on to church that day after we got through with the message. Who we were with, that didn't make any difference. Went on in that church house and listened to another good sermon preached. And the weather didn't bother us that day. We was interested in what was right, more or less than anything else.

During the pause, Rice asks, "On that day, were there some other songs sung?" Phipps continues, "There probably was at the beginning of the message. I'm sure there was some singing going on. I can't recall the songs that were sung at the beginning of it, as much so as on the last part of it, because it . . . The things were happening that would cause you to take more notice of what was going on normally than you would if the weather would have been fine. You know." Rice agrees with him, stating, "Uh huh," and then the tape moves on.[6]

In this story, a curious thing happens. Rain, song, and death are bound together to burn a memory in Phipps's mind. If he thinks of this memory, the song appears: it is "a-ringing" in his head. And it was the rain that made this memory so strong: the touch and sound of the rain was physically marking him, inscribing the townspeople's sung hymn in his mind, along with the preacher's intense and clear, quiet voice and the umbrellas gently opening over the silent casket. When Rice asked if there were other songs sung, Phipps's response reveals how that singular memory has remained while others have faded away; it was the combination of youth, weather, ritual, and song that made the moment so powerful and memorable.

The resulting piece on *American Winter* is called "I Was Interested in the Story You Just Told Me about the Funeral." When it came time for me to add my own accompaniment to the tape, I knew it must be subtle. I chose a toy piano and accordion. They are both static, moving over and through hymn-like passages. They are not competing with the voice but playing alongside it. Present, too, are the quiet pops and scratches from a record (also from the Berea collections); combined with the hiss of audio tape, their sounds evoke the funeral's rain.

What is astonishing to me about the field recording is that it needed very little intervention on my part. I did not feel obliged to chop up the voices or repeat phrases. Instead, the unaltered recording already contained a remarkable rhythmic, emotional, and sonic arc. The cadence of Phipps's voice carrying us along its trajectory, the emphasis of his vernacular speech, the rhythms of speeding up and slowing down, and his expert skills at telling a compelling, heart-filled story—these things were enough. Why should I alter them? I even left in the moment when Phipps adjusts his microphone, as it presents an intriguing interruption to the flow of the story; each time I listen to that moment, I find myself leaning in closer.

"The Soldier"

In other pieces, I eschewed the straightforward simplicity of "The Funeral" for a more complex collage of sounds, where many samples occupied the same space. In "The Soldier Pulled Off His Uniform of Blue," I sampled four women singers. I wanted the recording to feel as if they were all in a room together. The women—Berzilla Wallen, Dellie Norton, Mary Lozier, and (once again) Addie Graham—were recorded at different times and places. Sometimes we hear the song collectors, too. Throughout, the recordings are left alone, and we hear intersecting lyrics and melodies, in between banter and clapping and incidental noises.

The piece begins with an advertisement for a radio program called *The Commandos*. An announcer declares, "Join us again next Sunday night at 7:00 p.m. Eastern War Time, for another story with Chips Davis, American, and the men of the United Nations who share his exciting adventures in *The Commandos!*"[7] Dramatic orchestral music from the radio broadcast immediately follows. As it continues, we hear an accordion quietly emerging and overlapping; the historic music is then faded out, and the newly composed arrangement continues where the archival music left off. The radio program's gendered, militaristic tone and story situate us in the past, during World War II. But it is also advertising a dramatization and not the daily news. The new music carries this latter sentiment on, opening a larger mythological space, where the stories and voices overlap to point to deeper meanings. The music is slow, with a static, simple four-note pattern that all the instruments repeat and vary throughout. Here, and elsewhere, I learned that the harmonic stability of the music provided room to engage with the sampled recordings more fully; its variety and movement are textural and rhythmic and do not distract from the additional sounds and music contained on the tapes. In addition, the samples were chosen not only for their stories and the grain of the individual voices but for their melodies, too. Each song is roughly in the same or related keys (or modes). Sometimes, this creates new patterns and harmonies as we hear their exchange. When I assembled the samples, I was astonished at how the women's melodies and voices complemented one another, without my intervention. My process became more a matter of choosing and combining, rather than manipulating or chopping up the recordings.

What follows is a collage of ever-shifting songs, dialogue, and singers, flooding us with many stories at once. Addie Graham begins midthought, stating, "All their lives, all their lives, they've done nothing but sing. They all sang every night and every morning." The recording of Wallen interrupts, singing the beginning of a murder ballad, and we join in midverse:

> . . . marry me away
> She gave me trouble all my life,
> She made me work in the cold rain and snow
> Rain and snow, rain and snow
> She made me work in the cold rain and snow[8]

Graham returns, stating, "My goodness, since I've been sick, I haven't got my memory. Oh, let me see. I can sing it better than I can sing it. Here's the tune it ought to be to." Then, the clear voice of Dellie Norton begins the tale of a soldier visiting a woman on a moonlit night:

> A soldier traveling from the North
> The moon shines bright and clearly
> The lady knew the gentleman's heart
> Because she loved him dearly

> She took his horse by the bridle reins
> She led him to the stable
> There's oats and corn for your horse, my love
> Here to feed him, you are able[9]

Norton's singing is full of longing, and each phrase is embellished with subtle vocal turns and inflections. At first, I had thought the song's story was of an illicit love affair between a Civil War Union soldier and a woman from the South—and perhaps this was implicit in Norton's version of the song. But later I learned that there are many variations of this song, such as "The Trooper and the Maid," and in each, the "moon shines bright and clearly."[10]

Addie's voice breaks us out of the ballad's spell once more, and the recordings shift to Mary Lozier's version of the song "One Morning in May." Addie declares, "Barbara, let's me and you go into business," only to be interrupted by Mary Lozier preparing to sing, saying, "Well, there's just a lot of this I can't remember."[11] Lozier then begins:

> As I was walking one bright May morning
> Down by the riverside
> I spied a fair young couple a-courting
> That filled my heart with pride
> La la, la la . . .
> He asked her if she would marry him

Wallen's singing takes over, and we are lost in the voices and music. The words blend into one another and reach an emotional intensity. At the same time, the music's texture thins. The mood is melancholy and ominous, and when one song finishes to a crowd of people politely clapping, the juxtaposition is confusing, unsettling. Wallen sings,

> She went dressed like a lady in some town
> She come marching down the stairs
> Combing back her yellow hair
> And her cheeks, they were red like a rose
> Like a rose, like a rose
> And her cheeks, they were red like a rose
>
> She come marching to her room
> There she met her fatal doom
> And my cold, cold joints
> Trembled in fear

Dellie Norton chimes in, returning to the song of the woman and the soldier:

> I must go and meet them,
> O soldier dear, don't leave me here
> For I am thine forever
> . . . .
> When you and I get married
> O soldier dear, don't leave me here
> For I am thine forever

Addie joins and sings the ballad "Darlin' Corey." In this song, the narrator recalls a dream in which she tries to wake Corey from the sound sleep of death:

> Last night I lay on my pillow
> Last night I lay on my bed
> Last night I lay on my pillow
> And I dreamed darlin' Corey was dead
>
> Wake up, wake up, darlin' Corey
> What makes you sleep so sound?
> The highway robbers raging,
> They'll burn your building down
>
> Wake up, wake up, darlin' Corey
> With a dram glass in your hand
> Drinking down your troubles
> With a low-down gamblin' man

The ending of "The Soldier" offers a respite from the weight of war, murder, and unrequited love. As each song finishes, we are shocked out of its trance and brought back to reality. Addie immediately talks about how she enjoyed her song ("That was a good one!" she states). Barbara Kunkle and Loyal Jones begin to ask questions of the singers. And Berzilla and Dellie discuss whether they should sing another song. When Berzilla asks, "Do we sing tonight, too? Well, I guess we'd better rest up for tonight," Dellie quickly quips, "Oh, go ahead and sing!" The humor in this exchange provides much-needed relief.

The meanings that come out of "The Soldier" are complex. On the one hand, there are a series of overlapping stories rooted in folklore: a Cold War radio drama advertisement, a young couple in love, a Civil War soldier and woman in a night of passion, a harrowing murder ballad, and a nightmare dream of death. Heard together, the stories intersect and bleed into one another.

On the other hand, the larger themes of *American Winter* coalesce through a lens of metaphor: of winter, cold, rain, and snow; of the absurdity and pain of war and the small moments of humanity and connection that happen despite it; of loss and abandonment; and of the cruelty of murder. Much like in James Joyce's novels or Igor Stravinsky's ballet *Les noces* (The wedding), fragments of text and voices come together to offer a larger picture. Some of the stories send us to a place of memory or recognition, while others remind us of rejection, harm, and the grim and dark side of our humanity. Bound up with the character and humor of the singers, the songs show us a complicated past. Yet we cannot help but hear them in relation to the present, not as nostalgia but as cautionary tales.

Rawhead and Bloodybones

One day at Berea, I went to visit John Bondurant, an archivist there. We sat in his office, talking about nothing in particular, when the recordings of Leonard W. Roberts came up. Roberts sought out stories and folktales in eastern Kentucky throughout his career, many of which ended up in his 1955 book *South from Hell-fer-Sartin: Kentucky Mountain Folktales*. John then turned around and pointed to a reel-to-reel recorder on a top shelf. It was a careworn "Royal" suitcase model, tan and brown, with "Webcor High Fidelity" sound. It even had a broken tape partially threaded through its playback head. "That was Roberts's recorder," John said. We took it down to look at it, and I imagined Roberts carrying it around with him while visiting families and schools, to record stories passed down for generations. It was a reminder that a recorder is a medium between past and present, between telling tales and listening to them.

The transcriptions of the stories in Roberts's book are often fascinating and full of carefully rendered vernacular speech. There are fairy tales, "Jack" tales, myths, and local legends. But it wasn't until I heard the recordings themselves, with youthful voices and made in gymnasiums and homes, that the stories truly came alive. Some voices—like that of Jane Muncy—immediately captured my imagination and offered a glimpse at a new project of my own that would feature the Roberts recordings.

Years after I left Berea, I made that project, an album called *Rawhead and Bloodybones*.[12] It incorporates recordings from the Roberts Collection, additional samples from Berea, and newly composed music. The first track,

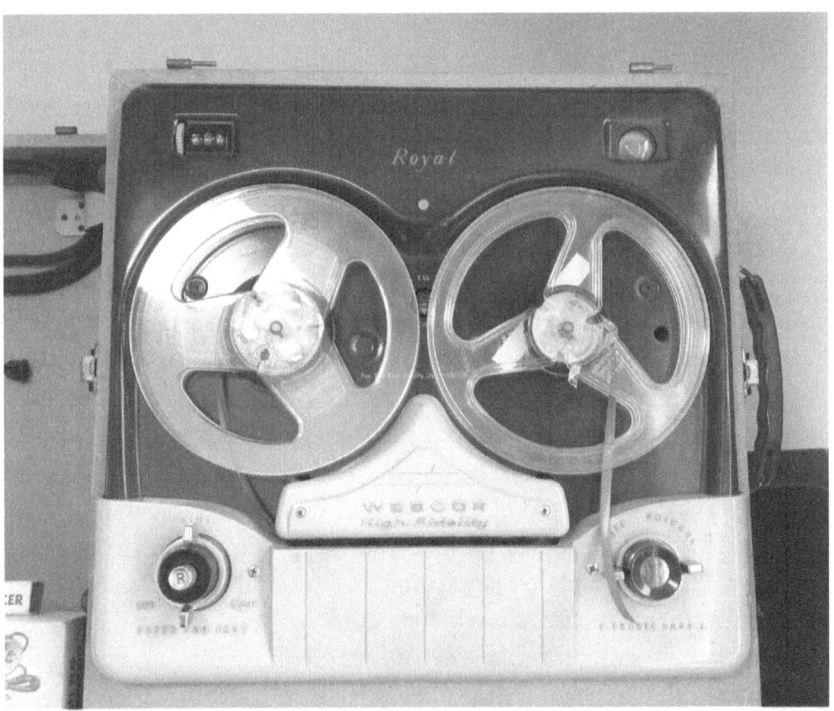

Leonard Roberts's tape recorder. Photo courtesy of the author.

"Merrywise," begins with Jane taking a deep breath and introducing herself: "My name is Jane Muncy, from Hyden, Kentucky, and the name of my story is 'Merrywise,' told by my grandmother."[13] Eleven years old when Roberts recorded this story in 1949, Jane is charismatic and a delight to listen to. In fact, I have listened to this passage so many times that I memorized not only what she says but how she says it—every pause, inflection, "uh," and "umm." Sometimes my wife would laugh at me as I walked around the house, reciting paragraphs from the story and faithfully rendering Jane's cadence.

On the tape, Jane speaks quickly, and the words tumble out. With a breathless excitement, she continues her story: "Once upon a time there was a little boy, and he had two brothers, Tom and Bill, and his name was Merrywise, and they lived in a little town, and their mother died." I am drawn in and racing along with Jane. I also hear a large and acoustically active schoolroom where the recording was made, at Hyden Elementary. As the story unfolds, I add to the mix an archival recording of Hiram Stamper playing "Lonesome Road."[14] Stamper's pounding foot acts as a wavering "click track," and sometimes other sounds are heard, too: coughing, an inaudible phrase, laughter. Gradually, instruments from my ensemble join in, including viola, flute, trumpet, vibraphone, bells, and Rhodes electric piano. The music builds and recedes, always making room for the story to remain centered and clear.

As the tale becomes darker, the music slows and grows somber to match. Jane tells of a witch tricked to mistakenly kill her own two boys, and the music grinds to a halt, making the shock of her words even more exposed. She states, "So, she thought he was asleep, and she went over and looked at the boys, which had the white caps on, and cut their heads off. She really thought it was Tom and Bill, but it was her boys." There is a striking contrast between the youthful innocence of Jane's voice and the ability to tell such gruesome events. Jane relays this moment with such matter-of-fact ease that the first time I heard it, I questioned if she said it at all and had to go back and listen again. Likewise, at the end of "Merrywise," it is remarkable to hear how quickly and calmly she finishes the story: "And she jumped down, and they put rocks in the bag and tied her up and threw her in the river. And killed her." And then, just as casually as before, "And they went back to their house and lived happily ever after." Jane's voice transforms in the same way as the story itself: from innocence to violence, a hurried chase, death, and then a carefree "happily ever after."

Later, when Jane tells another folktale, "Rawhead and Bloodybones," it feels as if she picks up right where she left off, with the same effervescent cadence.[15] To my ears, it sounds like a single run-on sentence, which only adds to its driving rhythm. She begins, "This is Jane Muncy again, and I'm gonna tell 'Rawhead and Bloodybones.' Once upon a time there was a woman, and she'd married a man that had a daughter, and she had a daughter. Her daughter was real ugly, hateful, and everything that she shouldn't have been. And his daughter was real beautiful, sweet, kind, and nice, and everyone loved her, but everyone hated the other woman's daughter, and she was jealous."

This time, it is the ensemble that first accompanies Jane: twinned banjos, vibraphone, electric piano, accordion, and viola. The music is harmonically static yet always rhythmic and active, adding and changing its texture. The story follows two girls—one kind and one definitely not. With the help of a witch, jealousy drives the mean girl to try to trap, run over, and poison the kind girl, but invariably her plans fail. There is a lot of walking and movement in the tale, so the music works to create a sonic world evoking a journey into the unknown. Eventually, a sampled archival recording of I. D. Stamper joins in, playing his rendition of "Redwing" on mountain dulcimer.[16] It, too, shares in the somber and thoughtful mood. However, when Jane talks about the kind girl returning from her travels, the music shifts, becoming vibrant and celebratory: "And so, when she came through the streets in her hometown, everybody smelled something so good, and they thought that a florist shop must be moving in or something, because everything was smelling so good. And they looked out the window, and there she came down the street, and they couldn't hardly look at her, she was so pretty. And the kindness just glowed out all over."

In these passages, I hear the confidence of an oral tradition in Jane's mind and voice. I can also hear that she truly enjoys the story and loves telling it. She is searching in her mind for the signposts of the tale, rather than translating from a written page. This is another quality that I have noticed across the Berea Archives: when I hear Jane speaking, I don't understand her words as text written on a piece of paper. Instead, the story blooms and thrives on the character and performance of the person recalling it, as much as (or more than) the plot or words.

Hearing this confident storytelling in a recording left me with the desire to do something similar with composed music. I worked to marry the qualities of oral tradition and field recordings within a structured composition. In the field recordings—and with Jane in particular—I hear emotion, personality, mischievousness, and awe leap out at the listener. I hear spontaneity and mistakes and an unforced complexity of sonic textures. When I began to place these attributes in the music, I focused on hybrids: between notation and improvisation, past and present, archival and live. I also searched for a structure that offered simple, articulated ideas that were malleable, allowing me to move between samples, performance, score, and recording. Eventually, I focused on three elements for each piece: a story from the Roberts Collection, an archival field recording of a single instrument (banjo, fiddle, dulcimer), and my own ensemble and music. The idea was to make the three elements integrated, as if they belonged together on the same recording.

I settled on a working process: first, I would spend most of my time researching and, above all, listening to the archival recordings. I paid attention to time, tempo, keys and modes, texture, instrumentation, what instrument was sampled, and whether the speaker was young or old, female or male. In my notes, I made brief descriptions of each tale, which read like Harry Smith–style newspaper headlines: "Granny chases brothers," "murder; bloody fingers," "bear eats everyone except squirrel," "asks God, digs well," and "mean girl, good girl."[17]

I then chose and transcribed each story and matched it with a field recording of a tune. The field recording, in turn, became a cue for the ensemble to follow. Only then would I compose and improvise additional melodic phrases for the ensemble, as a response to the field recording and story. These lines were complementary to each other as well as the sampled tune, offering interlocking rhythms around the archival materials. Next, I gave the recordings and parts to the instrumentalists to record on their own. This allowed the performers to play along as the field recording sped up or slowed down, while adding their own gestures and improvisations. The result was a parallel set of recorded materials, which I could add together with the archival recordings in the studio. I now had the materials and tools to collage the piece with sound and listening as my main guides, rather than a notated score.[18]

This process comes together in the track "Greedy Fat Bear," in which a boy named Estill South tells a story about a bear eating people and animals.[19] We first hear the tape recorder winding up, as the reels adjust their speed. Estill begins his tale: "My name is Estill South. I live in Hazard, Kentucky. Uh, I forget the name of the title of this story I'm gonna tell." Leonard Roberts then asks, "Where'd you hear it?" and Estill responds, "I heard it in my hometown. My teacher told it to me." At the same time, a field recording begins, of Manon Campbell playing fiddle.[20] This becomes a click track for the musicians to play along with, as if they were with Campbell and trying to keep up with his quick tempo.

Estill continues: "One time there was a little boy, a little girl, a mother, and an old man. They live out in the forest. There was a country store down the road apiece. The old woman asked the little boy to go down and get a can of kraut." Here, I take advantage of a slight pause to introduce the first of the ensemble's instruments—bells—which are soon joined by electric piano. In fact, each time Estill finishes a paragraph or phrase, the music texture thickens or changes, with more and more lines joining in the fray. Then, when the fiddle pauses, the ensemble follows suit, and the process begins again.

As the story unfolds, a bear chases and eats the boy, girl, mother, old man, and a rabbit, too. The music hurries along to match the action. I notice how Estill's speech seems to speed up as he reaches the tale's end, the story and storyteller each racing to see what happens next. Then, a squirrel manages to fool the bear:

There's a squirrel up on the limb. [Bear] said, "I'm gonna eat you, too." [Squirrel] said, "No, you're not." And the little squirrel stayed on the limb, and the bear climbed up on the tree. And the squirrel jumped off, and the bear jumped after it. Why, he fell to the ground, and his stomach busted open. Out come the little boy, said, "Ha ha, I'm out." The little girl come out, says, "Ha ha, I'm out." The old woman says, "Ha ha, I'm out." Old man come out, says, "Ha ha, I'm out." The rabbit said, "Ha ha, I'm out." And the little squirrel up on the tree says, "Ha ha, I'm out, 'cause I never was in to be out."

When Estill finishes, the entire ensemble joins in, including alto saxophone and two banjos. Everyone is following the fiddle's lead. The music feels chaotic; it is as if it is so loosely held together that it could fall apart at any moment. It also evokes the humor and commotion of people and animals tumbling out of the bear's stomach, as well as the spry, clever movements of the squirrel.

And then, the fiddle abruptly stops, with Manon Campbell saying, "gets tangled up, doesn't it?" At this point, the ensemble collapses. There is only Campbell rhythmically pounding his foot and playing fiddle together, then quickly moving on to a new tune, only to be cut off once again as the tape runs out. The fiddle and tape hiss disappear, and we are left in silence.

I DIDN'T FULLY understand it at the time, but working with the many recordings at Berea was a defining moment for my creative process. It cracked me open and pushed me to redefine what music is and how I made it. I still carry those lessons with me—of curiosity, community, and connection—in each aspect of my life. I saw that there were no boundaries between so-called high and low culture and that the music in the Berea Archives, made by everyday people, was as complex and rich and worthy as any other.

Later, I would come to see my work at Berea as archival ethnography, in which I understood people, places, and culture through recordings and documents. At the same time, I was also adding my own stories to the mix and then passing this new knowledge to others. The folklorist Jeff Todd Titon states in his book *Old-Time Kentucky Fiddle Tunes*, "Fiddlers do not quite possess the tunes, but, rather, use and care for them as a good steward tends to a fertile field."[21] In the Berea Archives, this applies not only to musicians but to everyone who encounters the recordings. The movement and exchange of the recordings do not end with the listener, with the collector, or with my own interpretations. Instead, they pass through us, with each of us caring for them and adding yet another layer of creativity to them as they continue, ever changing and expanding.

CHAPTER THREE

Junction City, Ohio: *Silent City*

Learning Silence

When my father, Paul, was dying, he lay in a hospital bed, restless and unable to walk. He was losing his ability to speak, and he desperately wanted to get up and leave. In and out of consciousness, he was between awake and asleep. His fear was to die in a hospital. And now we were unable to bring him home.

A week later, he died, quietly. In between, my family and I did everything we could to help him heal and waited for his signs to tell us what to do. He slowly became calm, and we then knew his answer. We switched to comfort and care. Upset and crying, I looked him in the eyes, and he gave me one last crooked smile. Then, it was a slow process of transition, eyes closing over a day, then labored sleep, then a softening stillness. The room became hushed, too: monitors turned off, lights dimmed, the endless beeping and warning sounds finally and permanently silenced.

Listening is the last sense to leave, I was told. Even when everything else fades, and even if my father did not understand, he would be able to hear voices. I talked to my father, letting him know I was there with him.

Throughout this process, my father's hands remained the same as they always had been: wide, strong, curious. Eyes closed, he would sometimes reach gently into the air and slowly grab an imaginary object. Often, his thumb and index fingers would come together, barely touching, moving back and forth. To the end, he understood his place in the universe through a sense of touch, picking up and examining whatever lay in front of him, even death.

This experience — one that so many others go through each day — touched me deeply, changed me. It also changed the way I think about silence. I had been enamored with silence my entire adult life; it was a background, a compositional tool, a concept, a philosophy, a spiritual practice, a mindfulness exercise. But never had silence felt so real and immutable as in those precious last moments with my father. I was confused and heartbroken. The silence in the room and from my father had not so much to do with sound but instead was a stripping away of everything I had ever known, only to reveal an absolute emptiness, an unknowing and sorrowful quiet.

I write about these moments because the album *Silent City* is about my father.[1] It was composed in 2008, shortly after my time in Berea, Kentucky, some thirteen years before my father's death in 2021. The album—of instrumentals, songs, and sampled interludes—came out of the same searching and experimenting that produced *American Winter* and *Rawhead and Bloodybones*. It is also tied to the Berea collections because of its use of archival recordings from there.

Silent City was the first project in which I focused on a particular place. The music is in conversation with the mix of history and mythology I hold in my mind regarding my father's hometown in Appalachian Ohio, Junction City. As a child, I relished visiting family there. In town, there was the "Mud Mill," where my father (briefly) and grandfather worked, making and firing ceramic tiles and pipes. The Top Hat was there, too, a local restaurant where my uncles had lunch every day. I remember eating sandwiches at the Top Hat with plastic swords pierced through them and marveling at my Uncle John, who always ordered a slice of pie before eating the rest of his meal ("In case I kick the bucket," he would say).

My father's house was on Route 668, situated on a hill overlooking the town and valley below. My grandfather Gus had an apple orchard, with barns and a tractor, fruit pickers, sorting machines, and cider press. He grew many old varieties of apples, including my favorite, Winesap. The trees were massive, and when they were heavy with fruit, the branches drooped over, like great heads of apple-braided hair.

The first memories I can recall were of visiting this orchard. I remember walking among rows of fragrant trees in September and early October. I would eat as many apples as I could stomach. And there were ever-present bees, drunkenly bumping into each other, attracted to the sweet, fermenting fruit that had fallen on the ground.

In the barn, there was the smell of grease and fuel, sawdust and old leather. Wooden crates were stacked up to the ceiling, some full of apples and some empty. Above a workbench, a 7 Up calendar was nailed to the wall, many years out-of-date. In the yard, I would step out into the sun and play a solitary, made-up game of running through and dodging mounds of my grandfather's spent tobacco in the grass. He often took me with him on the tractor to pick apples. Arriving at a tree, we donned canvas packs that fit on our fronts and, when full, untied them at the bottom to let apples fall into the wagon. Climbing high in the trees, much like my father used to do when he was a child, I would pull up against leaves and branches to grab the apples at the top. Up there, I could look down the valley to the north or across

An aerial photo of the Harnetty home and orchard, Junction City, Ohio.
Photo courtesy of the author.

the road to St. Patrick's Church; once, the early evening light was bright yellow, and there was a slight breeze across my ears and face as I took a bite of an apple.

St. Patrick's Church had a cemetery filled with our ancestors dating back to before the Civil War. In our family, this cemetery is simply known as "silent city," a parallel town of sleeping neighbors and kin. Another often-told family story is of my grandfather walking home from mass at St. Patrick's one morning and quietly lying down and dying in his front yard, under an old and shady tree, sleeping in the grassy driveway.

Sometimes, I would walk across the street with my father to "silent city" and move among the headstones, searching for names of relatives—Paxton and Spare—or of our own surname. Some of the tombstones were knocked over, and others were so faded that we could barely make out the words. And still others had variations of our name—Harnathy and Harnatty—chiseled into them at a time when spelling was fluid, and now no one exactly remembers which is the correct version.

And it was here, while walking around "silent city," that I first knew silence. This was the kind of knowledge learned from experience, arrived at innocently. It was not a silence that is merely an absence of sound but that deeper feeling that is at first unsettling but then welcoming and pregnant with something just beyond your grasp, a silence that, when you do reach out for it, allows you to extend faint tendrils of connection to everyone, everything. Among the gentle slopes and ancient oak trees that shaded the graves, a sense of silence was palpable, so much so that even a young child could feel it in his bones.

These experiences among the apple trees and in the cemetery stayed with me. It was around the same time that I began to find old trees to sit down underneath. Or I would climb up high in a tree and stay up there for an afternoon and look out. I couldn't have been much older than seven or eight. In hindsight, I see these youthful moments as a starting place for a particular way of paying attention, or mindfulness (a term I would not have known at that time). Combined with a deep sense of awe (that both the natural world and the spiritual traditions I was exposed to seemed to foster), these moments were the beginnings of what I now call contemplative listening.

It was these memories and the lore that accompanied them that shaped my adult sense of place and the past. I began to think of Junction City and its environs as a mythological town, one filled with personal and family history, as well as larger ideas and connections. I felt a deep recognition when I read of William Faulkner's Yoknapatawpha County or Wendell Berry's Port William—fictional places based on both memory and imagination and used as a novelistic canvas for the authors to come back to again and again. And there is also E. L. Doctorow's historical fiction novels that were like seamlessly crafted musical collages to me or W. G. Sebald's and Patti Smith's uncanny ability to bring together history, fiction, memory, and photographs into worlds at once observant, strange, and melancholic. As I grew older, I was determined to find ways to apply these models to my own projects. I was certain that sound could evoke similar emotions and connect us back to both an imagined and a real past.

Silent City is equally about the birth of my son, Henry. The project coincided with my wife Jen's pregnancy, in 2008. When we found out she was pregnant, I wrote in my journal, "This is a transition, a window, a doorway to a new place. Jump through!"

In those days and months, I often found myself thinking about childhood: my own, my father's, and now imagining our son's, too. I felt strong emotions at that time, full of warmth and sensuality. I often cried for no reason. I was also relaxed, as if I were a child. Music and sound became especially pleasurable, and I listened with the open and curious ears of youth again, playful and with awe. A few months into the pregnancy, I wrote, "I still can't—and may not ever—comprehend the fact that we have made, with intention, this being." That year had an air of mystery; and at the same time, it was perfectly normal, too.

That summer, we listened to Henry in utero. We gathered in our bedroom with friends. Our friend Jenna had a portable ultrasound machine, K-Y jelly, and towels at the ready. There was much laughter, and it felt like a party. There were no sounds at first, but as soon as the microphone touched skin, there were many at once: indeterminate rushing, a stomach growl, then blood flow and viscera moving in and out of the way. There was more laughter and searching, searching, and then woosh: the rhythms of a new heart.

Henry was born in September 2008. What began as a normal birthing process escalated into an emergency Cesarean section, and the situation was suddenly beyond our control. In the operating room, I remember Jen, laid out on a table with an anesthesiologist leaning over her head; monitors beeping, quiet talking, metal knocking on metal; and a white curtain hung low so I couldn't see. And then silently, Henry was held up, all blue and bloody and still tethered; he looked huge, with arms stretched out, fists clenched. And then he took his first breath, and I, six or more feet away, watched the blue skin disappear with a flood of oxygen and pink rushing in, accompanied by his first terrifying, joyous scream. Henry was inspected under a warm light. Notes taken, first judgments. He grasped my finger and calmed for a moment. Later I was told this gesture was merely a reflex, but I didn't care. Now quiet, I brought him over to his mother as she recovered, so that she might meet him face to face.

All of this is to say that at the time of making *Silent City*, I was keenly aware of cycles of life and death, of becoming and decay. I was searching to find connections and paths between the contradictions, sounds, and emotions I experienced; I worked to let them influence both the music I made and how I understood the world.

Sleeping in the Driveway

A few months earlier, I flew to San Francisco. I was spending a week at the Headlands Center for the Arts, located on an old, reclaimed army base in the Marin Headlands, north of the Golden Gate Bridge. I had been an artist-in-residence there in 2005 and happily returned several times after to work and connect with other artists and musicians.

It was early afternoon, and the long flight had made me stiff and groggy. And yet I felt rejuvenated as soon as I stepped outside the airport and into the sunlight and ocean-scented air. The landscape around me was foreign compared to Ohio; it was both disorienting and lovely. I found a rental car and started the drive through town to the Headlands.

Before leaving for California, I paid a visit to Berea, Kentucky. There, the archivist John Bondurant handed me a CD of recordings he recently digitized, including 1950s radio broadcasts from Renfro Valley and Barbourville, Kentucky. He thought that I would enjoy them and that the recordings might spark my imagination. As I drove through the streets of San Francisco, slowly making my way north to the bridge, I placed the CD into the car's player. A radio announcer begins:

> TED FOSTER: It's time now for your Sinclair Serenade, and here to introduce the singers is Mr. R. H. Hound.
> HOUND: Thank you, Mr. Ted Foster, and we're right here in the studio in Renfro Valley, and we have about—looks like about ten or twelve teenage girls right here. Gonna do some gospel singin' right now. And the group that's singing first is the Teenage Gosp—No! The Rhythmettes. And you're from Hog Creek, is that right? And Norma Jones, I believe, is the spokesman, or spokesgirl for these—this group right here. We're gonna let 'em start off singing, and then we'll find out who they all are.[2]

The teenagers began a gospel tune, their singing both sincere and awkward. Hearing vernacular Kentucky voices from the 1950s while driving through San Francisco some fifty years later was surreal. The recordings were completely out of context with the landscape. Yet experiencing this dissonance made the recordings poignant, as if I were in two places and times at once.

I arrived at the Headlands, and its remoteness and quiet put me at ease. I drove through clouds of ever-present fog to see a large building emerge, former barracks that were now a dining hall, offices, and artist studios. Further off, there was an old gymnasium, where my studio was years before. And then there were officers' houses where the artists lived, arranged in an arc and nestled among eucalyptus trees and rosemary bushes.

I loved meeting the other artists, hard at work and play. Communal meals in the cafeteria often yielded quickly formed friendships. After dinner, our conversations would continue as we walked in groups along rugged paths to the ocean, looking for the sunset. And then we would return to our studios to work, only to meet again late at night in the scruffy library-turned-makeshift-speakeasy. Finally, I would walk back to my room in the pitch black, singing to myself to make noise and ward off any nearby animals. As I slept, I could hear the distant ocean and the eerie wails of the tall, thin eucalyptus trees surrounding me as they bent and rubbed against one another in the wind.

While at the Headlands, I collaborated with the musician and actor Will Oldham on three of the tracks for *Silent City*. Oldham was an artist-in-residence at the Headlands during that time. He is from Kentucky, and his singing reminded me of the plaintive, subtly embellished ballad singers I had been listening to in the Berea collections. I thought his voice would be a natural fit for the album's tenor and feeling. I had already completed most of the music for the project before arriving in California; our focus was to add lyrics and melody.

At the time, I had been exploring how other composers found a balance between spontaneous and calculated music. I was thinking of Pauline Oliveros and Sun Ra, John Cage and Christian Wolff, and of musical scores that were more like poems or recipes instead of traditional notation. I was also listening to the loose yet intricate DJing of Madlib and especially J Dilla, whose music was always slightly (and wonderfully) out of sync, as well as the dub music of King Tubby and Lee "Scratch" Perry, whose studio editing took place live and was often a process of subtraction, stripping away layers of sound. At the same time, I wanted to allow the past—through memory and through the old recordings—to seep into the project. These fragments of the past gave us clues to understand and reside in the music and to make something new.

After many failed experiments, I finally handed Will a simple, handwritten series of prompts to follow. For the lyrics, I made two lists, one of gathered fragments of hymn tunes and phrases from the Berea Archives and the other of my childhood memories of Junction City. Will added a third list of his own. To assemble the lyrics, he chose phrases from the three lists and used them as the basis of each song. Then, he added other phrases or changed given words as he wished. The sung parts were made in much the same way. I gave Will a few musical notes—the faintest outline of a melody. The notes were based on the archival recordings, and to my ears, they went well together. Will then altered and developed them so that they fit his voice and the lyrics' phrasing.

When it came time to record, we hiked up to Will's studio, which was set apart from the main buildings. It was a quiet walk, and only occasionally a car would drive by. The smells of the sea, wild fennel, and musky animal scents were everywhere. If I listened carefully, I could hear the ocean down in the valley at nearby Rodeo Beach. When we reached the studio, I felt vulnerable and nervous. Even though it hadn't been said out loud, I knew that this kind of encounter needed to be simple, direct, and clear. And it needed to be done in one take.

Before recording, I only offered Will the drone of accordions to listen to in his headphones; I wanted the melodies to be rhythmically independent from the rest of the music. The accordions also created a suspended, ambient mood; and more practically, they were a reference for pitch. As he sang, Will repeated and altered the melodies, so that they were consistent yet filled with variety.

In the end, we shared only a skeleton of information with each other, and we did not work out everything beforehand. This collaborative process allowed for a looseness with the songs, inviting risk and experimentation. We moved quickly, without much deliberation or thought (these things came before and after). The constraints of this process encouraged a magic to happen in the studio, one of both spontaneity and economy.

The results were surprising and deeply meaningful. For example, in "Sleeping in the Driveway," I shared phrases based on memories from Junction City, where my grandfather lay down under a tree and died, and of the old farm radio my father listened to as a child. Will, however, did not know these contexts. Instead, he blended the phrases into a different story, one of a narrator coming upon a woman or girl asleep in a car in the driveway, with the faint sounds of radio coming from within:

> I see her sleeping in the driveway
> while the night is
> and lights are
> passing by
> windows unclear from
> the trouble in her
> breath
> windows closed
>
> I hear farm radio
> from the inside
> as the battery dies
>
> I see her sleeping in the driveway
> and as I did approach
> headlights rush past me
> and so silly I crouch to hide

> When in a low whisper I heard
> I see her sleeping in the driveway
> Mama's car
> when in a low whisper
> I heard
>
> How sweetly I sleep in here
> I heard how sweetly I sleep in here
> and I be still
> to hear still more

When Will added the three simple words "I see her" to the phrase "sleeping in the driveway," for example, everything changed. My childhood memory was turned into something else, a fictional story. But I did not mind; I welcomed the transformation. I liked that something new and unexpected came from words that had personal meaning. The process added depth and nuance to them, and they became greater in their exchange. I realize now that I was learning another way of performing an archive, of allowing archival materials to bloom and change, pushing their way into voice and music. And finally, I once again learned that giving up some control, through collaboration, can yield something rich and beautiful.

Well, There Are a Lot of Stories

At the heart of *Silent City* is the track "Well, There Are a Lot of Stories," which features a recording of my father talking about his childhood memories. Taking a cue from the many oral histories I listened to at Berea, I brought this technique home to listen to and document my family. I remember sitting in my parents' living room, along with my mother, Marilyn, and my wife Jen, as my father talked about growing up on the farm and orchard.

From the beginning, my father had an innate sense of timing and humor in his storytelling. He also placed his tales in a world between memory, myth, and truth. "Well, there are a lot of stories and a lot of things that are true, that happened," he began. "I can remember one of them. Now, this is not really a story—it *is* a story, but it's an *actual* story." We talked about my father's siblings and their skirmishes and disputes; we also talked about the apple orchard and working with the cows and other animals. I especially enjoyed listening to my father's cadence and how the grain of his voice changed as he slipped into a tale; he savored his role as a subtle performer.

Many of the stories I had heard before, but some were new to me and were shocking. In one, he talked about playing baseball with inmates at the local prison:

> But the prison yard itself—we used to play when I was a senior in high school and afterwards. We used to go out and play the prisoners ball—ball games. It had a very, a very small yard—prison yard—where the prisoners would roam around in, on their break time. Only trouble is you look up and here's this guardhouse up there. The prisoners weren't dangerous anyhow. They were—they were supposedly, uh, trusty, trustees—not trustees but *trusty* prisoners. Trust 'em that they wouldn't gonna be escaping. Although they did have a few escapes down there. And there were people that killed people too. They were *killers*. And I was never—never felt afraid all the time I was there. I thought, "Hell, I can run faster than any of 'em."

We laughed, and I was amazed at my father's confidence, which he had carried with him all his life, even when he was a child. My father then went on to another story, this time about his grandfather Sam Paxton, who had hired his grandkids to work in the fields:

> One hot day—and it was a hot day, too—now I had to walk about a mile and a half to get there. And he gave me a hoe, we went up into the field, to carry up to the field. And there was another half mile I had to walk to get to the field. And all day long—back and forth, cutting out weeds on this corn—the corn was about this high, and the weeds were just coming on, too. Some places they were about that same height. Uh, so we quit around lunchtime. Went in and had lunch. Went back out in the afternoon. At the end of the day, he would pay us. I had kept up with this man all day. And he didn't get ahead of me, and I didn't complain about a thing. Kept right on goin', truckin'. And, so he paid us, and he said, now he says, "I tell you boys, I'm going up there tomorrow, and I'm gonna check that field of corn. And if it isn't done right," he says, "you're gonna hear about it." And he says, "I'll let you know." Well, I told him flat out, right then and there, I says, "Well one thing about it, Granddad. If you go up there and check on that corn, the job was done right. *And you're not gettin' my money back.*"

At this point, we broke out into peals of laughter again. My father's gravelly voice and animated climax to the story was too much for us to hold our amusement in. Through our laughter, my father continued, with a slight smile: "'Cause I already had the fifty cents. None of the others said anything. We were all about the same age, a little older, a year or so." And then the story died down, and we moved on to another.

When I listen back to the recording now, I see myself yearning to understand my father, who always felt quiet and mysterious to me. I also recognize that the recording became an extension of what I learned in Berea; it was an early attempt to capture a person's history and focused on my family. And now that my father is gone, I appreciate hearing his voice all the more; even then, I was capturing it so that I could remember its imprint on me.

Listening to Photographs

While making *Silent City*, I went through old family photographs and slides of Junction City. Many of the photos were taken before I was born; I was the last of five children and at least a decade younger than my siblings. Perhaps this is why the people and places of Junction City remain intriguing to me yet just out of reach. I am grasping back into the past to piece together the lives and stories of those who lived there. But the older generations are no longer there, and there is no one left in Junction City to confirm their truth.

In several photos, my sisters are visiting my grandfather Gus and the orchard. It is the fall of 1967. In one photo, my sisters Karen and Jane are both eating apples, their hoodies snug around their heads. Behind them are stacked crates filled with red, yellow, and green apples. My grandfather is in between, leaning against the crates and with a slight smile, wearing brown boots, work clothes, a gray hat, brow-line glasses, and a cardigan sweater.

An older photo shows my grandparents' backyard. On one side of the photo, their white house sits neat and clean. It is summer, the grass is freshly cut, and the flowerbeds are in bloom. The cellar door is propped open. On the other side of the photo, a great, green-leafed apple tree is filled with fruit, standing perhaps thirty feet high. In the middle is my grandfather's turquoise car, its white-walled tires slightly turned, its door open onto the yard. Nearby is a wooden Adirondack chair placed in the shade of the tree. When I look at the photo now, it is striking how peculiar it is; there are no people, and I am left wondering why the car door is open and the cellar door, too. In my mind, I imagine my grandfather getting out of the car and admiring the day and yard enough to walk a few paces back and take this photo. And when thinking of the song "Sleeping in the Driveway," the photo becomes uncanny, and I wonder, Is there a woman sleeping in the car? Is the radio on, faintly drifting out into the yard?

Harnetty's grandparents' backyard, Junction City, Ohio. Photo courtesy of the author.

There are more recent photographs, too, of visiting "silent city" with my father, at St. Patrick's Church in 2008. We walked among the tombstones; and as he swept off leaves and debris, we snapped pictures of the names, and he told me who the people were. He told me stories, too, of having to cut grass between the graves as a child or of the harrowing day he got his brother's hand caught in the push mower. At the back of the cemetery, the oldest markers were of a white marble, now faded and knocked over.

In one of these photos, my father's head is turned away from the camera, and the tombstones rise and reach out across the hill. It is a clear day in early fall, and the trees are beginning to change. In the distance is the house where he grew up; the once prominently featured apple orchard is long gone. My father is looking out, and now I often wonder what he might have been thinking. No doubt he was filled with that strange, bittersweet, and melancholy feeling that settles in your stomach when walking on land that was so well known to you as a child. And certainly, he thought of his parents, grandparents, and brothers and sisters all buried there, too. At the time, I did not understand what he must have been feeling; he merely seemed quiet and thoughtful. But I think I am starting to understand now.

When we arrived at my grandparents' gravestones, I remembered another trip to Junction City. This time it was for my grandfather's funeral in 1979.

Harnetty's father, Paul, walking among the tombstones in 2008 at St. Patrick's Church, Junction City, Ohio. His family home is in the background. Photo courtesy of the author.

At the wake, the funeral director allowed me to hold the door open for visitors; I was six years old, and in my innocence, I was proud to be of service. I am sure I was unable to comprehend the complex emotions in the room. Instead, I heard informal chatter and watched my parents warmly greeting old friends and relatives. I can still see the formal polyester suits of a small rural town, the room's pale-blue silk curtains, the translucent Jadeite bowl filled with pastel butter mints, and the thick scent of cut flowers. At the funeral, I loved singing the hymns. Even before I learned how to read words or music, I would pore over the hymnals, imagining the shapes of the notes leaping off the page to fill the room with sound. And finally, I remember driving home in the family's 1972 blue Buick. We traveled along rural roads at dusk, somber and tired, with an old country tune quietly playing on the car's AM radio.

Each of these photos seeped into *Silent City*. The photos tell stories; they remind me of places, transport me through time, or rekindle half-forgotten memories. The moments the photos represent were often comforting and sometimes unsettling. It is not hard to see how they influenced the text of the songs. But I remember desiring to make music that felt the same way, too: of melancholic juke joints, hymn tunes, diner counters, and velvet-voiced disk jockeys on the radio. I worked to make the instruments and the music evoke this feeling without resorting to pastiche. For example, I deliberately chose an old, beat-up school piano as my main instrument. I loved its slightly out-of-tune sound, heard in a new way. Likewise, I borrowed fragments from hymns or chords from old tunes that, when placed in a new context, felt distantly familiar. This process taught me how to make music that not only is about a time and place but also becomes part of it, where it elicits not a representation or facsimile but a feeling of recognition.

THERE IS ONE other photograph from Junction City I cannot let go of. It is a portrait of my grandmother Florence; my mother, Marilyn; and two of my four sisters, Lisa and Jane. My father probably took the photo in 1967 during a respite between two yearlong stints quarantined at a tuberculosis hospital.

The photo is both posed and candid, staged and informal. The colors are warm: mauve shirts and soft sweaters to burrow into; homemade dresses and curtains of floral patterns; Jane has a cotton quilted blanket, and Lisa a purse proudly strapped across her shoulders; plastic flowers in the corner, matching the muted blues and pinks of backsplash tiles; a Formica table, knickknacks above the cupboards, a wall calendar from the local church, and a lone cooking pot. I am certain there is the smell of food here, of fried bacon

Harnetty's mother, Marilyn; grandmother Florence; and sisters Jane and Lisa. Photo courtesy of the author.

and eggs and baked bread—a smell that lingers throughout each day until the next meal.

The photo contains three generations of women. My grandmother looks wary, confident, comfortable, tolerant. But she is also apart, the only one sitting as Lisa and Jane cluster around my mother. Her cat-eye glasses reflect the light from the back door and shadow her eyes. A headband exposes a widow's peak even as it keeps hair out of the way while working hour after hour in that same room.

My mother's expression is composed, possibly strained: pursed lips, looking slightly to the side, strength and fatigue gleaned in her stoic expression. Somehow, I can't help but think this look is directed toward my father behind the camera; she is impatient for the photo to be taken. And perhaps there is something more underneath: I read in her eyes the everyday tensions of marriage, of his illness, of gendered work, of care labor, eyes revealing weariness in that exasperated way that parents (especially mothers) know all too well. Lisa's expression, in contrast, is innocently open and a little bemused; she is happy to be there, excited to participate.

Jane is elsewhere. She is looking out the back door, toward the daylight. She is probably four here, hair mussed, blanket in hand. She is the only one not to look at the camera or my father, her eyes wandering up and out, given to the distractions of somewhere else, of another place.

I can't help but read into this gesture, which was probably a brief, unplanned distraction, a wandering attention typical of a child. (In fact, I have another photograph, taken moments after, that contradicts my speculative reading of the image: Jane is engaged and smiling and showing off her missing front teeth.) And yet, when I look at this photograph, I am desperately scanning it over and over, searching for nascent clues and remnants, hints that might tell me why or how Jane would later develop early frontotemporal dementia in her forties, how a mind could erase itself, erase language and memory as she slowly transformed, moving from consciousness and the physical world to something and someplace else entirely.

The first thing to go for Jane was language. Words and sentences became scrambled, reduced to maddening phrases caught in repeated eddies of childhood memories, her work as a nutritionist, pop-culture references, and religious symbolism. Once, while holding a prayer book, running her finger along the text as if reading, she kept repeating to me:

Sugar, milk, and diabetes
Apostles' Creed

The Drew Carey Show
I think so

Even this eventually ended, reduced to a quiet, piercing stare and, finally, a delicate, frail, silent fist bump. She was young and strong. Her body was fine. She simply forgot to talk, to remember, to eat. Watching this process made me feel helpless, confused, sad, and upset.

If memory and presence are so easily wiped away, I angrily thought at the time, why do I even bother with photographs and recordings? What is the point? And furthermore, aren't unknowing and silence supposedly the ideals of contemplatives and mystics? To live in the present moment? The eternal now? To move into a cloud of unknowing? No, I concluded, these ideals are untenable if you cannot hold the past and future as well. Otherwise, you forget why and how to drink or talk or remember.

When I was a student in London, I stayed with my friend's Aunt Beatrice and Uncle Ralph. Ralph had Alzheimer's, and Beatrice said to me, "I used to think that as we got older our bodies might fail us but at least we could still share our conversations and memories. Now, even that is not possible, and all we can do is be in the presence of one another." This wisdom from Beatrice was true for Jane, too; but now that Jane is gone, everything has changed once again, and the photograph here becomes a weak, insufficient, desperate, and aching stand-in for her absence, steeped in memory.

How is it possible to not even be born during the taking of a photo or the making of a recording, yet now it is a physical object that has its own power to deeply affect me with memory? This is what another Jane—Jane Bennett—calls "vibrant materiality," where things have their own "vitality . . . not only to impede or block the will and designs of humans but also to act as quasi agents or forced with trajectories, propensities, or tendencies of their own."[3] Or, in older, more archaic language, the photo becomes a talisman, an icon, a relic. In this photo, memory spins out from the past to meet me today: memory obscured, blurred, false, approximate, and nevertheless concrete and real. Memory becomes a wish for presence in the face of absence. This photo of my family is an absurd and rebellious cry into the silence—however fleeting, however foolish—against the systematic erasure of a brain.

All of these relationships—first, of shared lives and conversation; and when that is gone, simply being present with another; and when that goes, too, the fragile and temporary lattice of objects and ephemeral memory—are waves of thought and connection overlapping and receding, resurging and also destined to disappear.

Memory and this photograph are both weak proxies for the connections between people, but they also mean something important and profound. A photo such as this is an object I can grasp and carry and touch, and it touches me back. (Roland Barthes would say this touch goes further, that it "wounds" me. I agree.) This photo, when held in tension with the past and with memory, is something that can offer a faint thread, a finger straining to reach beyond its grasp, pointing to an absent yet remembered presence. This photo: an archival stand-in, a place marker for a gentle, delicate, frail, silent fist bump, a way to make something new out of something old.

When I was working on *Silent City* in 2008, Jane was perfectly healthy. This photo did not carry any of the sadness or emotion it does now. At the time, it made me think of my grandparents' house and our visits there. I strove to make music that shared the same simplicity, colors, quality of light, smells of food, and the draw of family. Now, years later, I see that I inadvertently made something of a memorial for my sister, too. The music asks me to pause and reflect on the connections and friendship of family. And just like the photograph, the music tries and invariably fails to cross the impossible gap of time and space to the ones we love.

Some Glad Day

Near the end of *Silent City* is the song "Some Glad Day." Once again, the lyrics and melody are a combination of memory, archival fragments, and newly composed music. The phrases that I used from Junction City include the "Mud Mill," the informal name for the ceramic tile plant where my family worked; the ever-present "tobacco in the grass" from my grandfather's house; the apple orchard; and the Junction City Prison, built on the grounds of an old brick plant, where my father played baseball against the inmates. The song's lyrics—which Oldham once again selected and shaped—incorporate these phrases alongside fragments of hymn tunes:

> Mud Mill
> tobacco in the grass
> some glad day we'll all arrive
> this sweet comfort
> is had, even here
> I bid my anxious fears subside
> and they will, until

brick-making prison
tobacco in the grass
some glad day we'll all arrive
this sweet comfort
is had, even here
I bid my anxious fears subside
and they will, until

apple orchard
tobacco in the grass
some glad day we'll see we all arrived
this sweet comfort
would be had even here
I bid my anxious fears subside
and they will

The music begins with accordions gently setting the tone and mood, as they have throughout the entire album. Vibraphone, electric piano, and a bass line on an upright piano join in. The instruments feel as if they are suspended in air, never quite resolving; instead, they are free of one another, and independent melodies float between them. Slowly, a lilting melody from the electric piano takes over, alongside a single repeated note on the vibraphone.

The video for "Some Glad Day" reveals how I was thinking about Junction City as a mythological place, caught between fact, fiction, and memory. The video's locations were in three different places, none of which were Junction City. At that time, I was teaching at Kenyon College, located in rural Knox County, Ohio. Much of the imagery was shot in Mount Vernon, a few miles from Kenyon. Additional footage came from my then-neighborhood of North Campus in Columbus, Ohio. And finally, the video ends in Whitesburg, Kentucky, at a barn dance at Appalshop. And yet, all three places are joined together not only through the song but also through a shared melancholic tenderness.

As the video begins, the handheld, lo-fi camera lingers on a rural town. There is a stillness in each new image. Rather than people, the focus is on quiet streets, industrial lots, and local businesses: American Legion Post 136, Pond's Tires, Smitty's Carpet Store. When there is movement, it is brief or subtle—as when a car passes through the frame or heat radiates from parked cars and cracked blacktop or wind pushes through weeds at the side of the road or cottonwood seeds float through the summer air. There is also a contrast of textures and colors: green-glassed warehouses, rough concrete, yellow handrails.

The video transitions slowly from day to night, and we watch the light change: a street corner at sunset, empty parking lots and water towers, an old church with its streetlight flooding down at dusk. There is a brightly lit Saveway Mart, with flashing beer and lottery signs, and a propped-open door. Outside an old dive bar, the camera captures a man smoking, gesturing and stretching his arm like an orchestral conductor, before taking a drag off his cigarette. Now in the night, we see a lone porch light in a darkened lot or brilliant yellow and blue lights pouring out of empty laundromats.

And then the scene and mood abruptly change. Now there are people, coupled, smiling, and dancing under a large red-and-white-striped tent at night, young and old, men and women. They are moving with laughter and a sweet awkwardness, holding hands, imperfectly synchronized, trading partners, in jeans and dresses and boots, swaying and stepping into the center of the tent and back out again. They are clearly dancing to different music than what we hear, and yet the electric piano and vibraphone fit with their movements in a way that is at once free and thoughtful.

Looking at the video some fifteen years later, I cannot stop watching a particular old man who is part of the dance. Shirt tucked in and slightly formal, he stands out among so many young dancers, and yet he keeps up with his counterparts with delight and concentration on his face. As the music dissipates, he joins with a young woman, continuing their formal steps. Age and youth, across generations, sharing this moment together. The music runs out, and they continue, both smiling, both swaying into the night.

I remember this moment when I made the video, when the music and dancing end at two different times. Originally, I thought I would fix the problem and match the two, so that they both would finish together. But I did not; I became curious about the moment of silence that fell out of time—of both the music and the album—and I left it alone. Now, I understand this silence, born from happenstance, as the most important moment of the entire project. It is the silence of our shared humanity, exposed and naked, vulnerable and beautiful. Importantly, this silence is not contained within the music or anything that I made; it was found in the fissure of an out-of-sync mistake. I was merely a witness to it. It is a silence that is always present, always becoming; it is connecting us and touching us in its poignant and quiet dance.

CHAPTER FOUR

Chicago, Illinois: *The Star-Faced One*

Marshall

A recording begins: Half a dozen soaring, chaotic cellos slide and pluck from high to low. They settle into patterns—sometimes interlocking, sometimes erratic—moving in and out of metric time. Celesta, vibraphone, and electric piano join, shimmering and bristling with energy. A bass clarinet's melody rises above the others. Just as the instruments come together, a second recording interrupts them. Related in musical content yet different in tone, it is a rehearsal tape, and its hiss and room sound betray another location and earlier time. This audio tape offers a new band of instruments—flute, drums, bassoon, keyboard—that dovetail and take over from those at the beginning. A voice breaks in: "That ain't the sound! Let me hear your rim shot. It ain't powerful enough! Now, one, one, one, two—Marshall—one, two, three, four!"[1]

After this count-off, the two ensembles join, old and new, their sounds merging and pulling apart; and all performers are listening to and following the leader's instructions. Eventually, the texture thins. Then, except for the vibraphone, everyone stops at once. The voice continues to give instruction, talking and singing at the same time: "Now, now . . . Try this, uh. One, two, three. Bing, bong, bing, bong, dum-ba-da-lump-bump, bu-da-lum-bump. Four-and, two-and, four-and . . . No. One, two, three." At these last commands, the tape and its hiss are cut off, and we are left only with cello and celesta, still sounding as if they are playing along with the others. Finally, only celesta remains, and with two metallic thuds, the piece is over.

The voice on the tape is Sun Ra (1914–93; born Herman Poole Blount), a dynamic bandleader and experimental jazz composer. The "Marshall" that Sun Ra refers to is Marshall Allen, the longtime saxophone player and leader of Ra's ensemble, the Arkestra. This piece—called "Marshall"—is a sound collage I composed with archival samples of Sun Ra rehearsing with the Arkestra, and it is on the 2010 sound installation and 2013 album *The Star-Faced One*. As for the more recent performers, the musicians Fred Lonberg-Holm, Jeff Kimmel, Jeremy Woodruff, Aaron Butler, and I add to the mix. This piece makes use of in-between archival moments of Sun Ra

A postcard featuring a portrait of Sun Ra. This postcard was used for the opening of Harnetty's sound installation *The Star-Faced One* at Audible Gallery, Chicago, Illinois, in 2010.

counting, teaching, and adjusting as the music unfolds in the 1970s. My intervention brings these moments to the fore: what was initially a documentation of a rehearsal becomes the backbone of a new sonic work.

In 2010, Lou Mallozzi at Experimental Sound Studio (ESS) in Chicago contacted me about the possibility of creating an archival project there. I had already worked with ESS on mastering two previous projects—*American Winter* and *Silent City*—both released on Chicago's Atavistic record label. Mallozzi was generous and engaging, and along with several other artists, filmmakers, musicians, and writers, he offered me the chance to work with the Sun Ra/El Saturn Collection housed at ESS.

Sun Ra's life and works have increasingly been the subject of popular and scholarly interest, and his importance has grown from marginalized outsider to celebrated cult figure. Sun Ra's music is rooted in the traditions of American big-band jazz, experimental music, and free improvisation. The recordings at ESS connect with many disciplines and ideas, including US history, theosophy, Afrocentrism, memory, race, civil rights, and everyday life. In addition, Ra used and embodied mythology—specifically related to outer space—to subvert and circumvent racism against African Americans.[2] Ra's music and art have touched a new generation of artists today; their responses continue to develop what is now called "Afrofuturism."[3]

The Sun Ra/El Saturn Collection has approximately six hundred audiotapes, from the 1950s to 1993. It is housed in the Creative Audio Archive (CAA) at ESS. John Corbett and Terri Kapsalis acquired and stored the collection in 2000, and the recordings were donated to CAA in 2007. Then, the digitization of the collection was completed in 2010. Importantly, Sun Ra LLC (and not CAA) holds the collection's copyright, with Sun Ra's nephew, Thomas Jenkins Jr., as the managing director. The recordings are remarkably varied—including rehearsal tapes, live concerts, phone messages, lectures, and poetry—and Sun Ra's ubiquitous presence brings them together.

ESS received funding not only to digitize and preserve the collection but also to develop ways of interpreting it. As a result, ESS commissioned new works from the writer and musician Terri Kapsalis, the visual artist and musician Damon Locks, the filmmakers Cauleen Smith and Rob Shaw, and the musicians Todd Carter, Mike Reed, and me. I appreciated how the artists had different backgrounds and used different media; it ensured that the archival recordings could be interpreted from many viewpoints. I began to see each commissioned work as an archival performance: At once reflecting on the sounds of the past and revealing the subjective experiences of the artists today.

We were asked to sign a letter of agreement with ESS. The agreement protected the copyright holders, positioned ESS as a facilitator, and ensured a dialogue between all parties to use the materials. I mention this because it felt like a necessary and important part of building trust, and it established clear relationships around the recordings. I signed the agreement willingly and saw it as an integral part of working with the collection. The result is a series of works that highlight contrasts between access and restriction of the archive materials. It shows one possible way for an archive to navigate ethically between preservation, stewardship, power, authorship, and interpretation.

What the Hard Drive Contained

I did not at first go to the Sun Ra Collection; it came to me. A few weeks after talking with Mallozzi, a hard drive arrived in the mail, along with a three-ringed binder. The hard drive contained the entire collection. It was—to say the least—overwhelming. I remember the anxiety this small object produced. Once again, I was faced with the prospect of trying to understand a collection as a whole, even though I could not listen to everything in the amount of time the recordings were available to me. Remembering the lessons I had learned in Berea, I let go of control and of any systematic approach and began to listen. This is part of what I heard:

Rehearsals
live concerts
studio recordings
a beer commercial
room sounds
lectures
phone messages
poetry
poetry over the phone
radio DJs
self-help tapes
news broadcasts
recordings of television shows
preacher sermons
tape warble
distorted channels
church organ
clapping
muffled congas
Bari sax punching in and out
"Somebody else's idea, somebody else's world, it's not my idea of things as they are"
instruments warming up
cluster chords
aliens
synth freak-outs
entire ensemble freak-outs

Chicago, Illinois

"Nuclear war"
medical talks on acupuncture
"Neptune!"
heavily distorted percussion solos
reverse speaking
polka beats
"If you hear trees rustling in the breeze, that's music"
'80s hip-hop
speed hypnosis
sounds of space
"If the people had been alive, I could have enjoyed myself on this planet"
objects pushed around rooms
massive piano clusters
strange waltzes
"I gave up everything I never had"
a choir
a children's choir
Duke Ellington
tape hum
"Strange celestial grooves"
children lecturing on Hanukkah
ostinatos
a woman describing the "sociophonic key"
"Opening up the doors of the outer space employment agency"
a sermon on Luke
"There is no day, there's only darkness, eternal sea of darkness"
oboes in stereo with saxes added later
surf-like guitar with accordion
operatic singing
Claude Debussy's "Clair de lune" on electric piano
Fletcher Henderson
Jelly Roll
silence (hiss)

Readymade Tape

That time in my life was as overwhelming as the tapes were. My wife Jen and I were moving into a new house; our son, Henry, was just two years old;

I was teaching in an MFA program at Goddard College in Vermont; and I foolishly chose that exact time to enroll in a PhD program at Ohio University. Perhaps the chaos and busyness of those months forced me to concentrate my work on the Sun Ra project, to make decisive decisions with the material (knowing full well there were hundreds—if not thousands—of options to choose from).

What at first felt random in the recordings soon yielded patterns. I began to make lists of what I heard. For example, rehearsal tapes (like the one used in "Marshall"), performances, and some commercial recordings of the Arkestra were all linked together. Of these, the rehearsal tapes were most intriguing to me; the in-between sounds, mistakes, and conversations offered more information and sonic material to work with than the finished commercial recordings. I marveled at Sun Ra's ability to lead the Arkestra, stopping and starting songs to give out orders or make subtle adjustments. I began to recognize particular voices and was able to match them with instruments. The personalities and camaraderie of the performers became audible on the recordings.

On one such tape, Sun Ra is playing an electric piano and singing, "Close your eyes / Rest your head on my shoulder / And be."[4] At first listen, Ra sounds as if he is alone. Listening more closely, however, I hear him leading a rehearsal. I also hear the electric hum of the tape recorder; a drone that creates a persistent musical tension. A moment later someone in the background is whistling along—perhaps. The whistling seems related, but maybe the person happened to walk by with a different tune in mind. Still, I hear them in relation to each other. Ra sings his next two lines: "Close your eyes / And I will provide."

Percussion joins in, perhaps one or two people on conga and drum kit. Now, Ra starts another verse but stops; there is something he is unsatisfied with. He keeps the rhythm going, however, and in a voice between singing and talking says, "Uh, bing, bing. That's your trouble, Harry, you can't remember." The tape abruptly shifts. There is a brassy chord, heard in reverse, bleeding through from some other recording. Ra returns briefly: "You're slowing the process up! Lay out, Harry."

Then a succession of quick changes, swirling in and out of my ears: the electric piano comes back but now sounds as if it is at the wrong speed and in a different place; there are more reverse brass chords, and several voices are heard: "1971." "Look!" "Down button." More chords and percussion follow, alongside a brief blast of saxophone from a different rehearsal. Then, we are in a completely new place altogether. The room feels smaller and quiet. Ra says, "You see, it changes," and as he shuffles the microphone in his hand—perhaps learning how to use it—he continues: "Yeah, so this ought to be nice. It'd be a mean mic thing if I could get it working."

These sounds take place within the span of fifty-one seconds. It is confusing and feels as if we are moving between worlds: time traveling in sound. The tape reminds me of the fragmented, disorienting changes of experimental electronic music. Yet this effect is built in and embedded in this field recording of a rehearsal. It is not composed but "readymade," much like the everyday objects the artist Marcel Duchamp chose and declared as art. In addition, the tape was probably recorded over multiple times, with each new layer adding information and noise; so, there is some truth to the feeling of time travel. As I listen, I hear the rifts between times, places, and people, with the crunching tape head signaling each jump between them. Sun Ra's presence here is a thread through the stratified recordings; I close my eyes and hold on for the ride.

Archival Homophones

Another set of tapes focuses on Sun Ra's speeches, poetry, and spoken word. On one tape, he reads his own poems through a phone, only to be recorded on the other end. At first, we hear another man's voice talking to Ra over the phone while setting up a microphone: "Yeah, I'm gonna . . . Yeah, but I can't listen to you. I have to put it right on the thing. It's got the condenser microphone. I have a condenser microphone cassette. Yeah." The man places the phone receiver close to the microphone, and we hear Ra's voice as if we were listening to him through the receiver: "What can I . . . Ready? What can I say other than the music itself? Music—yes. To the ears that dare to hear, that dare to hear, that dare to hear."[5] The effect is mysterious, and Ra's voice sounds far away, with the quality of an old landline phone. His voice is then mediated through the glitches and hiss of tape and finally through a digital copy to reach my ears decades and worlds away.

On another tape, Sun Ra is giving a lecture during a residency at the University of California at Berkeley in 1971. Amid the sounds of Ra quickly writing on a chalkboard, he creates connections—however fragile—between words:

> Watch what you're saying, because you're going to have to give an account for it. In other words, you're going to reap what you *sow*. Now, that "reap what you sow" is another thing that is dangerous. You're

gonna "reap what you sow," that's what you think it means, but there's also the phonetic: you're gonna "reap what you *so*." Now, what is that? "So" means something. You say, "it is so"—it means something you make true; it's over there with this truth thing. Whatever you call the truth, you see, you're gonna get that back. Now, you're gonna "reap what you so." Now, what's "so"? It's represented by a plus, like you say . . . *So*, that's so, that's positive, a plus sign. As I said, when people die, they give them a certificate: something certified means something that is positified, something that is true, something that is so. It moves over into this, too: people get mad, and they say they "so." You see over there? And then, you've got this "soul" when people are ailing and they delve into their *soul*. Now, I'm gonna show you one more word on this thing, and then I'm gonna play you some music.[6]

Here, Sun Ra is using homophones—words that sound the same but have different meanings—as a philosophical technique to develop a personal, argumentative logic based in sound. Ra delighted in this wordplay in his lectures and writing, which are closely aligned with the practice of "street-corner preaching."[7] The writer and poet Amiri Baraka points out how these words have a homophonic power, stating, "Ra taught that a word is not only an idea, but a *sound*. It has force and power, and the way it sounded makes it open in the world of what it sounds like, and its many meanings manifest at once."[8] Ra's logic may be subjective and idiosyncratic, but it points to deep cultural, historical, and political insights. When Ra seamlessly joins the words "sow," "so," and "soul" together, he is showing us how he understands and navigates the world.

Applied to the entire collection, Sun Ra's logic of joining words together is also the link between each recording, no matter how tangential. So, archival recordings such as Sun Ra taping a television show on acupuncture, a studio session for a Busch beer commercial, and a Pentecostal preacher's sermon are archival homophones. The archive acts as a sonic network that allows us to hear Ra's critique of history, culture, and ideas. As listeners and remixers, we then follow our own paths along these lines. Exploring the recordings, no matter how loosely connected to Sun Ra, encourages us to understand archives as more than collections of objects. Instead, they have their own agency and vitality, with relationships and living contexts that extend out from the materials within.

A still from Jo Dery's animated video for *The Star-Faced One*, featuring images of tape recordings from the Sun Ra/El Saturn Collection.

Sounds at the Margins

Sometimes the tapes were confusing, their archival homophones stretched thin. Why, exactly, was there a Busch beer commercial, and did the Arkestra make that recording? Is that Sun Ra playing Claude Debussy's "Clair de lune"? News programs, television, radio broadcasts, talk shows, and UFO experts may have had Sun Ra as their common thread, but they were still strange and often contradictory ephemera.

These tapes were at the margins of Sun Ra's music and life, and yet they revealed something important: Sun Ra's curiosity, his searching for all things related to space and space travel, and his interest in current events. Often, the recordings were humorous, as in this self-help tape brimming with optimism about the Space Age and how it might transform our minds:

> This is Harold Sherman. Have you stopped to realize what an exciting time this is to be alive? Fantastic things have already happened, and more are getting ready to happen. This is because the planet you are residing in has entered the Space Age. It won't be too many years before man is going to travel thousands of miles a minute around the Earth, to the moon, to distant planets. In time, the speed of his rockets and spaceships will approach the speed of light, 186,000 miles a second. But there is something that travels even faster than that. It can reach the moon and distant stars in a flash. It is not limited by

time or space. It does not require liquid fuel or atomic power or any vehicle to transport it. That something is contained in man's mind. It is his thought.[9]

The announcer's singsong voice only adds to the tape's amusing quality. And yet, it also fits into the ethos of Sun Ra, in which space is used as a powerful metaphor, offering a radical change away from his contemporary world.

On another tape, what seems like a random program from the community radio station KMPX in San Francisco instead turns into an interview with Sun Ra. Here, I became interested in the moments just before and after the interview. The DJ, with a relaxed baritone voice, states, "We're sittin' in for Jay, who was going to go to the dentist, but Sun Ra just walked in, so Jay's gonna talk to Sun Ra."[10] It is shocking to hear. Perhaps it is so because two contradictory characters are thrown together: the easygoing, casual tone of the DJ and the mysterious Sun Ra, who "just walked in" the building, apparently unannounced. Before the DJ continues, however, he pauses to read an advertisement:

> Got a few things to get out of the way first, and uh, one of them is a trade school called Career Academy. If you're lookin' to get into a new job and, uh, don't quite know how to do it, you might look into trade schools. You know, if you go to college or something like that to learn a trade, you gotta take all this extraneous jazz that doesn't really help you in your work. But trade schools teach you like, uh, just what you have to do. Just be mellow and laid back. Well, Sun Ra's here and Jay's here. And uh, they're going to have an interview. First, we're going to hear a cut by Sun Ra, off of one of his new albums.

I can only imagine what the listeners tuning in that day must have felt. It is as if an alien came to visit the Earth, and yet he chose a community radio station to share his ideas and must wait patiently for a trade school advertisement to finish before preaching his message. This contrast between the everyday banter of the DJ and the deeply serious mythology of Sun Ra is fascinating. As I listen, I can imagine how Sun Ra moved through these different environments, bravely sharing his music and message. And yet, this moment also feels implausible, with two vastly different worlds colliding.

Archival Authorship, Archival Power

Making interpretive works from an archive such as this one leads to hard-to-answer questions: Who is the author? Who holds the power? These questions are never fully answered, and they never go away. Part of the reason for this lies in what archives are and how they are structured. They may appear impartial, but they are not. Power is part of each stage of the archival process: collecting, choosing, storing, and interpreting the recordings. And, because recordings taken out of context can easily have more than one meaning, there is power in how they are performed, too, and in what editing choices are made.

Musical borrowing—the creative act of appropriating previously composed music into a new work—has a long history, from medieval monophony to contemporary digital sampling.[11] However, if done without respect and permission, this process has the potential to become cultural appropriation, akin to theft. These tensions between authors and remixers can never be fully resolved. The writer and photographer Allan Sekula writes that each act of archival interpretation contains both a "liberation" and a "loss."[12] How, then, can we at least mitigate their effects?

The key here is to identify who holds the power and then determine if this power is being abused. There is a conflict: On the one hand, all creative endeavors involve some kind of influence and appropriation (earlier music, geography, class, place, race, education, interests, and so on), as well as an exchange, in which ideas are constantly in movement, picked up, discarded, and incorporated. On the other hand, this influence and exchange carry with them the potential for an imbalance of power. Making things more complicated are the subject and contexts of the archival materials used: Is the material a top-down bureaucratic document, for example, or is it a song from a marginalized group of people? Holding these issues together is built into the ethics of working with archival materials, of working with the past. They must be struggled with, and this struggle must become a central tenet to an ethical archival stewardship.

As I pursued this line of questioning, I became curious about the other commissioned artists working with the Sun Ra/El Saturn Collection. I wondered how they might approach the archival materials individually; I also thought about the cumulative effect of many different voices reinterpreting the same material. This shared approach—done with permission—offered a way to navigate complicated balances of power between creators, archivists, and remixers. Sekula once again came to mind, with his call to "listen to, and act in solidarity with, the polyphonic testimony of the oppressed and exploited."[13] This points to a way of thoughtfully and respectfully working with the polysemic archival materials that can all too easily be detached from earlier contexts and meanings.

Rather than being "anarchival," where there is an attempt to subvert or erase the power structures present, each artist approached the collection acknowledging Sun Ra and his work.[14] The detachment, distance, and irony often associated with postmodern pastiche and bricolage are pushed aside.[15] Instead, these new interpretations are deliberately anchored to the original works. This rootedness lends strength to the new works, and we can hear both together and individually. Finally, this process affects the artists and how they use the archival material: They move toward and away from the collection while always keeping it in mind. It becomes a balance between connection and freedom.

In an effort to bridge this gap, several of the commissioned artists understood their relationships to Sun Ra as akin to teacher and student. They followed and moved alongside Ra and his music. Cauleen Smith states, "I cast myself in the role of an apprentice to Sun Ra and made my work inhabiting this space. . . . [My work] is a direct response to the lessons offered in the archives from Sun Ra via his voice, his conversations, the things he recorded on the radio and TV, [and] his lectures to the Arkestra in particular."[16] Damon Locks also saw himself as a student and "not as someone that was trying to put [him]self in [Ra's] place and act as him." Instead, Locks looked for points of intersection, what he referred to as "crossovers," between his own interests and his perception of Sun Ra's interests.[17]

As listeners, performers, and participants, the commissioned artists and I heard the past and present together. Remixing the archive highlighted layers of subjective and historical counterpoint. Not only does the original author Sun Ra become a character in these new works, but each person who interacts with the archive is entangled and involved. The artists acknowledge the work of Sun Ra, while adding their voices as contemporary collaborators. Our memories, emotions, concerns, and histories are present alongside those gleaned from Ra. New listeners, in turn, become yet another part of the circular motion of an archive as it continues to unfold.

Making *The Star-Faced One*

With *The Star-Faced One*, I too was aware of the complex relationships present between Sun Ra, the archive, the other artists, and me. Sometimes, I was not sure where I fit in and questioned whether I should be interpreting Sun Ra's music at all. I knew that I could not claim to be an authority or to speak for someone else or to pursue my own gain at the expense of others. I cautiously moved forward, carrying this tension between remixing and

Damon Locks's album cover for *The Star-Faced One*, which was made during Locks's residency with the Sun Ra/El Saturn Collection.

stewardship with me. At the same time, I remembered the joy, curiosity, and experimentation that I heard from Sun Ra again and again on the tapes and resolved to follow his lead.

The process of making *The Star-Faced One* began with research. In addition to the sonic aspects of Sun Ra's music, it was important to understand the cultural and historical contexts in which it was made. Listening, too, was a type of research, and I spent the majority of my time becoming familiar with the recordings before writing a note of music. As I moved through the collection, I created a series of increasingly detailed, color-coded maps; sounds, tempo, rhythms, transcriptions, tonal centers (if any), and melodies were all highlighted. I recognized themes, too: tape collage, poetry, spoken word, space synth, tape warble, ostinatos, lectures, distortion, and more. I began to compose my own music in relation to the collection, and I

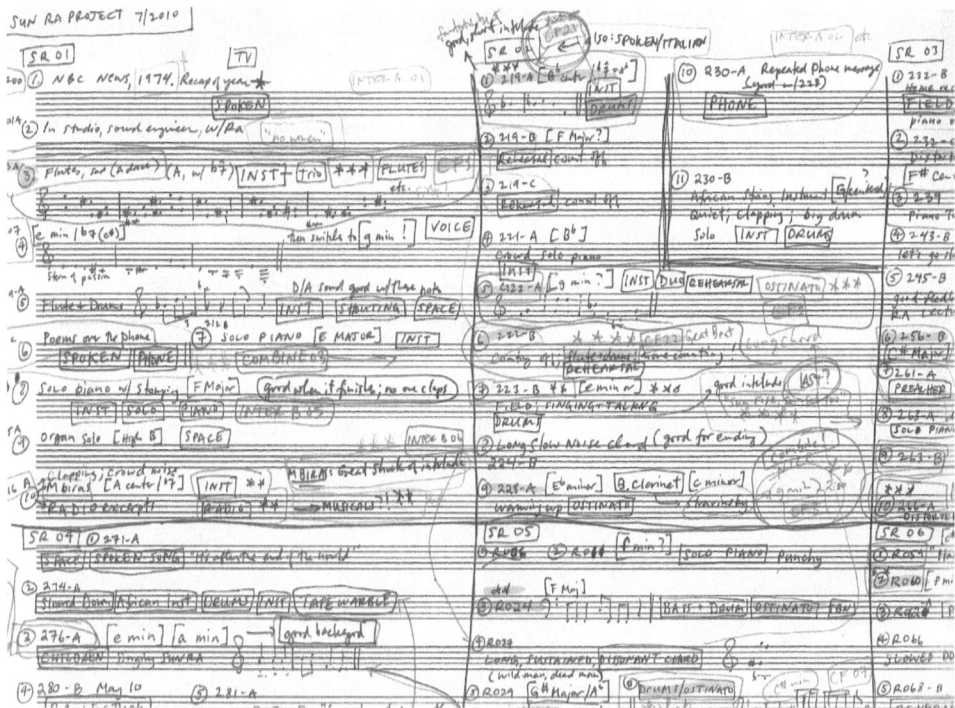

Harnetty's hand-drawn "maps" of archival recordings from the Sun Ra/El Saturn Collection. Photo courtesy of the author.

found myself moving around, between, and next to the Sun Ra lines. I wanted to make something that did not overshadow or erase the Ra material but instead complements it, allowing the archival recordings to be heard from many perspectives: from Sun Ra, the musicians, and me, too.

When it came time to share the newly composed parts with the ensemble, I expanded on the creative process begun with *American Winter, Rawhead and Bloodybones,* and *Silent City*. This included careful editing of archival samples as a loose click track for the musicians to follow along with. In order to reflect the spirit of the Sun Ra collection, the ensemble was invited to improvise freely over the parameters given to them. The musicians recorded their parts individually, in their own studios. They listened to the archival recordings on headphones while playing along on their instruments, reading the new music, and adding their own voices to the mix.

When I received the band's recordings, I was astonished. I could hear how they referred to the original Sun Ra recordings but also how they reflected the personalities of each performer. I heard remnants of the material I wrote, now transformed into something beyond what I could imagine alone. As before, it felt as if I had received a second archive in the mail. I began to organize and collage these recordings, along with the hundreds of Sun Ra samples that had become part of my daily listening.

The album was composed in four parts, roughly equal in size. Within the four parts, there are many contrasts: between long and short pieces, large and small forces, and textures and tone. The sharp differences between each piece were edited and spliced together just so, elided so that each track became a commentary on the previous one and a foreshadowing of the next. Finally, I settled on three distinct methods for working with the samples, distributed proportionally throughout the album: interludes, combines, and CFs.

Interludes, Combines, and CFs

First, there are "interludes," brief and carefully chosen samples of single recordings. The interludes provide quick, playful, jarring, or even unsettling moments of contrast to the project. Sometimes, the samples were left alone, as in "Humming," which captures Sun Ra by himself and playing for the sheer joy of the music.[18] Other interludes were minimally and carefully edited, as in "Cosmic Tones," "Rehearsal Side 1," and "I Would."[19] Here, the rhythms were spliced together with asymmetrical repetition and variation.

The interludes create thematic and structural cohesion for *The Star-Faced One*, as in four short pieces that reference a year, from 1971 to 1974. These interludes became the opening statements of each large section of the album. The first, "1971: Close Your Eyes" (mentioned earlier), has an unknown voice stating the year in the middle of the recording. Then, in "Chicago, 1972," another unknown voice is recording a performance of the Arkestra.[20] The tape is only eight seconds long, but we are given a lot of information. Amid crowd noise, a sliding bass note, and a screeching saxophone, a voice tells us the date and time: "Chicago, November second, 1972. First set. Saturday." A third piece, "5/2/1973," again shares a date, helps situate the album in a place, and gives listeners the impression that time is moving forward.[21] We are in a different environment than before; it is quiet and probably in a studio. A trumpet sounds three notes, and a voice says, "May the second, 1973." Sun Ra's organ begins along with a pizzicato bass. After a short phrase, they both stop, and a voice asks, "Are we going to start right there?"

And finally, a track called "1974: Not Ordinary Things" introduces the last section of the album. It features an NBC television broadcaster, speaking about the transition between 1973 and 1974: "Good afternoon. This is a program about a year nobody likes: 1973. It is also a program about a year no one knows anything about: 1974. The two are connected as most years are. But 1973 and 1974 are not to be regarded as ordinary years, because the things which have just happened to us and which are happening to us are not ordinary things."[22] Here, I was drawn not only to the authoritative and stoic voice of the broadcaster but also to the ominous and ambiguous language used. The broadcaster is probably commenting on the political upheaval that the Watergate scandal and the ongoing Vietnam War caused. Heard without any additional context, however, and in relation to the Sun Ra Collection, phrases like "not ordinary things" are mysterious. I also appreciated the extra sounds: notably the hum of the television and how we can hear the tape recorder being adjusted. It feels as if we are sitting in the room with Sun Ra as he is making the recording.

Then, there are "combines," pieces named after the artist Robert Rauschenberg's collage-like sculptures of found objects. The combines of *The Star-Faced One* use two or more edited and blended samples from the collection, akin to a "mash-up." Sometimes one follows after another, as in "It's Your Date, Simple as That." In this track, we first hear a piano solo from Sun Ra that is complex, dissonant, rumbling, and turbulent. Sun Ra then seamlessly and unexpectedly transitions into Duke Ellington's "Take the A Train."[23] Finally, a new sample emerges, with Sun Ra in the studio. The studio engineer is talking and asking Sun Ra if an intern can sit in while they are mixing a recording: "If it's all right with everyone, Cathy King is a student who's learning the room. So, she would like to watch the mix, if no one would . . ." Sun Ra's response is shocking, and he states, "Well, I can't function very well with women around, white or Black." The woman quietly says, "Okay," and the engineer responds to Sun Ra, "It's up to you. It's your date, simple as that."[24]

At other times, the samples are layered on top of one another, as in "After the Sound of the Tone," which contrasts an Arkestra rehearsal with an answering machine message. The Arkestra members are playing a melodic theme together, and I edited it in such a way that it becomes an ostinato, or a repeated pattern. Then, the answering machine reveals its own pattern, in which we only hear the greeting but none of the messages. An unknown woman states, "After the sound of the tone, please leave your name and telephone number. Your call will be returned. Thank you for calling 768-1390. After the sound of the tone, please leave your name and telephone number. 768-1390. After the sound of the tone, please leave your name and telephone number. Your call will be returned. Thank you for calling."[25] Together, the two patterns shift against each other, in and out of phase, and each repetition reveals something new: both a fascinating time capsule and a glimpse into the monotony of everyday life.

And finally, there are "CFs," pieces that bring together one or more samples along with the new ensemble. With this method, the sample became the central thread of each piece, and all of the past and present musicians were responding to it. "CF" is shorthand for "cantus firmus," a centuries-old music term that means "fixed melody." In early polyphonic music, a cantus firmus was a preexisting melody with additional lines surrounding it.[26] It was an example of "musical borrowing" and, to my mind, was an accurate way to represent the embedded archival samples of these pieces.

For example, in the track "Another Way," the first thing we hear is the high-pitched squealing noise of the tape, with the Arkestra quickly following.[27] Two flutes play the lead melody, with a strong percussion presence. The sample then settles into a repeating pattern at irregular intervals: an asymmetrical loop. This becomes the "fixed melody." I then join on electric piano, with contrapuntal yet static motives in the bass and midrange; it is filling in the open spaces of the Arkestra recording. Then we hear a new sample of a television talk show fade in, with the host Alan Burke asking a swami about his religious tradition:

> SWAMI: Yes, I think so because we are chanting from a spiritual platform. In a spiritual platform, there is no East and West; it is transcendental. Therefore, it appeals to everyone: experience and chanting. Perhaps I am the only Indian. All my disciples and students, they are American. And they very nicely take part; even children take part. So, I'm convinced that this transcendental sound is vibrated from the spiritual platform. It will be applicable anywhere, any part of the world—rather, any part of the universe.
> BURKE: Is the chanting the only method to achieve this cosmic consciousness?[28]

At first, the words are disorienting and only lead the listener to questions: Why is this part of the Sun Ra collection? What does it have to do with Sun Ra? The Arkestra sample slowly fades out while the electric piano remains, and our focus now is entirely on the exchange between the two people. The tranquil interview continues, until an audience member interrupts:

> SWAMI: Yes. Yes. We can utilize anything and everything for a preaching purpose.
> BURKE: Mmm hmm. There's a gentleman at the podium. May I have your name, sir?
> SUN RA: My name is Sun Ra.
> BURKE: Yes.
> SUN RA: And, uh, I want to say there's another way for the West.

It is only at this point that we realize Sun Ra is there, in the studio, during the taping of the program. When I first heard this recording, I was astonished. As soon as Ra says these words, however, I quickly added the sampled Arkestra back into the mix, with a different tune. In it, the performers are chanting:

> Sun Ra
> And his band
> From outer space
> Have entertained you here[29]

All other samples fade away, and we are left only with the singing, each Arkestra member adding their own inflections and personality to the words, until the piece is over.

In "Another Way," there are three distinct samples, plus my own electric piano. They all roughly have the same tonal center and tempo. They are also collaged together lightly; each sound gently fades into the others, and processing and editing are kept to a minimum. In addition, the electric piano's steady presence acts like glue between the samples as they transition in and out and fold onto each other.

It is important to note that "Another Way" takes place at the end of part 1 of *The Star-Faced One*. In the last track of the album, however, called "And as It Is Written," the interview continues where it left off. The exchange between the program's host and Sun Ra is remarkable to listen to:

> RA: And, uh, I want to say that, uh, there's another way for the West, that the East, uh, have things that haven't really proven themselves as far as making a happier world for the East. And therefore, for the West, there's another choice, namely, me.
> BURKE: You?! Sun Ra?

Chicago, Illinois

RA: That's right.
BURKE: Now, is this a given name or one simply created?
RA: Well, Sun Ra is my vibrational name.
BURKE: Your vibrational name.
RA: Yes. That people are what they are, and I happen to vibrate to the name Ra.
BURKE: Do these ancient Egyptians that you speak of have a spokesman other than yourself?
RA: Well, who should be a better spokesman for the ancient Egyptians than Ra?
BURKE: Well, I . . . I just don't know, Ra!
AUDIENCE MEMBER: That's why he said it!
RA: That's, uh, that's the way it is written, and as it is written, so it is.
BURKE: Well, I'll just have to take your word for it. I, uh, thank you for coming up, and good luck in your pyramid. Well, I'd like to have you back sometime and hear your space music. Would you make arrangements?
RA: Yes, quite so. It's time for America to hear.
BURKE: I don't know if we are ready for it, but I'd be delighted to listen to it. Thank you so much. [clapping] Swami, Krishna consciousness, you say, is partly the constant awareness of the Lord dwelling in all things.

Ra effectively, audaciously took over the program. He inserted his own message, one that contradicted the swami, and declared himself and the music of the Arkestra as the solution for the West's spiritual problems. When I first heard this recording, I couldn't believe that the host did not become argumentative or dismissive; in fact, he then invites Sun Ra to come on the program and perform at a later date. Then, remarkably, the host resumes his conversation with the swami (who had been silent up to this point), as if nothing happened.

Sunset in the East

Another track that makes use of the fixed melody (CF) technique is "Sunset in the East, Sunrise in the West." This time, my entire ensemble joins in with the sampled recording. The piece begins with an interlude: a field recording of Sun Ra playing a solo set in a noisy room.[30] He is quickly pounding his foot along with the music. The playing is fast and choppy, its energy frenetic. Strangely, when he finishes, there is no applause; in fact, the crowd's chatter increases in volume and takes over. In the background, a recording of 1980s popular music begins, and the cocktail-party-like conversations continue. Slowly, the archival sample fades into another, and the listener is transported to a different, quieter room, in the middle of an Arkestra rehearsal.[31] The hiss of the tape is prominent, and it sounds as if people are milling about. Out of muffled conversations, two flutes begin to play in harmony; sometimes, individual voices interject, but the flutes continue. This sample becomes the fixed melody that the new ensemble follows.

Bass clarinet first joins in with the old recording, with a plaintive countermelody. Cello and vibraphone quickly follow, each playing independently of the other, yet still paying attention to the rehearsal tape. Celesta and vibraphone come in later, creating antiphonal melodies that leap across the sound field. Finally, electric piano completes the ensemble, adding to the bell-like atmosphere. As with other tracks on the album, the new instruments split into twos and threes, their lines overlapping and in counterpoint with one another.

Slowly, the sample fades out, and the contemporary performers are left on their own. Here, the sample is used like the scaffolding of a building, with the musicians aligning their performance to it; when the sample is then taken away, the listener has the sense that the musicians are moving independently, drifting, and suspended in their own sonic worlds, yet with an unheard force connecting them. Or, perhaps a better analogy is of training wheels on a bicycle; the "wheels" are taken off, and there is a tremendous sense of freedom as the musicians move unencumbered and with momentum, balanced on and moving through the air.

When we performed together live, in 2013, I did not know if the magic of this moment would carry over. And yet, when the sample slipped away, the performers relished and responded to the openness. It was only then that I realized we were not imitating the Arkestra but were instead making a third thing, adding our own personalities and experiences together as a new performance. We were also listening carefully to one another, something that is not possible when recording parts individually. About halfway through the piece, all five of us became quiet at once. I remember it feeling as if the floor fell away from us; sitting behind the electric piano, I felt for a brief moment as if I were floating off the ground. And then, the sample quietly returned, anchoring us once more.

At the end of the piece, a new archival recording emerges. Here, Sun Ra is singing,

> Sunrise
> The sunset, too
> Sunrise
> The sunset, too
> Sunset
> The sunrise, too
>
> When the sunrise to the east
> The sunset in the west
> When the sunset to the east
> The sunrise to the west[32]

Ra is quiet and intimate, close to the microphone. Other voices are heard, too, and are sometimes louder than Ra's — "Tony? Yeah, Tony's in there" — lending to the inexplicable quality of the recording. It is as if they didn't know Sun Ra was even there, singing. The puzzling reversal of sunset and sunrise is an appropriate metaphor for Sun Ra's own contradictory nature. It makes sense; he is turning our biases and accepted notions about the world on their heads, so that we can break free from them. This may be one of the greatest gifts Sun Ra gave to us. At the end of the recording, only the contemporary ensemble's vibraphone remains, ending the piece with its repeated, metallic chiming toward silence.

CHAPTER FIVE

Shawnee, Ohio: Listening to Community

A Soundwalk in Shawnee

When I first arrived in Shawnee, Ohio, the forest surrounded me. I remember descending a long hill as the road straightened into a valley of oak and pine, dogwood and redbud. I paused to look up, and buildings and homes dotted another hill in front of me. Two opera houses stood tall amid storefronts and empty lots. Rows of buildings with second-floor balconies lined the street. Some balconies had chairs and swings; others were sagging and not fit to stand on. All around there were trees.

I walked onto Main Street. Even though I had never been there before, it felt familiar. The street was unusually quiet, even in the middle of the day. A man sat in a windowsill, eating his packed lunch. There was a restaurant, a community gift shop, and a furniture store that had been there for several generations. An occasional car drove by, breaking the stillness. I could see the Buckeye Trail headquarters at the end of the street; the trail is a hiking loop that traverses the entire state only to arrive back here in this tranquil place.

I decided to take a soundwalk along the length of the street.[1] Moving from north to south, it took all of six minutes. I heard a dog up the hill and distant birds. Gravel crunched underfoot. I even noticed the swishing of my own pant legs and felt my breath marking its own rhythm. Several buildings were uninhabited, and some were in disrepair. Later I learned that residents have worked for decades to hold these buildings up, an effort that visitors cannot easily see at first glance.

The first person I met on the street said hello to me. We began a conversation, and I told him my name. He said, "Oh, I knew your uncle Charlie! Everyone in Perry County did. He got a lot of people jobs around here when there were none to be had." I was surprised; this was a place where my ancestors and their deeds made me known and connected. We parted ways, and I continued my walk.

A tornado siren unexpectedly blasted even though it was a sunny, clear day. When I asked a local resident about it, she laughed and said the siren communicated different things to the all-volunteer services of the village, including medical help, transportation for the elderly, police, and weather. The siren signaled messages only known to the residents. My own bewilderment at the sound revealed that I was not a local. The siren, acting like a secular church bell, helped to sonically define and articulate Shawnee as a place. Its harsh, permeating sound both repels and attracts, and this push and pull also reflects the transitory space that its sound defines. The historian Alain Courbin notes that bells promote a sense of being closely tied to a location and ultimately time and again "recharge" that space.[2] The siren in Shawnee worked in a similar manner: it moved outward, disrupting the village with a sound most often associated with warning and danger, yet it also drew people in to serve and ultimately strengthen the community.

I returned to Main Street and passed an antique store with artifacts from the region on display. Inside, I picked up an old photo album. Only a couple of photos remained in the front. "They took the pictures out," said the shop owner. "But it's a nice album, very rare." The old corner tabs were still in place, and the paper was discolored where the photos used to be. The captions, however, remained: "Ron. Note his broken arm" was neatly written under an empty space. "Rex, the best dog" was under another. I thought about this gap — or silence — between the written text and missing images, between past and present. In my hands, I was holding a book of memory split apart, severed into partial stories and scattered to unknown places. These moments reminded me that sound does not stay put, and neither does the past. Instead, they emerge and dissipate; they bounce, return, and echo fleetingly. If lucky, we are left with the objects that they fill, resonate in, and depart from. They can be felt in an old photo album or in the kind words of a stranger who once knew your family.

We do not stay put, either. On this soundwalk in Shawnee, the combination of walking and listening was a simple and powerful way to experience the world around me. When we focus on listening, we allow ourselves to pay attention to sounds first. Our perspective shifts, just enough to open up a new insight, observation, or connection with another person or place. After the walk, I got into my car and headed back through the forest to my home.

Returning, Again and Again

After that first visit to Shawnee in 2010, I resolved to come back. Only later did I learn that Shawnee was where my mother's ancestors immigrated to in the 1870s as Welsh coal miners. Even though my father grew up in nearby

A view of Main Street in Shawnee, Ohio, in the early twentieth century.
Photo courtesy of the Little Cities of Black Diamonds Archive.

Junction City, we never came to Shawnee, since our relatives had all died or moved away. My connection to the place was a generation removed. But right away, I felt an immediate sense of familiarity, of being at home.

Shawnee is located in rural Appalachian Ohio. It is one town among many that quickly emerged around coal mining in the late nineteenth century, some forty years after the forced and brutal eradication of Native peoples from the land.[3] The towns are now collectively known as the "Little Cities of Black Diamonds," with "Black Diamonds" referring to the coal that once ruled their economies.[4] For two centuries, the region has been immersed in extractive industries, from coal, oil, and gas to timber, iron ore, and clay. The Little Cities are within the Wayne National Forest, where there is a common heritage of booms and busts, environmental destruction and recovery, and the formation of early labor unions. After nearly a century of economic and population decline, the communities that remain continue to work for environmental, economic, and cultural enrichment, to gain back some of what has been lost, and to make something new.

It felt like happenstance when I came upon Shawnee. I had been on a field trip with a graduate class focused on "sonic ethnography," which is a way of paying attention to culture and people through the lenses of listening and sound.[5] After visiting the nearby town of New Straitsville, I parted from the group and followed an instinct to drive on alone to the next town, whatever it may be.

It happened to be Shawnee, and I had no idea how it would change my life. I had some vague notions of where I was, but in all honesty, I was lost. And yet, I was open and eager to learn, which led me to a series of encounters with local residents that affected me deeply. I did not know it then, but I would go on to make Shawnee the foundation of a dissertation. And after leaving school, it would become the subject of many music, sound, and art projects, including an album of musical portraits of residents from the region, aptly called *Shawnee, Ohio* (2019).[6]

Before these projects happened, however, I began the long, slow process of understanding the town and its people. I was uncertain about what I was looking for or what to listen to. I only knew that if I kept coming back, something might emerge: a story, a familiar face, a clue.

Fortunately, sonic ethnography gave me a set of tools to help me bridge the gap between a community, an archive, sound, and the creative process. Here, I am indebted to the anthropologist and friend Marina Peterson, who, as my advisor, helped me to incorporate ethnographic methods—such as social engagement, observing, participating, listening, and writing—as part of my practice. I began to see how spending time in Shawnee and becoming curious about its sounds and people changed the way that I was relating to the place and the region.

This practice led to new friendships. Because I was not from Shawnee and yet I had family ties there, my presence confounded traditional notions of "outsider" and "insider"—I was somewhere in between. I cherished and relied on these relationships and am indebted to those who talked with and befriended me. Over the years, I continued to return. Eventually, past and present got mixed up, bled into each other. Two stories emerged: one of the region and one of my family ties to it.

And yet, I was wary that my work in Shawnee might become nostalgic. I had no desire to go back in time or to imagine that the past was somehow better than the present. The author and activist bell hooks, in her book *Belonging: A Culture of Place*, warned against a purely nostalgic reading of place, in which one "simply looks back with longing and idealizes." Instead, she used the past as "raw material" to critically understand where she was from, even as she continued to "return again and again to memories of family."[7] It is this balance—between my connections to the past and a sober understanding of the present—that helped me navigate the stories of residents and family in Shawnee.

The Archive, the Yearbook

At the time, the Little Cities of Black Diamonds Archive was located on Main Street. It was housed in a small two-room building with a painted orange exterior. The building was so small, in fact, that if you wished to go to the bathroom, you had to visit the theater across the street. Nevertheless, the archive was inviting: the walls had posters and artifacts hanging next to weathered photographs and local artists' paintings, and there were old musical instruments placed on tables alongside antique mining equipment.

I met a kind local historian there named Cheryl Blosser. I remember sitting in front of her desk, with its chaotic jumble of papers, musty books, and ancient computer. I began asking about sounds: Did she have any recordings? What were her memories of sound as a child? Could she recall the sounds of mining? Of recovery? I was pretty sure she thought I was crazy (she later confirmed this to me with a warm laugh), but she happily talked with me, showing me around the building, sharing books, and introducing me to other people who happened to walk by.

I kept returning to the Little Cities Archive. It was a place where I felt comfortable and where I could hear stories from residents. I began to look through all kinds of books, images, and documents. There were maps, too—mine maps, for example, revealing an underground system of tunnels that looked like Swiss cheese under the towns and hills. I also saw nineteenth-century maps of the larger region and could not believe my eyes when I spied "Harnethy" scratched across a small parcel of land in Perry County, just south of Junction City. This must have been the first place my father's family settled. It was just a name—spelled slightly different than now—but it unsettled me. In that moment, I could see my father's family among the local history: working and living, celebrating and mourning, learning and playing, and working some more. I could also imagine a larger picture of daily life, disasters, and labor struggles. I knew the longer I paid attention to these artifacts alongside the sounds of the present, the better I might understand the web of stories across the region, how they unfolded, and how they still affect us today.

One day while working in the archive, I accidentally found my maternal grandfather, Mordecai Williams. I was not even looking for him. Instead, I had been searching for documents on labor history and the culture of mining towns. I opened one of the many gray archival boxes and found two old leather-bound Shawnee yearbooks, from 1924 and 1925. Again, I knew little about Mordecai; I was the youngest in my family, and he died six years before I was born. Previously, I had only seen a single photo of him in his early sixties, just before his death. And yet, when I opened the yearbook to a random page, there he was, staring back at me with serious and youthful eyes. I still remember that moment of shock and recognition, seeing a person I had only heard of through family lore.

As I flipped through the yearbook's pages, I saw more and more of young Mordecai's life unfold in front of me. He was in the orchestra, captain of the basketball team, vice president of both the Literary Organization and the Junior-Senior Society, ran track, participated in the senior play, and was even the joke editor of the school's newspaper. Perhaps most importantly, these yearbooks displayed Mordecai's conspicuous talent as a visual artist. His fellow students often praised and remarked on his drawing ability. Mordecai helped design the 1925 yearbook, and his hand-drawn text and elegant ink illustrations were placed throughout. In both yearbooks, I found several photographs of him. They all suggested that he was poised, confident, serious, and full of a desire to apply these skills that he so clearly displayed.

I left the archive that day thinking about my grandfather and about his life as a young man. It was as if an entirely new person was introduced to me, one whom I could never fully know. I carried this knowledge with me. As I walked along the street and visited each building I wondered, *Did my grandfather walk here, too?* And with each person I met, I thought, *Did your ancestors know mine? Were they friends?*

Tonight: Basketball, Dancing

Across Main Street is the Tecumseh Theater. Built in 1908, it remains the tallest building not only in Shawnee but in Perry County, too. The first time I climbed a long flight of crumbling stairs and stepped into the second-floor theater, the room took my breath away. It was large, open, and full of light hitting the dusty air. I noticed the walls, where the plaster remained only in small patches. I could barely see intricate Edwardian stencil work on what was left, of ornate vines and dogwood flowers. The remaining walls were stripped down to their laths. As the light hit them, it revealed the building's see-through skeleton.

The theater was mostly empty and quiet. The faded and moth-eaten tapestry over the stage was still hanging. I heard wind blowing outside and occasionally voices of children playing in the street below. There were a few old chairs and signs alongside projector equipment, unused tickets, shattered records, glass bottles, and film canisters. Creaking sounds descended

The interior of the Tecumseh Theater in Shawnee, Ohio. Photo courtesy of Jonathan Johnson.

from the third floor above. A broken lightbox on the stage read, "To-night / Basket-ball / Dancing." As I stood in the theater, it occurred to me that I was not only listening to the present moment. I was also straining to hear sounds from the past, sounds that leave their traces in the building's bones and the objects surrounding me. I had the uncanny sense that the walls were speaking to me, that the floor's creaks and worn grooves were telling me the countless stories of the people who had been there before. The fact that my grandfather was one of these people only made this ghostly encounter more palpable.

Taking a cue from the lightbox, I looked across the floor and imagined the chairs pushed away. In my mind, I was brought back to the 1940s, and I saw awkward teenagers coming together to dance with one another. There was a band tucked into the corner—of piano, saxophone, and drums—playing music both rhythmic and sentimental. The dancers shuffled their nervous feet back and forth, and they held on tightly to each other. A young woman stood on her tip toes to reach her partner. Two older women danced together; their dresses swayed languidly to the beat.

And then the scene changed. It was now the winter of 1925. Instead of music, I heard the squeak of basketball shoes amid cheers and laughing and shouting. The theater was transformed into a basketball court, its elegant walls and stage now a backdrop to temporarily installed hoops and the sweat, bodies, and crowds of an intense game. The entire town showed up to watch, and the balcony above was bursting with fans.

Mordecai was on the court. In fact, he was the team captain, and this was his senior year in high school. I imagined the scene to be raucous, with the crowd cheering among the push and pull of athletes. Earlier, when looking through Mordecai's yearbooks, I found a collaged photo of the entire team. The players were cut out in athletic poses, their gestures exaggerated and without shadow or background and their expressions sincere. Mordecai is handsome and brooding, with his hair parted in the middle and slicked back. He holds the ball at an angle, staring intently into the camera. The caption states, "Mort is a popular Captain, and his team have had confidence in his headwork in the critical places. We are sorry to lose him this year."

The scene changed once more. This time, it was only a few days later: February 28, 1925. Mordecai was in the theater again, sitting next to his brother, Bill. Instead of a basketball, however, Mordecai was holding an alto saxophone. The event was a music contest between two county high school orchestras: Junction City versus Shawnee. The orchestras sat across from each other and began to tune their instruments. I imagined a jumble of violins, saxophones, piano, coronets, trombones, and drums clashing in an Ivesian cacophony. The sounds moved down the stairs and out into the cold, as the doors were opened and the audience filed into the theater. I stood in that place, listening for laughter, gossiping, feet shuffling, polite clapping. According to a concert poster, there were violin, vocal, and piano solos, as well as numbers with the full orchestras. After each school performed its selections, the judges tallied scores, and cheers and stomping resonated from the balcony as Shawnee won the contest. (Years later, a local man told me, "You know, there are only two things every person from Shawnee loves: music and basketball.")

Some fifty years earlier, Mordecai's grandparents arrived in Shawnee, on August 4, 1872. John E. Williams and Jane Howell were immigrants from Wales, and they were part of a large migration of Welsh mining families to the region. John worked in the mines during the height of a coal boom in the 1870s. At the time of their arrival, the town of Shawnee was newly founded and dramatically expanding in population, seemingly overnight. As a result, the town was referred to as "The Magic City."[8]

I climbed another set of stairs to the top floor of the building, perched above the theater. I could tell there had been water damage, and the only

A piano sits among stacks of theater chairs in the Tecumseh Theater, Shawnee, Ohio. Photo courtesy of Jonathan Johnson.

thing remaining of the walls and ceiling were structural beams. There were holes in the floor, with some boards dangerously sticking up. I cautiously walked across them, making my way to the front of the building. Beer bottles, old theater props, and bits of newspaper lined the walls; pigeon droppings were everywhere.

And yet, when I came to a large ballroom at the front of the building, light poured in from windows along the wall. I was high enough to be among the treetops, and I could see the forest stretching into the distance. A piano stood in the middle of the room, keys warped and strings missing. Rolls of plastic, paper, and trash sat on top. A hundred old theater seats were propped up against the piano's sides, with ornate patterns and moth-eaten velvet cushions. They were in a heap, like a pile of discarded crutches. I waded through them, my legs tangled and twisted in the thicket of chairs. Reaching the open-faced piano, I played a note to watch the instrument's inner workings come to life. Sound filled the dusty room. I played another and another, each time paying attention to their sounds—out of tune and sometimes only making a dull thud—and the ways they bounced from wall to wall. I closed my eyes and strained to listen further. A car passed below. The floor creaked. The sounds of the piano hung in the air for a long time. I couldn't help but think, *Did my grandfather play this piano?*

I imagined yet another scene in the theater. At the end of April 1925, Mordecai graduated in a class of twenty-seven. The graduation, more formal than the previous two events, had music that included performances of light orchestral songs, including Fritz Kreisler's "Fair Rosmarin" and Percy Grainger's "Country Gardens." A program of the event shows music was woven between and through an "Invocation," a "Salutatory," an "Oration," a "Class History," a "Valedictory," an "Address," a "Presentation," and a "Benediction."

A local history book took note of this particular graduation. There seemed to be a palpable sense of excitement at that time in Shawnee: "The new graduates went forth to make their mark on the world. . . . In 1925 the time was ripe for 'something' to happen. The town seemed ready to burst onto the scene once again and become a 'boom town.' There was a certain energy about it, a low pot on the stove about to boil."[9] For Mordecai, this excitement must have meant that there was a hopeful and bright future ahead. Perhaps there were jobs available and a way to create and shape a prosperous life in Shawnee.

And yet, similar to sounds, we are neither fixed nor stable over time. It turns out that the immediate years after 1925 were a dramatic turning point in Shawnee, an antecedent of the Great Depression to come only a few years later. Since then, Shawnee and the other "Little Cities" have experienced a lasting economic downturn. As the boom of mining turned to bust, mining companies reduced pay, union disputes followed, mines closed, unemployment soared, and the coal industry moved out of the region for fields in Kentucky and West Virginia.

Mordecai took part in this migratory movement, but instead of south, he traveled with his family north to Columbus, Ohio. There, the Williams family weathered the economic depression as well as they could. Mordecai took classes at the local high school but always felt differences between himself and the "city kids." He fell in love and got married and over the years took on a number of jobs: in factories, desk jobs, and even moonlighting as a clothing designer.

Strangely, as he raised his own family, Mordecai actively discouraged his children's artistic abilities. Perhaps he saw his proud moments of achievement in high school as folly, child's play. I am grateful that my own parents did not do the same, allowing me to find my own way through music and art. It is a reminder that the regional mining bust of the "Little Cities," followed by the Great Depression, must have had a profound impact on many people, including my grandfather. It was an impact that, despite his talents, he could not have been prepared for.

At the theater, I looked out the windows again, at the street and forest below. I remembered how—when Mordecai walked up and down a busy Main Street in the 1920s—most of the trees were not planted yet; the hills would have been barren, clear-cut, open. And now, the forest had returned, but the streets were empty. It was a switch that gave me the feeling that the forest would eventually take over, swallow the town, and return it to its wild nature, covering the wounds and scars of the mines.

As I walked down the stairs and onto the open street, I traced my grandfather's life as one among a constellation of histories and interactions. I listened for his voice, straining to make sense of his choices, insofar as he could make them. I heard and felt deeply how his past still affected me, even as my feet stood firmly on the exact same ground as his own did a century before.

Making a Sound Archive

On another trip to Shawnee, I walked into the community gift shop on Main Street. It had a tin ceiling and an ornate ceramic-tiled mosaic floor. Antique wooden bookshelves with glass doors lined the walls. Even though it was a warm day, it was cool inside and still. I met the owner, John Winnenberg, and he showed me around the building. I had been inquiring with residents to see if they had any family histories or old tape recordings they would like to share. When I asked John, he got up and took me to a back room and then into a walk-in closet. There were metal chairs, piles of old furniture, posters, cleaning supplies, and dozens of unlabeled boxes with newspapers and books poking out. After a few moments of searching, he returned with a single box filled with cassette tapes. "Here you go," he said. "It's probably better for you to have these than me. You'll take better care of 'em!"

At the time, I had no idea how much these recordings would affect me. The box was old and dusty and did not seem promising. I wasn't even sure if the tapes would still work or if they had deteriorated beyond rescue. But in hindsight, that box of tapes was a treasure trove sitting quietly dormant in the closet and latent with meaning and mystery. The tapes became the heart of my work in the region, offering a window to the past and a connection with people in the present, too.

I gratefully took the recordings home and began to listen to them. Most of the recordings were made in the 1980s and 1990s. Some were earlier. There were several interviews with local residents and a few answering machine tapes. There was even one recording of homemade church music

The box of cassette tapes that Winnenberg gave to Harnetty in Shawnee, Ohio. Photo courtesy of the author.

of an older woman singing devotional hymns. Her cracked voice could be heard alongside a synthesizer playing premade arpeggiated chords over an oom-pa-pa waltz. Her singing had a sweet quality; and like all these recordings, her voice was earnest and without irony.

Many of the recordings were from history groups. Later, John would tell me how local historians (including him) traveled from town to town to record residents telling stories before they were forgotten. I found these tapes to be particularly powerful. The residents were talking and listening to one another to reclaim and redefine their communities. They used this process to create a new history, one that was proud of its diversity and advances in labor rights. They also pushed back on the regional, rural stereotypes of homogeneity, backwardness, and poverty.

As I listened, I was astonished to see how the humble tape recorder became a community organizing tool. I learned that, as a young man, John would drive around in his car, listening to and memorizing the tapes. Together, the community wrote a local history book based on the recordings that shared the stories. At the same time, local nonprofits popped up in the region to help restore the environment and repair the economies of the Little Cities. I realized that these humble recordings became a seed for future change. As the residents' stories were told and shared again and again, a sense of pride in the land and people arose; efforts to save old buildings, communities, and the land itself soon followed.

Over the next year, I went through the slow process of digitizing and cataloging each recording. I also took extensive notes as I listened and transcribed dialogue that seemed important, or simply interesting, even if I didn't fully understand what was happening. Without meaning to, I was making a sound archive.[10] I also had an inkling that these tapes would become the basis of a new music project, one that told the stories of Shawnee and the Little Cities from the voices of people who lived and worked there.

The Anne Grimes Collection

Despite the richness of the Shawnee tapes, I found myself searching for archival recordings of a different character, recordings that might tap into the folk traditions of the region that were celebrated and plentiful in Kentucky and West Virginia yet seemingly sparse in Ohio. I turned to the Anne Grimes Collection, from the Library of Congress. Anne Grimes (1912–2004) lived and worked in Ohio and spent a great deal of time traveling around the state to make field recordings of local songs, ballads, and stories. Many of these recordings took place in the 1950s, and they have often been compared to those of John and Alan Lomax.

I traveled to the Ohio History Connection in Columbus, which had an antiquated cassette copy of the Anne Grimes Collection, along with many of the original papers and notes that Grimes made. When I arrived, I sat in a large reading room and was presented with boxes of dusty tapes that appeared to have been copied in the 1980s and not listened to since. I was also provided with a small tape player, and judging from the strange looks I got, I gathered that requesting audio recordings was not a popular activity there.

Nevertheless, I relished the collection. I loved listening to Grimes's introductions to each tape and to the grain of her confident and articulate voice. I also admired reading through the original typed transcriptions and notes of the collection. Many pages had handwritten corrections and marginalia. The paper was thin, aged, and semitransparent; typewriter ink bled through so that I could see layers of lyrics and text at the same time, much like my experience of listening to overlapping voices on the tape recordings. As I listened and read, it felt as if Grimes were talking directly to me and letting me know what her experiences were as she traveled throughout southeastern Ohio. Often, she would give detailed descriptions of the towns I had grown to know so well: New Straitsville and Gore, Gloucester and Carbondale,

Nelsonville and Murray City. Once again, I had the uncanny feeling that the tape player was a time machine, allowing me to experience something of these places as they were some sixty years earlier.

Some of the recordings had humorous titles, such as the song "Seven Beers with the Wrong Woman." Others were political, like "Vote for the Local Option" or a "Campaign Song," about the 1898 presidential contest between William McKinley and William Jennings Bryan. Still others offered harrowing news accounts of local murders in song form, such as Amanda Hook singing "Terrill" and Ina Simmons singing "Pearl Bryan." Both songs were murder ballads from the aptly named town of Gore, just a few miles from Shawnee. A common practice in the folk tradition, both are adaptations of earlier ballads, with the lyrics swapped out to tell a local story. "Pearl Bryan" begins with Grimes introducing both Simmons and the song:

> Next recording made January 15th, 1954, in Columbus, Ohio. Mrs. Ina Simmons, now a resident of Columbus. However, she was a native of Hocking County, as was Mrs. Neva Randolph. Nelsonville, which she mentions as being the place where she spent her young girlhood, is in Athens County. That's where she learned many of the songs that follow. "Pearl Bryan," however, seems to have been a Hocking County version of that gory ballad. She thought that this particular version was made up by a local editor there, uh, near Gore. Her reminiscences of the Terrill murder, at Gore, which is another murder, of course, earlier, which happened in that section, uh, are interesting.

When Grimes asks Simmons where she was born, Simmons responds, "I was born in Carbon Hill, Hocking County, twenty-second day of March, in eighteen hundred and eighty-three." Grimes quickly moves along and assures her, stating, "Okay, well, let's hear you sing this, Mrs. Simmons. It'll be fine," and the singing begins:

> Pearl, come to your lover
> A villain once cried
> Pearl, come to your lover
> And stroll by his side
>
> Though I have betrayed you
> I'll make it all well
> So none will upbraid you
> Or know what befell[11]

On another tape, I was astonished to listen to the Affrilachian musician Reuben Allen sing a song about a mine fire in New Straitsville. The mine fire was most likely started over a labor dispute in 1884, and according to residents, it continues to burn today. The recording begins with Allen's tenor voice and slightly out-of-tune guitar. His playing is intriguing and imperfect; he provides both chords and accompanying bassline, but sometimes the notes buzz or are missed. The tape warbles and pans slightly back and forth from speaker to speaker, qualities of the tape's age. Reuben's voice warbles, too, and I could not help but laugh a little; perhaps it was the combination of his heartfelt, amateur singing against the song's serious content. These contrasts made me love the recording. Allen sings,

> A man who fights for his honor, none can blame him
> May peace be with him wherever he will roam
> No child of his could ever go to condemn him
> A man who fights for his honor and his home
>
> It was a frosty morning when the fire was set
> The band was playing in the snow
> But nobody knows except the union leader
> That what was taking place in the hole
>
> When they heard the boom
> When they heard it boom
> And the men come running up

After he finishes, Anne Grimes continues to talk with Allen about the song:

ANNE: What do you call it?
REUBEN: Uh, "Homestead Strike."
ANNE: "Homestead Strike," and this, you say, it dates from the fires down here in, uh, is that Morgan County?
REUBEN: No, uh.
ANNE: Is that Licking? It's, it's, uh, it must be within twenty miles of Zanesville.
REUBEN: Yeah, that's right.
ANNE: And the fire started at that time. They set the fire?
REUBEN: They set the fire. The mine's been burning ever since.
ANNE: And you say it's about sixty years ago, when you were a young man.
REUBEN: Yeah. It was . . . I'll tell you. It was right after the Spanish-American War.[12]

Shawnee, Ohio

Later, I learned that the song "Homestead Strike" was not originally about the mine fires at all but instead was a labor song from Pennsylvania, documenting the fight between striking steel workers and the steel company in 1892.[13] In addition, the Spanish-American War took place in 1898, fourteen years after the New Straitsville mine fires began. Even so, the lyrics appear to be adjusted to fit the mine fires. They serve as another example of how folklore can move, change, and adapt to different places and times.

After listening to these recordings, I knew that they, too, would contribute to the growing puzzle I was already working on in my mind, of voices, songs, and sounds coming together to tell the stories of Appalachian Ohio. And while the Anne Grimes recordings are mostly from neighboring towns (and not directly from Shawnee), they nevertheless fit within the spirit and tenor of the region. They uncover a rich and complex musical past of Ohio that is often overlooked.

What Does a Photo Sound Like?

Just as I had done with my family's photos in Junction City, I began to pay special attention to photographs in the Little Cities Archive. I imagined what they sounded like and heard all kinds of stories: the sounds of industry, machinery, trains, and horses; the intense fire of brick kilns; the bells of cattle wandering through town streets; and, of course, mining and its unintended impact on the land. The author and musician David Toop calls this a way of listening for "auditory artifacts."[14] I decided to find as many photos as I could that might reveal sounds from the region, sounds that had not been captured on a recording.

Many of the photos are of landscapes and cityscapes now largely gone, showing the prosperity and buildings of the nineteenth and early twentieth centuries. There are black and white and sepia-toned photos of Main Streets, crowded and raucous or ghostlike and mysterious, with quiet storefronts and faceless people standing on second-floor balconies. I can imagine the busy sounds of rowdy bar fights and church hymns or of the industrial churning and rumbling of moving earth in nearby mines. There are pictures of children playing in the streets, young and joyous and mischievous, brandishing popguns and marbles and wearing baseball hats and newsboy caps. I cannot help but wonder what it was like to walk along those sidewalks or to talk with passersby. Or, there are photos of public events that an entire town would go to, such as the 1909 funeral for Ann Davis Ricketts in McCuneville, with horses and buggies lining the street on their way from the church to the cemetery, slowly moving in mourning and respect.[15] The photo looks as if it were once folded, and so there is a vertical crease close to the middle; somehow, this only lends to the image's somber and pastoral softness.

There are many portraits of people, too: posed and candid and of groups and solitary subjects. I found myself drawn to Grandma and Grandpa Ashby posing outside in their yard, both wearing their Sunday best, with Grandpa sitting in a straight-backed wooden chair.[16] They lived in Rendville, a town known for its racial tolerance and integration. Or, there is a photo of a man standing across the street and under the Corning Theater marquee, posing for the camera. He is wearing a white apron and cap and is next to a popcorn machine.[17] I can hear in my mind his calls of "fresh popcorn!" as he tries to entice people to come in and see the latest movies. A small boy sits behind him, barefoot, staring intently at the camera, too. In another photo, I studied the dusty faces of workers at the New Straitsville Brick Plant, with their overalls, upturned collars, and all manner of hats, with hands at their sides or resting in camaraderie on each other's shoulders.[18] They are standing in front of large beehive kilns, and the photograph's visual noise of dirt and scratches against the kiln's smokestacks and crisscrossing wires creates a hazy, blue-purple patina.

And then there are some of my favorite photos, of musicians: string bands with fiddles and basses or wind bands of neatly dressed men with matching hats and jackets. In one photo, there is a trio of fiddle, dulcimer, and banjo.[19] Wearing their best suits, the men are all performing; the dulcimer player is missing an arm, perhaps due to a mining accident. In another, there is a quartet of string players — three fiddles and one double bass — with the peculiar addition of a small child sitting in front of four neatly arranged bottles of dark beer.[20] Or in another, I see a school parade in the town of Corning, with tuba, trombone, French horns, and saxophone, each child proudly playing their instrument.[21] Throughout these images, there are girls and boys, and men and women, and they are often racially integrated, refuting the stereotype that Appalachian towns were homogeneous and segregated.

In these photos, there are all manner of parades — Fourth of July, graduations, Halloween, Decoration Day — featuring bands in uniforms and eager spectators. One captivating photo is of a Memorial Day parade, perhaps in the 1930s.[22] In it, there is a band wearing maroon uniforms and marching uphill at the Shawnee Cemetery. Two flag bearers and a trio of young women lead the way. Cars line the road, and behind them is a stand of trees, lush with silver-green light. There is a dreamy quality to the photo; it is both sharp

A Hungarian band. Photo courtesy of the Little Cities of Black Diamonds Archive.

and soft at the same time. When I look at it, I imagine what music the band might be performing, its sound drifting out among the gravestones. I also think of the ambient sounds, of cars and wind, trees and people talking.

And as I continue to look at the photo now to write about it, I realize that the perspective of the camera is up on a hill overlooking the people below and that the person taking the photo is standing exactly where my great-great-grandparents John E. and Jane Howell Williams are buried. Only a short time ago, I stood in this same spot, reading their shared tombstone and feeling the tug of ancestors and imagining what it must have been like to be there at their funerals. And now, looking at this photo, I can feel the warm sun and the uneven, grassy ground beneath my feet and the light breeze and the birds flying by and the silent hills.

In many photographs, I saw the pride and struggles of workers. An early photograph simply called "Miner" shows a man guiding a horse-drawn cart out from underground, highlighting the use of animals and the sounds associated with them. The miner has muddy feet and clothes, which point to the dampened acoustic space of the mines and the difficulty of moving through them. Another photo, titled "Women Miners," poses a crew of

A Memorial Day parade at the Shawnee, Ohio, cemetery. Photo courtesy of the Little Cities of Black Diamonds Archive.

men and women together, a rare sight in a field where men were dominant. Their faces sooty, the women are proud, smiling, and determined. A later photo, "Miners at Meigs," depicts a group of men—perhaps from the 1960s—crouched below the heavily scraped roof of the mine, revealing an aural scar of the machines used to cut a path through the earth. Likewise, photos of the "Congo Mine Belt" show large chunks of coal crashing down into the back of a rail car. Running continuously, the large and noisy belt moved and sorted the coal; its sounds were a permanent fixture in the mines.

Photos from the early oil and gas industry also reveal a distinct soundscape, one above ground as opposed to the underworld of coal.[23] "In the Hills of Shawnee" shows a single oil well nestled in a valley, with a tipple in the distance. Trees and nothing else surround the well, and in operation, it would have provided a rupture to an otherwise natural soundscape. Another photo from the early twentieth century reveals a group of men standing in front of an "Oil Well Supply," some in suits and others in coveralls, with a desk clerk seen working inside the building.[24] The storefront becomes a place of class tension in a coal town, where commerce, management, and mining labor converge. Miners must come here to interact and to purchase explosives and other equipment from the company store.

Perhaps the most striking oil-related image from the Little Cities Archives is a postcard depicting a hand-tinted landscape of the New Straitsville oil fields from a hilly vantage point.[25] Conspicuously absent are trees, which were removed over the course of the nineteenth century. Dozens of derricks can be seen fading into the background. Here, the aural essence of the photo is one of machines and engines echoing through the valley without any forest to absorb their sound. The fact that this image is a postcard indicates the novelty of this landscape, once seen as a sign of progress, domination over nature, and wealth.

There were several photos of the New Straitsville mine fire that I found myself mysteriously drawn to. In one blurry photo called "Picture from Mine," there is a black hole in the bottom center, with steam and smoke seeping out.[26] There are no animals or plant life around and no sounds to hear other than the fire below ground. Another image shows the gimmick of residents frying eggs in a crack in the ground, where the fire is breaking through the surface.[27] In my mind, I hear the sizzle of the eggs and smell the strong odor of sulfur from the mine, making for an unpleasant meal.

One of the more iconic archival images of the mine fire involves a scene of two men erecting signs that say, "The World's Greatest Mine Fire," "Plummer Hill," and "Scene of 'Bob' Ripley's Broadcast."[28] They are advertising the mine fire not only as a tourist curiosity but also as a place significant enough to capture the attention of a national radio broadcast. Cars are parked in the background, and what appears to be a lemonade stand or ticket booth has customers standing in line. Strangely, there is an intimidating figure of a large man in a pork pie hat standing to the right of the signs, holding a shotgun. He is looking directly at the camera, his eyes squinting and uninviting. It is odd how the photo depicts attempts to attract novelty seekers yet pushes them away.

In the end, it was the mining and its corresponding infrastructure that became novelties, and the mine fire remained the permanent fixture. The fire revealed the instability of an economy and community built solely on extraction. Mining has its own rhythms of a quick buildup followed by an abrupt decline, leaving destruction in its wake. This photograph strikes at the heart of the strange situation New Straitsville found itself in, not only after the fires began but from its origins. Built on the optimism of a coal boom, the town attracted laborers while ingenuity and creativity fueled development. However, from the perspective of the miners, the mining industry would never provide environmental, health, or economic sustainability; it was designed from the beginning to be wealth generating for a few and untenable for everyone else. The miners who conspired to set the mines on fire in 1884 were faced with the impossible choice of either the ruination of their work and lives because of unfair pay and unfit working conditions or the ruination of their work and that of the mining company, too. It appears they chose the latter, damning the land to over a century of fire as well. The mine fires may have created an environmental and economic disaster, but disaster was already inevitable due to the nature of mineral extraction. The fires hastened the rhythms of destruction already in motion.

Old Films: Jack Shuttleworth

One hot summer day, I went to the Murray City Mining Museum. I had been searching for any historical films of the mines or of the daily lives of miners that I could find. After inquiring with several people, one said, "You've got to go down to Murray City and talk with Jack Shuttleworth. If anyone has films of miners, it's him."

When I arrived, Jack was waiting for me. His wife Mildred had just dropped him off at the museum and stuck around for a while, perhaps to make sure I was friendly. After saying hello, Jack took me inside an old white building, with its outside paint peeling away. There was nothing fancy about it, save for the hand-drawn sign on its side that included crossed mining picks, shovels, and a helmet with a lamp on it. Inside, it was the kind of organized chaos that I had come to recognize in the region, a passion project realized with a solitary vision and little money.

Jack was well into his eighties, and despite being unable to move around easily, he was full of life. He wore a neatly pressed shirt, gray slacks, and a baseball cap with a Mining Museum patch on the front. He enthusiastically showed me old mining equipment, clothing, helmets, photos, and memorabilia. When I inquired about a particular photograph on the wall, he took it down and insisted on giving it to me.

I asked about any films that Jack might have. He first shared with me copies of a series of films from the local resident Jack Simon, made in the 1950s. They were silent and in color. They showed everyday life in the town. I could see right away that the subjects of the films—people on the street walking up to the camera—knew and trusted Simon. Their faces revealed smiles and a comfortable familiarity. Even though Simon was an amateur, this camaraderie between photographer and subjects was remarkable to see. Jack simply handed the copies of the films to me, saying it would be better for me to have them than him. It was certainly an unusual move for a museum to give its objects away! In hindsight, I think Jack was a trusting and perceptive person and was happy to share with anyone who sought out his stories and museum.

Finally, I asked Jack if he might know of any early mining films from the region. He took me into a back room and dug through a drawer. Producing a single VHS tape, he handed it to me and said, "Well, this is either the oldest mining footage I've ever seen—from 1910 or maybe earlier—or I may have accidentally taped over it with a show from the History Channel." He went on to tell me that the original film reels had been lost. He gave the tape to me, and I thanked him. I was amazed at his generosity.

We stepped outside, and he took me across the street to an empty lot full of weeds, rubble, and brush. "This is where an old bar stood," he said. "At one time, they used to have a dozen bars in Murray City, one for every church!" I paused to look at the lot, and I started to see a footprint of the building. On the ground, there were hundreds of tiny ceramic circles. They were the last remnants of a colorful mosaic floor, now partially covered with dirt and slipping back into the ground. In my mind, I could see the building: a honky-tonk filled with smoke and music and the sounds of glass and laughter.

Mildred returned in their pristine, decades-old sedan. She and Jack both insisted that I join them for lunch. So, I followed them to their house, only a few blocks away. Murray City is a fraction of the size it once was, and it, like many of the Little Cities, has struggled economically for many decades. There are run-down buildings and unkempt houses, and the streets have the worn look of an old town. So, it was a shock to arrive at the Shuttleworths' fastidiously neat house, situated in the middle of a struggling neighborhood. There was a picket fence, and the yard was perfectly trimmed (later, I noticed that it may have been artificial grass). Jack and Mildred were by no means wealthy; they just took care of their house and property in a way that contrasted shockingly with their surroundings.

We went inside, and Jack offered me coffee. It had a faint smell of sulfur from the well water. It was also strong, oil thick, and burned from being brewed early that morning and kept warm for hours (just like my father made it, incidentally). When we had been at the museum, Mildred had quietly gone to Miller's, a favorite restaurant in the region, and brought back fried chicken for us. The interior of the house reminded me of my childhood when I would visit my family in nearby Junction City. Everything felt worn and yet cared for. There was a pride in simple objects. Nothing was thrown away that could be used again for some new purpose.

We talked of family and of my parents' connections to the area. We also talked about Neva Randolph, an Affrilachian singer who had lived in town in the early and mid-twentieth century. I had listened to recordings of Neva more times that I can remember, each time marveling at her voice and the conversation around her. On one recording, "My Station's Gonna Change," Neva was ill and, according to the tape, was on her deathbed.[29] And yet, when she began to sing, she revived and sat up and became full of life again. Mildred and Jack remembered stories about Neva and noted that she had lived a few streets over from them. I was astonished to hear these details, and once again a recording—made sixty years before—became a conduit between the past and the present moment.

As I sat with this kind and generous couple in a tidy house in an old coal-mining town, I thought about the many connections I had made with people living in the region. From that first soundwalk in Shawnee, I knew there was something special there, something I felt deeply but could not yet identify. And then working in the local archives and stumbling on my grandfather's yearbooks sent a shock through me, and I saw I was bound to this land in ways I hadn't known before. This recognition was only reinforced when I stood in the middle of the old Tecumseh Theater, imagining the daily lives of residents a century ago. And when I was given the box of audio tapes, the connections and insights became tangled in recorded sound; as I listened, I intimately came to know the voices of people who lived in the Little Cities. I learned their cadences, speech patterns, rhythms, and accents—and their music, too: of murder ballads, marching bands, jazz groups, and protest songs. All were lodged in my mind. The archival photographs and films only added to this knowledge. Together, they revealed a proud and complicated landscape of people living, working, dying, and sharing their stories. I found that over the years, I had been assembling my own archive, one so mixed up with family and history that they were blurred together, were one in the same. Sitting with Jack and Mildred, I realized I was experiencing something beyond research. I was seeking and finding connection: real connection with people and with the land. I hadn't admitted it out loud yet, but somewhere inside I also knew I was preparing to join these experiences together, to begin working on *Shawnee, Ohio*.

CHAPTER SIX

Performing *Shawnee, Ohio*

Putting It Together

It took six years of listening, research, scholarly writing, and meeting with residents before I could figure out how to make *Shawnee, Ohio*. During that time, my creative process shifted once again: I slowed down, paid closer attention, took in more details, and waited for the right moment. Unlike the Berea Archives or the Sun Ra Collection, I had to first define what the sound archive was, and then help preserve it, before I could think about performing it. I also recognized I was no longer working with archival materials alone; instead, it was an entire town, or even many towns, with complex histories that intersected, overlapped, and were still in motion, evolving.

After those years, I was itching to begin composing music to accompany the archival tapes; I had waited as long as I could. In hindsight, it seems absurd for me to take so long to complete a music project, but I am glad I did. It allowed the material to develop organically and in collaboration with local residents. My understanding of the archival recordings became more nuanced.

This process also changed how I thought about audiences. I began to consider the communities I had been working with. I thought of our friendships as I was composing. I found myself imagining them sitting in a theater and listening to the music and voices. I wondered what music I could make that would satisfy both the interests of the towns' residents and my own. The simple act of asking these questions changed and molded the music I made.

Years later, I was at a festival of new music. I began talking with another composer about writing music based on material from a specific community. The composer said to me, "I have to ignore what any audience might think. I can only write for myself, and if they like it, that's great; and if they don't like it, so be it." I understood this rationale, and depending on the project, I use it myself. As I stood there, however, I realized I could no longer think this way with the communities in Appalachian Ohio. If I earn the trust of residents, and they share their music and history with me, we are now in a relationship with one another. They have become my main audience. I cannot think about myself alone or an abstract audience. Instead, the music becomes a medium for a living, concrete exchange between us.[1]

This conversation helped clarify my role within the town of Shawnee. Once again, I found myself deliberately creating ties to a community and anchoring my creative projects there. I did not want my work to be detached. Instead, I wanted it to find a balance: a connected interdependence. I wanted it to touch the people who had touched me with their stories.

What does it mean, then, to say that a community can become a project's cocreator? In this case, it began with the relationships and the trust that emerged over time. Each of the people I have already mentioned, and more—John Winnenberg, Cheryl Blosser, Jack Shuttleworth, Skip Ricketts, and Ivan Tribe—offered their input on the project. As I gathered material, residents shared their stories, helped me choose which recordings and photographs to use, and pointed me to the music made there over the years. And while I worked alone on composing the new music, I did share it with residents for their feedback, making sure that I had not misinterpreted their contributions. In fact, I always kept them in mind as I worked. And finally, I found small ways to give back to the community—volunteering at the Little Cities Archive, helping with community events, digitizing and returning the recordings, bringing copies of the finished music and writings to share, and even spending a year as an AmeriCorps volunteer in Shawnee—so that our relationships were based on exchange and I was not only taking materials from them. I saw these activities as part of my responsibility toward a community.

Sometimes I felt lost, as if the larger goal of collaborative work swallowed up my own identity. In fact, when I spoke to my former teacher Michael Finnissy about it, he was concerned for me, that I might lose my creative voice at the expense of others. And yet, I gradually noticed I still had much to offer. I shared insights on issues, people, the past, and the current moment, all from the perspective of an artist. And because I was an outsider, I could listen to others and present a new approach. I could also help with retelling the stories of the region through music and tap into what was common between us in our shared human experience.

Preparing to make *Shawnee, Ohio* was a process of gathering, finding, seeking, fumbling, learning, and listening. During this time, I was occasionally corresponding with the artist and musician Steve Roden. In one email to me, he said, "Value is not inherent—it is awakened!" This resonated with me. I understood how the archival materials could be overwhelming or confusing. It was not always easy to see how they might come together to make something coherent. Roden reminded me of my role in this process: to listen, to witness, to interact, and then to "awaken" the materials so they could be absorbed and inspiring to a new audience of listeners.

Obviously, the audio tapes were at the heart of the project, alongside my grandfather Mordecai's yearbooks, my own field recordings, and archival photos and film. Together, the sounds, music, words, and images created a map of the town. In working with this material, my guiding principle was to always pay attention to its physical and emotional content: Does it affect me? Does it move me? Does it make me feel? I once again thought of Roland Barthes's concept of "punctum," a photographic image that inexplicably moves us, or "pierces" us.[2] I applied it not only to the archival photographs but also to the films and recordings.

Some photos—such as the one of Mordecai's high school orchestra—offered clues for the album's instrumentation. Here, we see Mordecai holding an alto saxophone. The other students are playing piano, strings, brass, and percussion. For *Shawnee, Ohio*, I chose several of these instruments and added bass clarinet, banjo, and vibraphone to the ensemble. Other photos—of concerts, graduations, and event programs—showed the styles of music played at the time, which was more varied than what one might think of for Appalachian music. This included popular tunes from the 1910s and 1920s, such as "Rose in the Bud," "The End of a Perfect Day," and "Memory's Garden." I also came across labor tunes, going back to the nineteenth century, such as "Come Join the Knights of Labor" or "Eight Hours," a song about the fight for a standard workday (I especially enjoyed the lyrics "Eight hours for work / Eight hours for rest / Eight hours for what we will"). I transcribed these recordings and identified fragments that caught my ear. I would then turn the transcriptions into short patterns and riffs that could form the basis of the new pieces. Now, each aspect of the music had its own logic, it had roots. This new music was born from and connected to the music that residents listened to a century ago or more. It was then turned into something altogether different and combined with the stories and voices from the archival recordings.

I thought of *Shawnee, Ohio* as if it were a novel. Specifically, I used Sherwood Anderson's aptly named *Winesburg, Ohio* as a loose model for the project. The book, published in 1919 (exactly a century before *Shawnee, Ohio*), is organized as a series of short, interconnected stories that are not overly reliant on plot. Each story is powerful by itself, and yet the whole becomes greater than the sum of its parts. I applied this strategy to *Shawnee*, with each track as a portrait of a local resident. Since this was an album and not a novel, however, I also focused on the "noisy memory" of those who were recorded and the music that moved around and alongside the voices. In

The Shawnee High School orchestra in 1924. Harnetty's grandfather Mordecai Williams is holding an alto saxophone and standing in the back row, sixth from the right. Mordecai's brother William is standing to our left of him. Photo courtesy of the author.

addition, I deliberately avoided Anderson's concept of his characters being "grotesques," which always made me feel as if he distorted them solely to suit his own needs, rather than letting them speak for themselves, too.

I also thought of *Shawnee, Ohio* as a companion album to *Silent City*. This time, it would be a project that focused on my maternal grandfather's hometown instead of my father's; yet it would remain in the same area, Perry County. Once again, this approach harkens back to the idea that "place" can become a connector between the albums; they are interrelated but without an overarching plot or scheme.

I began to focus on eleven portraits, each named after a person who lived or lives in the area. In their own voices, we hear about events from everyday people—birth, relationships, work, death—directly and without mediation. These people speak in their own voices, unrehearsed. They talk and sing of mining, disasters, murders, social life, protest, and hope. They include women and men, are Black and white, are not famous or wealthy, and span across generations and centuries. Their agenda is to share, remember, learn, and find ways to move forward.

The portraits were brought together with the same techniques I had been developing over previous recording projects. After choosing the instrumentation and the musical material, I gave newly composed melodic fragments to the performers. They, in turn, recorded themselves three times: first, as a straightforward rendering of the written notes; second, with slight alterations (such as octave transpositions, rests, or rhythmic changes); and third, with additional improvised elements that go further afield (such as experiments with texture or extended techniques). Then, the musicians sent their recordings back to me. As with earlier projects, these recordings became a second archive, one full of both familiarity and the excitement of the unknown.

My workflow for each portrait took on a regular pattern. I first gathered material, including samples, scores, text, historical documents, and field recordings. I then composed parts based on the material, which the musicians recorded. Once I had the new instrumental recordings, I cleaned up each part, focusing on tuning, timing, rhythms, extra noise, and equalization. Then, I collaged the parts and lines into a music portrait, creating a structure that revolved around the voice. Next, I placed each portrait in relation to the others. I focused on the global structure and the different tempos and ensured there was variety and flow between each piece (this part of the process often felt like I was making a mixtape, like the ones I and so many others used to make as teenagers). At this point, I would share the recordings with friends and community members; their feedback provided essential insight into the pieces, insight that I would have otherwise missed.[3] And finally, the mixing and mastering took place, offering one last chance for adjustments. I also drew maps of each portrait: of its instruments, shape, and textures and how they unfolded.

Only after this process would I make a musical score for the project, so that we could perform it live. This seems like a backward way of composing music! But for me, it meant that I was always prioritizing sound—of the archival recordings and of the instruments—over a concept or the score's appearance. And listening was placed at the forefront of each stage, from the earliest conversations with residents to archival research to composing and recording and even during performance.

Jim Bath

To organize the portraits, I placed them into one of three themes: "Town and People," "Mining and Disaster," and "Protest and Hope." The two categories of each theme felt like different sides of the same coin: you cannot have a

The cassette tape of Jim Bath. Photo courtesy of the author.

town without its people, mining without disaster, or protest without hope. These themes not only shared many of the central tenets of the history of Shawnee since the 1870s but also contained a built-in expressive arc, moving from everyday life in the town to the people's jobs and hardships to the ways in which the residents made their voices and dreams for the future heard.

It seemed fitting to begin *Shawnee, Ohio* with a recording of Jim Bath, a local resident.[4] The recording is from the 1980s, and on it, Jim remembers the Main Street of Shawnee as a child, building by building. He also recalls the names of each shop owner: Yank Hartson, Hazel Matthews, and Doc Hill. As I listen, I can see the street in my mind, bustling with people. I can also imagine Jim finding each place and person in the depth of his waxing and waning memory. There is something about his voice and demeanor that capture the languid, earnest atmosphere of the town.

As the recording begins, the first thing we hear is the noisy old tape, full of distortion and hiss; the recording itself becomes one of the characters in the story. The interviewer Dot Dishon begins the conversation, asking, "What, uh, what did you do when you was a kid growing up that you had the most fun doing?"

> JIM: Well, I uh, told you. Playing basketball and shooting marbles and knocking the can and stuff like that.

DOT: What did you do on Saturday night as a teenager, growing up?
JIM: Uh, I used to like to get out, out on my grandmother's and grandfather's front porch and watch the people go up and down Main Street.

The piano sets the musical accompaniment in motion with a two-note repeating pattern. When I first imagined what this piece might sound like, I thought of Jim's description of the buildings, and I made the tempo of the music match a leisurely walk down Main Street. In fact, I used my own field recording of a soundwalk in Shawnee as a guide, and I matched the music to the tempo of my stride and the time it took me to cross the town. This field recording was eventually removed, but it helped provide the framework for the piece until the piano and other instruments captured the right tenor to match it. I also knew that this initial melodic pattern needed to be as simple as possible. Anything virtuosic or emotive would only distract from the mood the recorded voices and tape already established. The slowly repeating notes of the piano continue with variation until the end and offer a clear starting point for the rest of the music and album to develop. As more instruments join in—saxophone, viola, cello, and bass clarinet—they each have their own rhythmic and melodic patterns, sometimes independent, sometimes together. Jim continues:

Believe it or not, on a Saturday night, the people in town—the town was crowded. But then you had, uh, you had . . . Senator's was a restaurant. Then you come on down, then you had, uh, Peytons had a Red and White store. You come on down, and Yank Hartson had a store for various things. Come on down to Eddie Welch's or Charles Welch's, and he had a little bit of everything in that store. It was mainly, uh, mining supplies and feed. But he had a lot of other stuff in there, too. And if you went in there and asked for something, and he didn't have it, he'd probably have it in there in the next week or two, like pottery and different things like that.

Uh, but I would be up there on the front porch. The fire station was knocked down there. There was, uh, Nicolas's store. It was still standing, maybe. It might have fallen down by the time you get this printed, but right now it is still standing. And then you, uh, there was another building in there, Daugherty's. They had a music store in there at one time. And then when the bar across the street burned out, they moved the bar—and the music store had been out of business for years—they moved the bar in there. Uh, Hazel Matthews, that was before she bought the bank and moved everything up to the bank.

And then, the next building to us was the funeral home and furniture store, mainly a funeral home and the furniture on the side. Sam Coin was the owner of it, and Doc Hill was the undertaker from, uh, Zanesville. He's dead now. He came into Shawnee, and he met and married the Richards girl in Shawnee, here.

And uh, he, uh, and then there was my grandfather's two buildings. And then there was, uh, at one time, years ago, there was a real jewelry shop. It was in the other building that burnt, Dogherty's side. Shore, Mrs. Shore had a jewelry store in there. Up there in Hannah's building was a restaurant, and it was run by, uh, oh shoot, he's from Hemlock, and Peyton's.

As Jim tells his story, I feel as if I am there with him. I hear the grain of his voice—old, gravely, matter of fact, full of character, with a slight speech impediment and a vernacular tone revealing his Appalachian roots. I imagine how he must have walked to school or to the store or how he might have strolled down the street slowly on a Saturday night with a date.

The video for "Jim" begins with a series of archival photos of Shawnee, black and white, or sepia toned. The photos progressively reveal the town's landscape of buildings, houses, and churches ascending the hill, up to the water tower. Then, a view of Main Street from about 1910—of restaurants and storefronts, carriages and young children, lamp posts and balconies—transforms into a contemporary video shot from the same place. My friend and photographer Jonathan Johnson and I stood in the middle of the street, positioning the camera so it would see Shawnee from the exact spot as in the earlier photograph. The new video shows that many of the buildings are gone, the carriages are replaced with cars, and what was once a barren hill in the background is now covered with green forest. The video is still, but the longer one looks, small details emerge: slowly floating clouds, subtle shifting light, an American flag gently moving, a faint breeze. This transition happens several more times throughout the piece, and the effect is one of disorienting jumps in time, where past and present do not feel quite so far apart anymore.

Near the end of "Jim," the video switches to a series of Johnson's photographic details of Shawnee buildings: salt-fired bricks and peeling blue paint, angular lines and warped wood, and shadows that mirror and distort. Here, the saxophone—played by my friend and composer Jeremy

Woodruff—breaks free of its patterns and begins a thoughtfully improvised solo, loping and bending, melancholic. I love this solo. To my mind, it completely captures the spirit of the music and video. It makes me imagine my grandfather soulfully playing the saxophone, and it instantly connects me to him and to the town. As the last still image of Main Street returns to the past, the passage of time leaves me disoriented and confused, and the aesthetic pleasure of the photographs, alongside the irrecoverable loss of family, the unsettling awareness of mining's destruction on the land, and the inevitable process of death and decay, are all acknowledged and made audible with the saxophone's mournful line.

I wish I had composed this piece just so; but in truth, its elements came together as if they were gifts. This is the magic of working with archives and with focusing on community, collaboration, and listening. The archival recordings, contemporary video, and musicians' performances presented many details and elements outside of my control, which turned out to be the most profound moments of the piece. I was merely there to collect, arrange, and join them and to marvel at how they fit together.

Boy

"Boy" is the second track of the album, and it features my friend Anna Roberts-Gevalt playing the banjo. Shortly after she begins, we hear the click and hiss of tape, and an anonymous boy states, "May third. I'm going to ask my grandma questions of the olden days. Um, Grandma? In the mines, um, do you know how many people died?"[5] A second banjo joins in. I had given Anna two different melodic patterns to record, and she freely improvises with both. They are in counterpoint, circling around the looping melodies. The boy continues: "Um, do you know anybody that was in the mines? Uh, can you tell me three people? Can you name 'em? Yeah, yeah, yeah." Piano, vibraphone, violin, and viola enter, playing bell-like long tones. They do not stay for long, however, and the boy continues his unanswered questions: "Who else? Sean Henton? Oh. Do you know a couple people that died in the mines? Can you name 'em, too?"

This back-and-forth process between the banjos and the rest of the ensemble becomes a feature of the piece. The texture thickens and thins accordingly, so that we can clearly hear the boy's words. With spoken text, it is too easy for the words to become obscured, or the music can become too distracting. I often found myself taking more and more parts out in service of the story. I did not want the vernacular grain of the voice to get lost in the music. The boy continues: "Uh, okay, uh, when you was little, what kind of chores did you have? Um, did you ever wash on a washboard? You did? Did you ever feed the cows and the yard animals? What about the other animals? Uh . . ." As he trails off, the entire ensemble enters. By design, the harmony of the piece stays static. As with the music's texture, frequently shifting harmonies can distract from both the voice and the sonic atmosphere. What some may see as a defect, or a too-simple harmonic language, to me is a central part of each piece's structure; it keeps the listener's focus on the archival recordings and allows more of their details to shine through.

At this point, the music thins out one more time, and the boy finishes his questions: "Did your dad work in the mines? How much did he get a day? A dollar? Uh, well, I hope you give me an A, Mr. John Winnenberg. Thanks for letting me do this. Bye." When the boy mentions "Mr. John Winnenberg," I always laugh; this is the same John who provided the box of tapes to me all those years ago. It must have been for a class assignment (John couldn't remember who the boy was, when I asked him). The piece ends as it began, with a solo banjo, still working within the given melodic pattern yet also imbuing a feeling of moving toward an ending and a slight, unsettled melancholia.

When I first heard this archival tape, I was confused. On it, the boy—perhaps ten or eleven—is asking his grandmother about the "olden days," coal mining, everyday life, and miners who died. But often I couldn't hear the grandmother's answers. I thought she might merely be reticent or reluctant to be recorded. After listening again, I guessed that the boy must have placed the tape recorder near himself and away from her. The effect is ghostlike, and we are left wondering what her answers might be. However, this turned out to be one of the most interesting recordings in the collection, for this very reason. What I originally thought was a defect in the tape or just a poor recording now became a feature. The more I listened, I found myself wondering about the grandmother's life, and the absence of her voice only made my intrigue and curiosity stronger.

The video for "Boy" is made entirely out of archival photos and film. If "Jim" is focused on the town and its buildings, then "Boy" is exclusively portraits of people. We see a grandmother, a paperboy, couples, miners, a family out for lunch after church, children dancing in a circle to "Ring around the Rosie," a group of old ladies laughing, factory workers posing in front of their equipment, class pictures of Black and white grade-school children, church groups, a meter man, a gas man, baseball players, bikers, farmers, old ladies with shawls, and old men in suits that have become too large on their shriveled frames. In these portraits, every person is aware of the camera. Most are looking directly at it. We look at the people of this region, and they are looking back at us.

The video is formal and follows its own additive logic. It begins with single portraits of people, both in still images and in film. Then we see two people, then three—and steadily more and more are added until there are large groups. Then, as the music recedes, so do the images, quickly reverting back to twos and threes and finally a single young girl breathlessly running toward the camera. Throughout, the video does not correspond directly to what the boy is describing; instead, it is telling its own story, related and overlapping, which adds to the complexity of the region. And yet, I cannot help but hear the boy's questions and then connect them to the people in the video. How many of these people died in the mines? Did they know three people who died in the mines? Could they name 'em?

Judd Matheney

"Could I tell you a little story about that?" asks Joshua "Judd" Matheney on one of the archival recordings.[6] This recording begins part 2 of *Shawnee, Ohio*, which is focused on mining and its related disasters. The recording was made in 1988, and on it, Matheney speaks of his family, childhood, and work as a state mine inspector. His voice is deep and melodic, and its grain reveals his age and regional accent. The recording makes audible an unstable and changing past, and Judd's voice moves through time to meet us in the present. Judd describes working in the mines and a typical day of loading coal. He also speaks of his experiences as an inspector and of getting along with men and women working in small family mining operations, mines often located on private property. "I didn't crowd the law on them too bad," he states.

When it came time to compose the music for "Judd," I knew it needed to be related to his work in the mines. I adapted a melodic phrase from "Hold the Fort," a nineteenth-century Knights of Labor song. The recording begins with bass clarinet and piano offering a simple waltz-like melody, which becomes the foundation of the piece. Once again, I found myself creating music to complement the speaker's voice: both formal and conversational and firmly between a sense of pride and wistful storytelling.

The video for "Judd" makes use of the archival film Jack Shuttleworth gave to me of mining at Sunday Creek Mine Number 5. The footage could be from as early as the first decade of the twentieth century. At both the beginning and ending of the piece, what at first appears to be abstract white circles on a grainy black background in fact becomes the reflected light from miners' carbide helmets deep in the mines. Then, a flash of light illuminates the space, and we see a mine car on tracks coming toward us, sparking and blazing as it passes. An unknown interviewer begins the conversation, asking, "Judd, what is your full name, just for the tape, so we have it for the record?" "My full name is Joshua Edward Matheney," he responds. "Very few people know me by Joshua, though. Judd is much easier to say." Here, vibraphone and violin strike long notes that add to the lilting piano, and a viola plays a rhythm that makes the waltz slightly out of sync.

The imagery periodically reveals its own history, too, and we see remnants of it being a film, then copied to VHS, and finally digitized. Rather than erase that history—of frayed edges, distortion, tape warble, and the occasional "PLAY" indicator in the top corner—I decided to let it remain, each layer adding to its visual story. The interview continues:

> INTERVIEWER: What did your father do? Where did he work at?
> JUDD: My father was a miner.
> INTERVIEWER: He was a coal miner?
> JUDD: He was inclined toward farming. He enjoyed farming very much, but he owned no land or anything. He, uh, would plant every foot of ground he could have access to, but living on company ground, like we did, it was very limited.
> INTERVIEWER: Now, do you—did he ever own land himself, own a farm?
> JUDD: Never owned a foot of ground in his life.
> INTERVIEWER: I see.

I notice a sadness in Judd's voice. It must have been difficult for his father, who desired to farm but was forced to spend his life underground. Then Judd continues, describing the tension between him and his father over working in the mines:

> INTERVIEWER: When did you start working, uh, Judd, when did you start . . .
> JUDD: In 19 . . .
> INTERVIEWER: . . . working at a job?
> JUDD: In 1928, when I finished, uh, high school at Murray City. And my father never wanted me to work in the mines. He, uh, worked . . .

insisted against it all of the time. If this story isn't gettin' too long, why . . .

INTERVIEWER: Oh, no!

The saxophone prominently plays a melody as the entire ensemble comes together. The video continues with old footage of a coal tipple and miners exiting from their underground tunnels in twos and threes and alongside their ponies and mules, which reminds me of the Lumière brothers' famous films of workers leaving factories in France. I was so drawn to this grainy and out-of-focus footage that I found myself pausing it often, trying to catch a glimpse of the miners' faces: old or young, mustachioed or covered with soot, hardened or smiling. As I assembled the film for the piece, I decided to formally incorporate this instinctive process, and I created short pauses in the video every time I felt the desire to linger on a person's face. This only added to the asymmetrical rhythms of the music, creating a complementary visual cadence. The process reminded me of the relentless searching and exploration of archival film in the work of the filmmaker Ken Jacobs. Jacobs once noted that he was determined to "get to the grain" of the film, and after working with this archival footage, I understood his sentiment. But I also felt an intense desire to get to the people, to see them and their lives and contexts with as much intensity and clarity as possible and to let their humanity move me.

Now, Judd tells a story of "sounding" the roof of a mine with a pick to check for safety:

JUDD: I was working Carbondale Number 2.

INTERVIEWER: Yeah?

JUDD: Yup. Hand loading.

INTERVIEWER: You were hand loading there.

JUDD: Could I tell you a little story about that?

INTERVIEWER: Yeah, I'd love anything. That's the thing I'd like to have.

JUDD: I went in a little mine up Pittsburgh Holler one day, a couple of men working by themselves. And I looked up at the roof, and there was just like a circle around it. And I said, "Fellas, what do you got up there?" And they said, "Ohhh, they call 'em 'pots,' but it's all right." And I said, "Let me have your pick a moment." And, uh, I sounded it with a pick, a customary way of checking the roof. And it sounded a little drummy, and I said, "Fellas, I believe that's dangerous." "Ahh, no, don't think so." "Let me have your bar for a moment." One of 'em handed me a pinch bar, and I pinched a little bit and finally got a pretty solid hole. I chipped in, gave a good pry on it, and there was big circle of slate, at least six foot across, and there was this cone shape. It would've mashed those two men easily, if they'd . . .

Judd's voice briefly trails off. It is as if you can almost hear the thought passing through his mind, of what might have happened either to those overly confident miners or to himself if that cone had fallen on them. The music follows this cue, becoming sparse and allowing Judd's story to breathe. The pauses and silences between the words take on meaning, offering chances for the listener to reflect. The "drummy" quality of the roof indicated—to Matheney's trained ear—an unsafe mine. The author Hillel Schwartz refers to this process of "sounding" the roof of mines as "jowling," a term used in the United Kingdom and dating back to early coal mining there.[7] Matheney's ability to listen to the mines as well as to the people operating them served as a means of not only maintaining mine safety but also building a rapport with miners in the region over his lifetime.

At the end of the piece, the music disappears, and we are left with Judd alone and finishing his story, with a plaintive tone and an old-fashioned turn of phrase: "Of course, all men didn't escape them kind of conditions. Many men got tangled up with them and lost their lives."

Sigmund Kozma

In 1930, an explosion at the Millfield Mine Number 6 killed eighty-two miners and became the worst mining disaster in Ohio. When I read accounts of the explosion from the Little Cities Archive, it became apparent that the Millfield disaster was not only a scene of death and destruction but also an intensely sonic event. These accounts depict a vivid yet troubling soundscape ranging from mayhem to stunned silence.

In the days following the explosion, newspaper headlines and photographs reverberated throughout the country and portrayed it repeatedly in sonic terms. "We had just started to work when there was a terrific noise and a wall of flame," reported Walter Porter, a miner in the explosion.[8] Other miners offered testimonies that described the pressure of the explosion followed by yelling and commotion. *The Dayton Daily News* reported, "Rasp said he was blown almost 100 feet from the place where he had been standing by the force of the explosion. He heard a roaring noise and then the shouts of his fellow underground prisoners."[9] Grief and silence later followed the initial chaos of the explosion at Millfield. *The Dayton Daily News* reported,

"A silent crowd of women and children whose husbands and fathers met death stood throughout the night, hoping against hope that their loved ones had escaped the choking gas, but broke into tears when body after body was brought to the surface in a cage that dropped down into the depths of the mine."[10]

Sigmund Kozma, who died in 2009 at the age of ninety-seven, was the last living survivor of the Millfield Mine disaster. His story is both a lament of the past and a cautionary tale for today. During an interview for Justin Zimmerman's 2008 film *Meeting Again*, Kozma recalled being in the mine at the time of the explosion: "We went down inside the mine. . . . So, we heard through there. The way we noticed it is a—a pressure came on our ears. I said, 'Dad, what was that?' He said, 'That was an explosion.'"[11]

In a related article from *The Athens News*, Kozma further expands on the physical experience of the explosion as a wave. He states, "We were loading a coal car, and we felt the pressure (much like diving) and then it was released. All you could hear was the force of air (in your ears). There was no sound of an explosion. . . . The force of the explosion hit them and rolled them. . . . As long as we had good air we would have lived. We followed where the good air was leading us."[12] Kozma's two descriptions impart the physical impact that the explosion had. There must have been a tremendous emotional impact as well.

Heard together, these reports of confusion, screaming, crying, and grief depict a series of sonic shock waves spreading out across the region in the explosion's aftermath. This sonic boom did not end when its sound waves exited the mine. Instead, it continued on in a series of sounds, testimonies, and social waves that were all in direct relationship to it. They can be heard in the absence of those who died, in new friendships formed out of grief, or in the memories handed down to subsequent generations. The explosion sonically altered the soundscape of Millfield and continues to resonate today.

When I began composing new music to accompany Sigmund's interview, I carried this knowledge and sadness with me. Sigmund's words became more than an individual recollection. They were a story for the entire region and its history of damage to its land and people. The film for the piece begins with a close-up image of Sigmund, speaking unaccompanied. It is delightful to witness Sigmund's kindness, expressiveness, and innate charm as he speaks. At the same time, it is harrowing to hear his story as he describes the events from that day. "It's just the enormity of the thing," he begins. "After we got outside and realized how bad it was and, uh, how many friends—almost every man in there was of course a friend of mine. There were a few that I was more acquainted with than others, but—some of those people that I grew up with and I went to school and played with and worked with and everything, and it was just—it was just hard to realize that they were gone."

The music enters with long, pensive chords based on a fragment from "Rose in the Bud," a song performed at Shawnee's high school graduation in the 1920s. The accompanying instruments have a still, mourning feeling, without any vibrato. Visually, excerpts of Sigmund's interview are contrasted with archival photos and newspaper reports from the explosion. Throughout, Sigmund's voice and image, the music, and the archival documents each tell a different side to the story. Sigmund resumes as the photographs slowly unfold:

> Immediately after the explosion, it was chaos, as you can imagine, because so many of the families had lost a member of the family in the explosion. And of course, you know how even when one person dies, the rest of the neighbors and the friends and relatives and all those are all—they, they try to support them the best way they can. But when there's so many, so much of it, so many of it, you can imagine what a chaotic time that was in that town, in that camp. It was just a terrible. . . . It was so huge, so much death and so huge that it was, um, everybody was numb for weeks.
>
> But, of course, eventually—mining towns being what they are and how they're situated and everything and as far as work and living is concerned—things get back to normal. The mines opened up again, and they started working. And eventually, gradually, why, people begin to live normal lives. Miners' lives, coal miners' lives.
>
> And, uh, I don't know, you, you, kind of get a—a kind of numbness or something. It's not that you get insensitive, but you just don't . . . It's just hard to realize that everywhere you look—you look around through the camp—and almost every house was touched by death.

One archival photograph powerfully illustrates the event. *People at Millfield Mine Disaster* shows a loud, chaotic scene: hundreds of people are crowded around a building, jostling to see if their family members are alive, anxiously awaiting any news. Others—perhaps journalists—are standing about, talking with one another. The piece switches back to Sigmund's interview, and he continues, "And, uh, it's just like I say, you get kinda numb to the fact that there were so many dead people in one place like that and that it happened that suddenly. That was the thing that bothered me more than anything. It was hard to realize that could occur like that, young as I was."

At the end, we are left with flute and bass clarinet, each somber in tone. Their melodies are separated and broken, moving slowly in tension with each other. One last image is shown, of uniformed men carrying one of the victims out of the mine. The men are young, and their candid stares are haunting as they look directly at the camera.

Jack Wright

Part 3 of *Shawnee, Ohio* focuses on the themes of protest and hope. It begins with a portrait of Jack Wright, a local musician and filmmaker. Out of the eleven pieces on the album, the archival footage for "Jack" is the most recent, focusing not on the distant past but on current struggles. I was interested in Jack's work because he embodies both protest and hope; his serious yet optimistic efforts to protect the land in the forest show that you cannot have one without the other.

In 2012, nearly one hundred residents gathered outside the Wayne National Forest headquarters to speak out against proposed hydraulic fracturing (or "fracking") wells. Their purpose was to urge the forest authorities to delay issuing permits to drill wells on public lands and instead perform additional evaluations on the environmental impacts of fracking. Many of their concerns were related to environmental and economic damage to the region, including disruption of the watershed.

Jack Wright stood up in front of the group, holding a piece of paper.[13] "Fresh off the press," he said, to the laughter of the crowd. He began to sing a modified, unaccompanied version of the well-known Florence Reece song "Which Side Are You On?," which was originally written in response to striking coal miners in the 1930s. Wright sings,

> You rulers of the forest, this song to you I'll tell
> Do the impact study, save us from fracking hell
> Which side are you on, boys, which side are you on?
> Which side are you on, girls, which side are you on?
>
> Come all you good people, good news to you I'll tell
> If we stick together, we'll save our water wells
> Which side are you on, boys, which side are you on?
> Which side are you on, girls, which side are you on?

> We're fighting for the future and for our sons and daughters
> To make our world secure and leave them with clean water
> Which side are you on, boys, which side are you on?
> Which side are you on, girls, which side are you on?

After he finishes, Jack references a 1967 Billy Edd Wheeler song against strip mining, saying, "One more thing: they can't put it back!" This turns into a chant that the entire crowd repeats; each time it gets louder and with more force: "They can't put it back!" I loved hearing Jack's earnest voice and seeing his bravery in standing up to sing in front of a group of strangers.

Later, I talked with Jack to learn more about his experience at the protest. The idea to alter the song's lyrics came quickly, and Jack wanted to convey a clear message, just for that day. "My wife and I composed that song on the way to the gathering," he told me. "We knew what the issues were. We weren't experts, but we knew what was about to come down. My wife was driving, and we were making up the verses as we went, and I think I wrote it down on a paper bag. It wasn't something I set out to do. It was very spontaneous."

Jack's adjustments to the lyrics and creative reuse of the songs are part of a larger folk tradition of adapting music to fit a local place. In this case, it was the Wayne National Forest, including Shawnee and the Little Cities. The changes are also a form of musical borrowing with a historical awareness and stewardship. The lines of history for the Reece song go back further, however. The tune is based on a previous song, the Baptist hymn "Lay the Lily Low," or "Jack Munro." Jack's connection to the Florence Reece song is also personal, as he was able to meet and know her before her death in 1986. Taken together, Jack's performance was a deeply intimate way to speak out against a current issue. At the same time, he was embodying and connecting to the past, through song.

I understand Jack's new lyrics and singing as an archival performance, or as part of a continuum of archival performances. To change aspects of an older tune to fit a contemporary issue is to move through time and space in two directions at once. When Jack directly referenced fracking in the forest, he made a connection to the place where he was standing. It was a deliberate attempt to make regional, national, and global issues smaller, personal, and local. Jack's process of adaptation is also a way to absorb and comment on past and present issues at the same time, with each influencing and altering the other. It is a way to hold past experiences and present threats together.

Not only did Jack give voice to the people gathered to protest, but he also played the role of a mediator. He addressed the song both to the crowd and to the forest authorities. When Reece begins her version of the song, stating, "Come all of you good workers / Good news to you I'll tell," she is directly addressing the miners, urging them to join the union and imploring them not to become "scabs" (workers who cross a picket line). She continues to do so throughout the song, and it is clearly meant to help organize, inspire, and encourage the miners to stay unified in the face of violence from the coal companies. Jack, however, first addressed the people in power, the "rulers of the forest"—including the US Department of Agriculture Forest Service, Ohio Department of Natural Resources, and then-governor John Kasich—to directly ask them to go ahead with proposed environmental impact studies. When Jack then paraphrased the Reece lyrics, singing, "Come all you good people, good news to you I'll tell," he was opening his address to include both the people in power and those who were meeting that day to protest against the wells. In doing so, Jack was asking his fellow protesters to sing together and the forest officials to listen to and act on their request.

Threading throughout Jack's lyrics is the issue of water. In fact, water continues to be a central issue in the region, and it is even more so with the increase of fracking. Importantly, the fracking process not only makes use of millions of gallons of fresh water but also takes this water out of circulation: now contaminated, it is injected back down into spent oil wells. It can no longer be a part of the exchange between people and environment, unless its containment under the ground fails and it seeps back into the watershed as poison, replete with chemicals harmful to the ecosystem.

"Right now, it seems like the most pressing issue is fresh water and keeping our water clean," Wright commented to me. "I think there's some people that have this strange view of how the world is and how it works in terms of how mysterious water is [and] just how much we're all in the same boat. It horrifies me to think they can just shoot this poison back into the ground and nothing will ever happen to it. [They think] it will just be out of the way forever." Contaminating the water and taking it out of circulation is an act of silencing, removing its life-giving function and reducing it to poison. This silencing is also applied to political interaction connected to the water. Water flows, and money and influence flows, too. Once the water (or the voice of resistance, for that matter) is silenced, it is no longer able to be a part of the forest. Wright's warning, "You can't put it back!" takes on new meanings beyond its original protest against coal. Now, it refers to both the extraction of gas and the injection of the wastewater back into the wells.

"That was a good day," Jack said about the gathering at the Wayne National Forest headquarters. "I wish they could have listened a little bit clearer to what we had to say. We still have to insist that what we believe *be listened to*." His assessment of the event, tinged with a mix of emotions, points to the struggles of raising one's voice not only to be heard but to change the course of events. Singing became a forceful act of resistance, and listening was the hoped-for goal. Ultimately, however, federal officials deemed that the proposed fracking sites would be allowed, and the back-and-forth fight over the land's use continues to this day. "It was just for the moment," Jack told me, "to try to help get those people together and let the Wayne Forest people know we were there in force. If they could hear the force of the song and hear us shouting, that sort of made our crowd a little bit bigger. Even though in the long haul it didn't change their minds, at least they knew we were there to contend with their violations."

Neva Randolph

The last portrait in *Shawnee, Ohio* is of Neva Randolph, a singer from Murray City. She was the same person whom Jack and Mildred Shuttleworth had known, back in the 1950s. Neva's grandparents were freed slaves who settled in the nearby town of Logan.[14] She sang several songs for Anne Grimes in 1953, each with a religious theme, including, "After Death Judgment Will Find Your Soul," "You'll Go and I'll Go with You," and "Shine on Me." I found Neva's rendition of "My Station's Gonna Change" to be particularly moving. I appreciated the sense of hope embedded in the lyrics and her voice. I saw this as a metaphor of the resilience I encountered again and again of the residents of the region. It felt like a suitable song to end the project.

The recording begins with Anne telling the story of meeting Neva and recording with her.[15] I like how Anne rolls her *r* when pronouncing the number "three." Meanwhile, the video opens with slowed-down archival film. It must have been at the beginning of a spool, and it only shows an ever-shifting pallet of green-hued light along with the scratches, splices, and detritus of the film, like a found version of a Stan Brakhage film. Anne begins her introduction: "Murray City, Hocking County, November 1953. Mrs. Neva Randolph. When we went to her home, we found her sick in bed. In fact, her daughter and her neighbors thought it was her deathbed, and a number of people had come in. But she, before we left—although she had been down flat in bed when we went there—before we left, she was sitting up in bed, singing, and asked us to come back again."

When Neva begins to sing, my friend and musician Katie Porter joins her on bass clarinet. On the other Neva recordings, Anne Grimes sings harmony with Neva, and this gave me an idea: I loved the thought of singing (or playing) along with Neva across the decades, so I composed a short melodic pattern for Katie that feels related yet independent from Neva's voice.

The video shifts to a garden filled with colorful tulips blooming on a hopeful, sunny spring morning. The focus is on the flowers, but we also catch glimpses of people and houses, humble and proud. Neva begins to sing:

> Oh, the station's gonna be changed after 'while
> Oh, the station's gonna be changed after 'while
> When the Lord Himself shall come
> And shall say, "Your work is done"
> Oh, your station will be changed after 'while

The tape jumps in the middle of the verses. Some of the words are cut off, only to be added later. I decided to leave the tape alone and let its imperfections and skips become part of the piece.

Piano and then flute and viola join with the bass clarinet, adding new patterns to the music. With each repetition, the music ebbs and flows but also steadily increases in texture. The video now shifts to a series of archival and contemporary images, each shot in the same places, reminiscent of the opening minutes of "Jim." The photos steadily move through Shawnee today and then slowly return to the past. Neva sings,

> The gospel train is coming
> It's coming around the curve
> Stopping at every station
> After 'while
> When the Lord Himself shall come
> And shall—
> Straining every nerve
> Get your ticket ready
> Prepare to get on board
> For your station's gonna be changed after 'while

The music swells, and multiple piano and string lines spread out in stratified and augmented canons. Here, the film shifts once again. It returns to the spring flowers, but now they are roses, their deep red color saturated against the greens and purples of the leaves. The emotional content of the singing paired with the roses made me think of Bruce Baillie's experimental film *All My Life*, which contrasts red flowers with a soundtrack of Ella Fitzgerald. Here, however, it is a local resident's homemade film, spontaneously and proudly made on a bright spring day. Neva continues:

> Oh, your station's gonna be changed after 'while
> Oh, my station's gonna be changed after 'while
> When the Lord Himself shall come
> And shall say, "Your work is done"
> Oh, your station will be changed after 'while

The music recedes, and we are left with interlocking piano patterns as an accompaniment to Neva's final verse. Moments before she finishes the song, the music and video both abruptly stop, and we are left with Neva's last line amid the sounds of her room. The tape phases in and out, and as it is shut off, Anne whispers with astonishment, "Wonderful!"

I have watched and listened to this film and tape again and again, and each time, these last moments touch me deeply. I cannot help but think about the flowers and people, full of such color and vitality, and how they are now gone. I think about Neva and how the power of song seemingly brought her back to life from her deathbed. I think of the emotions rooted in her voice and how the tape captured and remembered them and her humanity. I could not imagine a better way to end this project—just as it began—with the unadulterated voices of extraordinary everyday people of Appalachian Ohio.

Performing at the Tecumseh Theater

In late October 2016, I traveled with my band to the town of Shawnee to perform at the Tecumseh Theater. It was a stunning fall day, and the eight of us had just finished a series of three performances of *Shawnee, Ohio* in Columbus, at the Wexner Center for the Arts. I was relieved and happy that the music worked (I am never fully sure if it will until it is over).

We arrived in Shawnee in the early afternoon. The other performers were excited to see the town. I felt a sense of pride in introducing them to the residents who showed up to help with the event. Our first task was to record a video upstairs in the old theater, the same room my grandfather Mordecai performed (and played basketball) in a century before. We set up on the floor, just below the stage, and recorded a live performance of "Boy." It was such a pleasure to perform there; it felt as if the building came alive, with the sounds of banjo and piano, strings and flute, bass clarinet and vibraphone echoing off the walls. As we performed,

Harnetty and ensemble performing "Boy" at the Tecumseh Theater in Shawnee, Ohio, in 2016. Photo courtesy of Kevin Davison.

I think it was fair to say that we felt what can only be described as an unadulterated joy.

Afterward, we returned downstairs to the ground floor. A group of local residents had set up a community potluck. As the audience walked into the building, they were greeted with the smells of homemade food, as well as the laughter and conversations from people enjoying each other's company. I was astonished at how many people were there; it felt like half of the village showed up! Even just moments before the performance, the band was happily eating and talking with residents, sipping coffee or beer, or vying for a last slice of homemade pie.

When the performance began, I still felt the relaxed spirit of a small country town. Any pretense of "high art" slipped away, and I no longer experienced the pressures of a formal performance in a fancy concert hall. This was more honest, to my mind, and more fun, too. I loved catching glimpses of the audience sitting only a few feet from me as we performed. In fact, the audience became an integral part of the evening. I would occasionally hear laughter or the shock of recognition as someone saw an old relative or perhaps even themselves. They were talking back to the video and music and, in an important way, completing it.

When the performance was over, everyone stayed. More food and drinks were passed around. We talked together as a group, to process what we saw and heard. Residents asked questions about certain photos: Where was that picture taken? Was that so-and-so? Was that your grandmother? "When I was young, I came into this space right here every Saturday night to see a picture show," said Skip Ricketts, a local resident who purchased the theater for $500 decades earlier. "It wasn't a movie; it was a picture show—and thank you for bringing back a Saturday-night picture show." John Winnenberg was there, too, and he chimed in, "This is the first time in fifty-six years that people sat here in a crowd and watched [together]."

The residents' comments and questions nearly brought me to tears. I have never experienced anything like that night, before or since. It stayed with me. In that moment, I saw differences between people vanish, momentarily, into a shared connection.

We drove home late in the evening, moving slowly through dark country roads to avoid any wayward deer. I couldn't stop thinking about the powerful connection that had taken place. It was an echo of my earlier creative process of returning to share a work with the community it is based on, but this time it felt different. It was celebratory and profound. I could see the interest and pride in the theater growing; I could feel the town responding to the performance, just as I had been responding to them.

That night planted a seed for all of the regional work I have done since. Later, I went on to do *Forest Listening Rooms* (2018–present), a socially engaged sound project focused on bridging differences between people and ending fracking on public lands. I also joined AmeriCorps for a year, helping to rebuild the economy and restore the ecology in the region. Now, I serve on the board of a local nonprofit in Shawnee called Sunday Creek Associates, which focuses on positive, equitable, and sustainable community development. Only a short time ago, I proudly introduced community members, politicians, architects, and construction workers in that same spot where we performed, to celebrate a community-led, multimillion-dollar refurbishment of the theater. In each of these endeavors, I see hope, a deepening of friendships, and a renewal of the exchange I witnessed all those years ago, on a beautiful October night in Shawnee.

CHAPTER SEVEN

Trappist, Kentucky: *Words and Silences*

Thinking Out Loud in a Hermitage

In 2017, I traveled again to Kentucky in search of recordings. This time, I visited the Thomas Merton Center in Louisville, which holds an archive of the Cistercian monk and writer Thomas Merton (1915–68). In 1941, Merton entered the Abbey of Gethsemani monastery, located near Bardstown, Kentucky. While there, he went on to write many books and become a celebrated author and spiritual leader. Later, he moved into a small hermitage on the grounds of the abbey and worked in solitude. I was attracted to the Merton Center, curious to explore the materials of his life: journal entries, photographs, drawings, books, a typewriter.

I listened to audio recordings, too, of lectures, talks, even Merton's funeral ceremony. I noticed that there was an outward, public quality to them. I kept listening, uncertain. I listened for different kinds of sounds: emotional sounds, environmental sounds, sounds that might betray a field or room, extra sounds beyond the message of the text. An archivist pointed me to reel-to-reel recordings Merton made in his hermitage during the spring of 1967, late in his life. *A hermit alone with a tape recorder is odd*, I thought. The tape began, and I heard something unusual, the first words fired off quickly and without pause or punctuation: "Okay now I hope we can go on recording like this I think it will stay down good let's go."[1]

There is a distinct delight in Merton's voice. He is not lecturing or pronouncing; instead, he is curious and experimental with the tape recorder. "I am abashed by it. I take back some of the things I have said about technology," I later read in Merton's journal dating from the same April day.[2] I listened closer: a clock was ticking, and the cinderblock room of the hermitage came alive in these recordings, made audible. I chose another tape and listened in. Merton was now recording outside, noting the birds he heard: "The sound of an unperplexed wren. No comment necessary . . . A cardinal, meadowlark, cardinal, flycatcher. Voice of the tape, a comment on the silence of the hermitage. The silence commented on also by birds."[3] There is no audience except Merton, and his candor and ease with the recorder is unsettling. I felt as if I were in the room with him.

I heard contradictions in Merton's words: voice and silence, comment and no comment, perplexity. I heard him creatively making use of the tape recorder. And I heard what the recorder reflected back to Merton and revealed to him. The tapes began to show something to me, too, twice removed and some fifty years later. I had an intuition that there was a project present in these tapes, one that might bring together the recordings with music as an archival performance, to bring Merton's interior voice out of the archive and into the world.

Playful Perplexity

Two years later, I was at an artist residency in Vermont. My studio—alone and up the road from the other artists—was a temporary hermitage. There was a piano, a desk, a chair, a coffee maker, and a place to sleep. An occasional car passed by. I listened to the Merton tapes again and again. The recordings filled the room. The windows were open, letting in summer air, a lone bee.

I began the tedious process of transcribing Merton's words on the tapes; there was no need to make choices about what to use, yet. I noticed that he was systematically moving through many texts—Sufi mystics, Michel Foucault, Samuel Beckett—and he offered commentary on and analysis of each, directly into the recorder. I also made note of the sounds I heard: creaking chairs, bells, laughter. Slowly an aural image of the hermitage took shape in my mind. I stayed as open as possible and listened for clues between the words, just after one thought and ahead of another. Or I listened for brief pauses where Merton didn't seem to know what to say (which was rare): breathing and silence, humor, laughter. I liked hearing him turn the recorder off after finishing a last thought; each time, the gesture felt definitive, sure.

There was something more: Merton was using the tape recorder as a creative, contemplative tool. This reminded me of the ways in which he used different media—writing, poetry, photography, drawing, and painting—to explore his own experimental, spiritual practice.[4] Each medium offers its own unique approach, each trying to reach for the same ineffable thing that can't quite be described: the silences between words, images just out of frame, sound beyond the tape.

Merton began to make brief field recordings, noting sounds around him. He listened to birds and rain and how sound carries from the monastery to

Photo of Thomas Merton standing in front of his newly built hermitage at the Abbey of Gethsemani in Trappist, Kentucky. Used with permission of the Merton Legacy Trust and the Thomas Merton Center at Bellarmine University.

the hermitage. During the night, he mused about recording far-off sounds of shooting at Fort Knox, wondering if the microphone could pick them up. Merton also used the tape recorder to experiment with language and his own voice. On one recording, he suggests, "To perhaps make a tape in which all the intonations are unfamiliar, in which I intone things in an unfamiliar, unacceptable way."[5] These words of curiosity point to the creative process. Throughout, Merton listened back to his own voice "to see how it sounds," to hear if the recordings could show him something new.

At other times, Merton read his own poetry and journals and the poetry of others. After he finished reading a Samuel Beckett poem, he commented that the words had "a strange effect, like a message of *spies*. Definitely affected by the media that we use."⁶ He then decided to listen back to the recording, connecting Beckett's poetry with his earlier musings on "perplexity" and silence and admiring the openness and "flatness" of the words heard aloud:

> Sounds very good. What it brings out is the monotony of the language and of the syntax evading complicated statements, simply stringing together nouns and adjectives and so on seems to emphasize the metaphysical silence behind the persons that he is talking about. And in the end, the silence is emphasized as being metaphysical. This is a piece that *does* manifest the silence. The perplexity is very subdued in it. And this is the right kind of perplexity. Not an emphatic perplexity but a subdued and deep awareness that everything is perplexed. And that in this getting back to a concrete elemental awareness of the things, without anything that we have added to them, without any comment of our own, seeing them in their bareness, their way of merging into each other, their flatness. Taking away the perspective that we have put into everything. Seeing them again as *flat*. Allowing them to make their own different perspective of something underneath which we have not presupposed, which we have not put there. Honest, Beckett.

Here, Merton was preoccupied with how Beckett's even and featureless language—arranged as a simple, stark mosaic—points to a silence behind the words. "Well, I think the tape will shake things up a bit," Merton later noted in his journal. "Read a bit of Beckett on tape and played it back—it was illuminating and helpful. Beautiful simplicity in drabness."⁷ It is this act of reading aloud into the recorder—and then listening back again—that makes this silence audible, known. I was reminded of another Samuel Beckett project: the short, one-person play *Krapp's Last Tape*, in which a solitary man at the end of his life speaks to himself through a tape recorder. Krapp listens back to his past, grasping for something in his own voice and the hiss of tape. I wondered if Merton could have known this play.

Sometimes there are moments when Merton used a more performative, formal "poetry voice," as is the case with this Beckett poem, and it made me laugh, uncomfortably. At other times, the recordings felt too intimate, too personal, as when Merton begins to sing with such earnestness that I shut the recording off. These moments reminded me that Merton's experimentation necessarily goes in many directions, each feeling for connection, never fully certain that it will work. I decided not to include these moments, instead choosing others before or after. In doing so, the main content of the recording is obscured, and I listen in at the periphery, where different things are revealed: anticipation, nervousness, confidence, curiosity, fatigue, calm, transformation.

This peripheral listening guided me as I sat with another tape, on which Merton improvises what he calls an "experimental jazz meditation."[8] Here, Merton speaks out against racial injustice happening in Louisville and across the country, and I realized that he is using the recorder in another new way: now it is a political, social tool. In the recording, it is late at night. Merton plays records of the organist Jimmy Smith and simultaneously records himself responding to the music, what he calls a "montage on jazz and bible." It is surprising to hear Merton's inventiveness, his openness to trying something new. I found myself drawn to brief periods of time when Merton seems to be at his most vulnerable, uncertain. Before the meditation, Merton offers an introduction: "There've been riots in Louisville for the last two or three days. The subject of the meditation is: Who are you identified with? It's not a meditation with points in the background. It'll speak for itself, and if I get some ideas, I'll speak them, too. If I don't get any ideas, I won't say anything. Outside the moon is full. It's very quiet here. In other parts of the world, people are being killed. We'll see what it sounds like." I listened to the clicking of the tape and the chill and quiet of darkness. I heard Merton's direct, short utterances, full of curiosity: he is preparing to dive in.

I continued to listen. As the meditation unfolds, I began to recognize a pattern, one used many times in these tapes and in Merton's journals, too. Throughout the recording, he states, "The moon is shining, and the wheels are turning." I noticed that he continually returns to the present and grounds himself in simple observations of the natural world; then, sufficiently anchored, he follows his creative impulses, the wheels turning in his mind. When Merton finishes the mediation, he continues: "After I got through recording that, I went out in the night. The beautiful smell of the grass, full moon. Cool. Dew on the grass. Dark. Lovely cold, quiet night. . . . Tonight is a very beautiful night, and I'm celebrating a feast of liberation. Now perhaps we might read at this point one thing I want to read, but first I want to turn back a little bit and see how that sounds, see if it works, see if we're knocking out some stuff that I recorded before; that's important to know."

I became attuned to the grain of Merton's voice, hearing that it has subtly changed. The experiment has affected him: his voice is calm, thoughtful, vulnerable, and perhaps he has become tired. As before, he returns to the present and offers sensorial observations of what is around him, followed by an inquisitiveness about how the recorder and the experiment are working. In between, Merton cryptically notes a "feast of liberation." I can only speculate about this. Perhaps it alludes to a recent love affair with a woman referred to as "M." His journals indicate how he was struggling in the months after the affair ended, torn between their relationship and his solitary life. Maybe Merton was attempting to definitively let go, trying to convince himself the relationship was over. Or perhaps he was thinking of something altogether different. Maybe it was the recorder that offered him a "liberation," one that allowed his words to become freer, more open: a montage of sounds, without judgment, full of playful contradictions.

What Does the Tape Reveal?

My family was with me in Vermont. During the day, my son went off to a camp to play with the other children, so that I could work in solitude. In the evenings, the artists and families gathered for dinner or to swim in the quarry and talked of projects and ideas and nothing in particular. I loved listening to everyone's stories and how conversations grew and receded throughout the night. Other times, I sat in the garden, and listened to insects and chickens or wind through the raspberry bushes. If I sat long enough, I began to think I could even hear the vegetables grow, roots stretching through soil below, tendrils curling in the open air.

In the studio, I continued to transcribe the Merton hermitage tapes. One begins like this: "It's Monday morning, April 24th. Some ideas about the use of tape, something that just occurred to me. Tape can be used to speak on in such a way that you say nothing and hide everything, or it can be used in such a way that something is revealed. What is the point of using tape in the hermitage so that something is revealed? There's no point using tape here in such a way that everything is hidden. That is to say, simply saying things for the sake of saying them. But what is revealed?"[9] I noticed the recorder influencing his imagination; spontaneously, he shifts his focus from using it as an experimental, playful tool to an interrogation of the medium of audio recording itself and its own absurd contradictions. The fact that he records himself while doing so only highlights this absurdity of speaking into this quiet listening machine, even as he is searching for meaningful reasons to keep using it. He continues: "But what should be manifested in thinking out loud in a hermitage is not simply the mechanical operation of the mind itself, mechanically recorded on another machine, two machines recording each other, but a speaking which will somehow bring to the surface this metaphysical perplexity of man in the presence of his own being—or being in the presence of other beings—in such a way that the unity has manifest of the one and the many."

Even now, when I reread this passage out loud, I get tangled up in it. Merton is twisting and turning the language; it is alliterative, repetitive, and his words seem to deliberately complicate and obscure the mirror that the tape is, how it is always reflecting what he says. It is as if he is attempting to do the thing he warns against: overrunning the tape with words in order to find out what does and what does not have meaning. As I listened, I was sure Merton was aware of this, yet another contradiction lying at the heart of these "two machines." I thought about how this line of questioning is connected to the "perplexity" he mentions so frequently: underlying speaking and hearing is a deliberate, bewildering confrontation that forces him to grasp for something beyond language. The tape recorder offers a sonic mirror to him; in his need to fill the tape with sound and words, he risks getting lost in them.

After speaking nearly a thousand words, Merton's ability to attentively move through this line of questioning struck me, and he reached a conclusion imbued with its own contradictions. He states,

> The purpose of the solitary life is to be totally free and spontaneous and manifesting God with the inmost grain of one's own being and not to live against the divine grain, so to speak. Hence, the danger of simply speaking as if one *knew*. And when the tape is moving, you have to keep talking, and you have to keep saying something, and you have to keep pretending that you know something. In which case, you hide the fact that you don't know. You get away from the perplexity, and perhaps the danger of tape is that it takes you away from the inner mulling over of what is not yet formulated, to let the inner word really grow and develop and expand in you before it is uttered, in other words, the danger of speaking constantly from the top of one's head instead of from the heart.

Merton is speaking urgently, quickly, thoughts streaming onto the tape. As I transcribed them, it was hard to keep up; I had to go back many times and listen again, and I often didn't know where sentences began or ended. This process of listening and relistening brought out patterns in my mind, as the freely improvised spoken words became solidified: knowing and unknowing, inmost grain and divine grain, head and heart. I thought, *Did Merton make an entire tape in real time that is improvised, from the top of his head? And yet, is it also from his heart?* Funny, confusing, and moving, it occurred to me that this is an absurd performance; Merton is performing for the tape, once again dangerously doing exactly what he cautions against, yet navigating through it to reveal a paradox beyond the surface of words.

In another recording made three weeks later, Merton offers a commentary on the philosopher Michel Foucault's *Madness and Civilization*. This is another opportunity for Merton to think deeply about the medium of tape and how it might offer a new way of writing and being in the world: "The salutary effect on me is to see suddenly how partial and how limited my own preachments are, my own temptations to say that such and such a thing is because of such and such a phenomenon, and this is right and this is wrong, and so forth. It is polarizing, it is a very limited, a very weak approach to reality. And it's much better, instead of polarizing, to make mosaics of all the material that is there, to take the material as it is—natural and social."[10] While listening, I heard a shift, a flattening of hierarchical thought, a purposeful uncertainty. When Merton states, "Let there be a moving mosaic of this rich material. And perhaps tape can help to do this," he is letting go: judgment, certainty, and preaching fall away, and he is left only with the "material" in front of him. Let the material be—Merton seems to be saying—let it "speak for itself." I was reminded of the composer Morton Feldman, who likewise refused to "push the sound around" in his music.[11] It is interesting that Merton sees the medium of tape as a way to create these mosaics. Tape continues to spark his imagination; he perceives how collaged sounds might be assembled: "thrown together" and allowed to arrive and dissolve ambiguously, without explicit answers.

In this recording, Merton once again steadfastly strips away artifice and surety in favor of an open, playful, and complex uncertainty, increasingly rooted in silence and perplexity. This ability to reconcile contradictions is the key mark of the mystic, according to the philosopher and psychologist William James, where the "opposites of the world" are "melted into one another."[12] But to carry all of these qualities together, unresolved and without judgment, and then to create something new with them—this is the mark of an *artist-contemplative*. It is no coincidence that the author James Baldwin's description of an artist's role—to face one's own silence alone and to find ways to "illuminate that darkness"—is strikingly parallel to Merton's own words and deeds.[13]

An Uncertain Self

One night in Vermont, I skipped the evening social gathering and walked back along the road in the pitch black to my studio, aware that my time there was ending. There were no cars, and I made my way by feeling the asphalt underfoot, waiting for my eyes to adjust to the night. It was still hot, and a chorus of crickets and katydids sang antiphonally from fields on either side of the road. There was a rustle in the bushes; I jumped and then laughed at myself, realizing it takes a long time to become comfortable with the night and with the noisy stillness of rural places. It was as if I too often hid in the light and did not pay attention to what I could not see. Here, I was forced to listen, to feel, to touch my way to the studio, and slowly I became accustomed to this world and slipped in. In the studio, there was a solitary light on at the desk. Insects clamored at the window. I tried to embrace the unnerving quiet of solitude and got back to listening.

I played another tape. On it, Merton reads the prominent Sufi mystic Ibn al-'Arabî (1165–1240 CE), from a book recently given to him.[14] It occurred to me that much of the content on these tapes was due to coincidence: what Merton happened to be thinking about during that spring in 1967. Still, he takes this opportunity to read passages and then uses the tape to explore "out loud" what the words sound like and how they influence him.

In one passage, Ibn al-'Arabî unifies pairs of opposites—inward and outward, speaking and hearing—as two sides of the same thing, both pointing to the presence of what Arabî terms the "Absolute." Merton then shifts to his own preoccupation with the medium of recording and how the tape itself illustrates both this contradiction and its reconciliation. And then, a remarkable moment—Merton states,

> To return to Ibn al-'Arabî then: "The inward belies the outward when the latter says 'I' and the outward belies the inward when the latter says 'I.'" Who is this "I"? I speak. Here I am speaking. And a moment ago the birds were singing. And the gas just turned off. Who is this I? Who am I who sit here? [pause] It's very difficult to say. Because the I who speaks outwardly, who uses this tape recorder, who speaks back to itself in the tape recorder is to some extent an illusion, and to use a tape recorder is to perpetuate this illusion.

At first glance, this text shows a detached exploration of Ibn al-'Arabî's words, which is then applied to Merton's personal observations of the hermitage and to the tape recorder. But this written text obscures an affective layer of meaning, only heard on the recording. When Merton says, "Who am I who sit here?" his voice wavers. Something *is* revealed, something deeply emotional—an uncertain "I"—and the tape recorder is there listening. In fact, it is the presence of the recorder that disrupts and destabilizes Merton's sense of self; it mirrors and splits not only his wavering voice but also his wavering identity. There is a pause, and we hear the silence of the hermitage—the ticking of a nearby clock, the hiss of tape, the faint sounds of the furnace—and each is now part of a profoundly charged silence, full of meaning and bewilderment. All along, the tape recorder quietly clicks on, reflecting Merton, unsettling him, forcing him to remain both between and uncertain.

In that instant, I heard an acute sadness in Merton. Only three days earlier, he notes in his journal that he is in a "hole of despair," almost certainly as a result of his recent love affair with "M."[15] They had only stopped seeing each other a few months before, and Merton talked with her on the phone two days before; she is still on his mind. I hear confusion and doubt and searching—a moment of inner conflict. It is as if the unlikely combination of Ibn al-'Arabî's words, Merton's emotions, and the presence of the tape recorder so deeply touched him that he is physically, audibly shaken.

Psychologists use the phrase "speech reveals and text conceals," because many layers of information are built into the sonic qualities of the voice, information that is often hidden or obscured when written down.[16] I am sure that Merton, as an author, would have found additional words to convey his meaning clearly. But here, emotion and affect work to convey something beyond the text, allowing us to *hear* exactly what he is talking about: between opposites and contradictions is a still point, a silence embodied and made audible. The remarkable thing is that we are able to witness this unguarded openness through the tape. Perhaps the agency of the tape recorder even encouraged him to open up.

Lasting only thirty seconds or so on the recording, this moment is brief. A moment later, Merton finds composure and continues his analysis of Ibn al-'Arabî; but to my ear, he remains transformed. In using the recorder as a critical lens on himself, he makes a piece of his own memory and experience known, and he recognizes his own uncertain self.

This passage reminds me of how much sound can *touch*. In fact, each time I listen to it, I am deeply, physically affected. As if on cue, my spine tingles, starting at my head and below my neck. Waves of nerves radiate across my back and shoulders and down past my knees. My body is detecting and responding to the slightest emotion: a fever chill of joy.

Listening With

Six months later, I was alone in a cabin in Knoxville, Tennessee. It was late at night in December, on the fifty-first anniversary of Merton's death. There was no one around, yet the cabin was anything but still: snow and rain fell on the roof and clung to every tree. I sensed the size of the room, the pressure of air against my ears. I felt dizzy. I had a desire to fill the cabin with sound: radio, music, anything that could be a distraction from settling down with my thoughts and this unceasing, unsettled silence of being alone.

Still thinking of *Krapp's Last Tape*, Merton's experimental jazz montage, and his comments on Michel Foucault ("Let there be a moving mosaic of this rich material"), I began to collage the transcriptions of Merton's words. I asked myself, *What if I write everything out like a play, not only of text but of sounds, too?* I wove long passages together, focusing on in-between moments or beginnings and endings or times before or after the main events. I roughly structured the passages in the order they were originally recorded, mapping the spring and early summer of 1967, plus a single winter night, on New Year's Eve. I followed the contrasts that Merton alluded to: night and day, sun and rain, jazz and sacred, theoretical and emotional, contemplation and action. Together, these tensions mapped Merton's movement from silence to words and back again. I enjoyed listening to the collage of different writers and thinkers Merton presented, and I made sure to allow them to become characters, too.

I began to transcribe the music Merton had listened to and loved. The cabin had a piano in it, and I played fragments from the transcriptions and spun them out: slowing them down, stripping away rhythms, and adding new notes and lines. I did this so the music had its own logic: it was tethered to Merton, and yet I could still share my own voice alongside, allowing the music to change and grow. I imagined that he might even recognize some of the material. It was not hard to see how this music impressed Merton. An avid music fan, he grew up playing piano, and there are numerous references to music in his journals. I took delight in the variety of performers: John Coltrane and Bob Dylan, Wes Montgomery and Jimmy Smith, Bix Beiderbecke and Louis Armstrong. This music was playing through my head, and I pictured Merton absorbing it, listening closely, searching for its inner spirit.

Merton talks of music on the hermitage tapes, too. On New Year's Eve 1967, he states, "I'm up late. It's seven o'clock, and instead of going to bed, I'm going to sit around and play some records. And, uh, so you are invited to participate in this New Year's Eve party of one or, rather, two: me and my girlfriend, Mary Lou Williams, but Mary Lou Williams is on a record."[17] You can hear him celebrating, laughing, not really caring who his audience might be. And exactly one year earlier—New Year's Eve 1966—music triggered a different emotion for Merton, a sonic "anamnesis," in which sounds from the past viscerally affect the listener in the present.[18] As he ate lunch at Cunningham's Restaurant in Louisville, Merton notes in his journal, the jukebox played Buck Owens's song "Together Again," and he acutely felt a longing for M.[19] It was their favorite song, and it opened powerful and complex emotions in him as he struggled to reconcile their relationship.

It occurred to me that I was listening *with* Merton: eavesdropping on these innermost words, trying to find and conjure and compose yet another meaning, another layer of connection, manifesting itself as music. I wondered, *What does it mean to listen closely to a specter, a recorded shadow of a man?* The dead speak, and I listen.

In the headphones, every inflection of Merton's voice was audible, his thoughts made concrete, his solitude and confidence and questioning all laid bare—a voice full of childhood and youth, jazz, Europe, New York, Kentucky, and finally the quiet of the hermitage. I heard breathing, rain and thunder, water dripping, ticking, throat clearing, records, laughter, morning birds and evening stillness, bells, snapping fingers, sighing, and singing. Each hesitation, laugh, and pause held meaning; each fumble or confidence of words betrayed his humanity and intelligence and vulnerabilities.

So close, so far. Merton was not listening back to me. It was a one-way conversation; it was, as he says, "an illusion." But this is the point the recordings make: listening is *both* intimately close and impossibly far, both illusive and real. And my equally absurd response—through music—strains to complete an exchange across the silences of death, geography, and time. These two sonic worlds—voice and music—may be a mirage, but they are also folding into each other, overlapping in "widening circles," as the poet and novelist Rainer Maria Rilke writes, that "reach out across the world."[20] Or perhaps they are more like artist Paul Klee's drawn spiral (from his *Pedagogical Sketchbook*) that turns upward and outward to ever-increasing freedom, connections and movement pointing to both return and release, active and radiating and sparking with life.[21]

Breath and Liberation

In the spring of 2020, I was sitting in my garage in Ohio during the first weeks of the pandemic, composing. I felt anxious. Like so many others, I was in a forced solitude, facing the uncertainty of viruses and shutdowns and shortages and life and death. Sitting in the open air, I relaxed. Outside was the one place I was not stifling my breath, where I was not afraid to breathe deeply and fully.

I was finally ready to assemble a sonic portrait of Merton with the collaged tapes and fragments of music he listened to throughout his life. Loosely following the dates on the tapes, I observed my spring in parallel to his, fifty-three years later. In one recording, Merton notes the far-off evening sounds of Fort Knox, and I became receptive to the world of sounds around me—wind, new leaves, a squirrel, my son Henry playing in the yard, laughter—all made unusually audible against the pandemic-induced quiet of empty streets and skies. In another recording, Merton hears bells ringing down at the monastery amid a dark and gray morning, and I, too, was listening. There was a light rain, and the water dripping from the gutters reminded me of my own heartbeat. I was in my garage and Merton in his hermitage: two people attending to greening springs, ever separated yet folding into each other.

Slowly, Merton's words and the music came together to make the first drafts of what would become the album *Words and Silences*.[22] I began to assemble a mosaic. I had a wall full of sticky notes, and I paired different fragments of composed music and tempos and rhythms with the sounds and words of the Merton tapes. A few months before, I sent these music fragments to an ensemble of performers. I intentionally sought out flute, clarinet, saxophone, trumpet, and trombone to balance the piano; it felt important to think of wind and breath made audible, even as COVID-19 rendered the air around me tangible, and breathing a symptom of illness. These instruments also indirectly referenced the jazz, folk, and spiritual music Merton admired and the slow breathing of meditation and prayer. I asked the musicians to record their parts several times. With each new iteration, they made subtle changes to rhythms, textures, and notes. Now, the resulting recordings constituted my own unusual archive that I drew from—something known yet unfamiliar—full of sounds that might resonate with the archival tapes of Merton.

Sometimes the music closely follows the auditory cues laid out on the tapes, as in "Breath, Water, Silence," where Merton comments on several passages of Ibn al-'Arabî. Arabî's notion that all of nature is "grounded in the divine breath" moved me, where each of our lifetimes are contained within a single breath, and where we are breathed out and then back in again: "Nature is described by Ibn al-'Arabî as 'the breathing of God': all being is grounded in the divine breath. The Prophet says, 'He who wants to know the divine breath must try to know the world, for he who knows himself knows his Lord.' We seek our Lord, then, in the midst of the creatures which he has breathed out and which he breathes out around us, and he breathes us out also. And then he will breathe in and take us all back into himself, and we will realize that all the time that we were he."[23] This long breath permeates each aspect of the piece. I began with a transcribed fragment from "Boogie Woogie Prayer," a blisteringly fast Meade "Lux" Lewis and Albert Ammons piano duo. Merton's commentary, however, seemed to stretch time out in my mind, so I dramatically slowed the fragment down and spread it out across several octaves. Now simplified, it expansively resonates and helps create a pocket of space for the words to inhabit. Trombone and clarinet play long tones, the length of a breath. Along with the trumpet, the instruments color these notes with tremolos, bended notes, and buzzing sounds. When Merton speaks, the texture of the music thins, as if accompanying a singer. Sometimes the musical phrases nestle between words, and sometimes the rhythms of words and music match or mimic or are in counterpoint with each other. And then, there are times when the music reflects or comments on what Merton is saying, as when I pulled a triplet figure from "Boogie Woogie Prayer" and spun it out to correspond with the archival sounds of water dripping in a bucket and wrens outside the hermitage. Merton continues: "Uh, for Ibn al-'Arabî, water is the most appropriate symbol of life. He says, 'The secret of life is in the act of flowing peculiar to water.' The watery element is, for him, the most fundamental element. Of course, what he's saying there, he's simply expressing an intuition, of dynamism, movement, and becoming in all things, a sense of vitalism and life in everything." For Merton, breath and water become symbols of his own "hermit life," in which he is immersed in silence as if it were water. As the piece unfolds, these two elements—breath and water—wax and wane and then join with saxophone, which plays a melancholic, wavering three-note melody to the end.

In another piece, "A Feast of Liberation," I got stuck trying to set Merton's "experimental jazz meditation" to music. No matter how many times I tried, it fell apart; my attempts were too obvious, and the recording did not need my intervention. I impulsively decided to replace Merton's meditation with music. I created a "cutout" of the tape, only allowing the listener to hear the moments before and after. To my surprise, this not only allowed the music to evoke the emotional intensity of the meditation but also allowed the silence beneath Merton's words to come to the fore. At the beginning of the tape, Merton talks of racial unrest and protests taking place that night in Louisville. I thought of the suffering then and the suffering now, too: the murders of Breonna Taylor and George Floyd were still raw and ringing in my ears, and once again breath had been made palpable. I added a repeating, solitary, sparse line to Merton's voice, built on three notes evoking John Coltrane's album *Ascension* (another favorite of Merton's). It gave enough space to provide a lilting counterpoint with Merton's voice, and it swelled into a cloud of dense piano lines, suspended in the air. The music then abruptly stops, and Merton's voice returns. His words are calm and oddly quiet yet powerful. It is as if he is tired and emotionally spent from the evening's experiment but also now in a new place. It is the audible remnants of reflection and repose.

Visiting the Hermitage

Because of the pandemic, it wasn't until after I finished the album that I was able to visit Thomas Merton's hermitage in person. In June 2022, I received permission from the monks to come to the Abbey of Gethsemani in Kentucky. My friend and videographer Kevin Davison joined me, to film the hermitage and its surrounding landscape. I also brought a keyboard to record solo live performances of the music. I wanted to listen to Merton's voice in the same space where he made the recordings. It felt important to hear it in the acoustics of the room but, perhaps more importantly, to pay attention to the contexts of the hermitage.

In the spring of 1967, a young monk named Brother Paul Quenon gave Merton a reel-to-reel tape recorder to use at the hermitage. It just so happened that the same monk was standing outside waiting for us as we arrived at the Abbey. Paul was wearing the traditional robes of a Trappist monk, plus gray sneakers (no socks). Kevin and I felt like Keystone Cops as we scrambled to move our mountain of equipment in the car to make space for him, so that we could drive to the hermitage together. As we traveled over dirt roads and bumpy terrain, I was worried a pinned box of cameras would come crashing down on his head (thankfully, it didn't).

Brother Paul was direct, quick, alert, and funny. He improvised on the keyboard while we set up. He was nice to talk with, and he never let a conversation go on too long. (Later, I read Paul's poetry, which is beautiful, simple, and spare, and to my delight, it often describes the sonic world around him.) He was also not afraid to help us. In his eighties, he insisted on carrying equipment into the hermitage. "I work," he said happily. When we thanked him for being with us and for the permission to be there, he said, in his matter-of-fact way, "Well, it was something new."

The hermitage was bigger than I thought it would be. Brother Paul noted that this was so Merton could have guests and conferences there ("poets and writers, mostly," he said). The porch was as big as the main room. I felt totally, surprisingly comfortable there; it was familiar. Perhaps seeing earlier pictures from the photographer Ralph Eugene Meatyard prepared me for the experience—of the building and woods, picnics, empty fields, and a conference with the writers and poets Wendell Berry and Denise Levertov and with Merton agreeably playing bongos.

I performed for Brother Paul, playing three pieces that included recordings of Merton speaking on Samuel Beckett, Michel Foucault, and Ibn al-'Arabî. Paul leaned back in his chair, his arms behind his head, listening intently. After that, Paul allowed us to stay and work on our own. He said that he may not see us the next day but encouraged us to go about our business. "There's more work to do," he said and took his leave.

The landscape surrounding the hermitage was all that I imagined: remote, quiet, wooded. But it was also more dense and hillier than I had expected, humid, too, and teeming with insects. Sonically, it was lovely. I heard the bells down the hill, the wind in the trees and grasses, birdsong, and only a few cars on distant roads. The sounds were welcoming, subtle, and active.

The experience felt a bit like a pilgrimage. It was something akin to Patti Smith's travels in *M Train* or even the obsessed fictional characters in A. S. Byatt's *Possession*: visiting places of writers, sensing the landscape and soundscape they wrote in and how these places influenced their words. But I was also an uncertain and skeptical pilgrim, careful not to get lost in reverie or nostalgia, wary of placing Merton on a pedestal. It felt good just to be there, to take it in, and to simply get on with our tasks.

I performed alone both inside and on the porch of the hermitage, for no one (except for Kevin). My audience was an empty field, mature poplar trees, an occasional wild turkey, a pair of skittish deer, many birds, and a million mosquitoes. This was yet another form of silence, one where I was performing, yes, but also deeply paying attention to the land and sounds, to the weather and humidity and trees and wind. It felt surprisingly good, comfortable. There was no need to worry, no pressure to entertain; my anxieties fell by the wayside. I imagined that Merton felt particularly free here—a freedom to be silent, to make mistakes, to not have to perform for others, and to come closer to one's most authentic, spiritual, naked self.

In one of the Merton recordings, he states, "It's a dark, gray morning. It may rain later." As I played alongside this recording at the hermitage, a thunderstorm came in. The sky got progressively darker. Partway through the piece, the hermitage door slammed shut. The trees became a collective of white noise, steadily getting louder. It was soon pitch black in the daytime. As I was playing the last notes, the rain began. I finished, and we scrambled to grab the cameras and microphones, dangerously exposed to the elements.

When we later told Paul about the storm, he said, "Now, that's a real Merton moment!"

The storm was beautiful. After we retrieved the equipment, we stayed on the porch and continued to film and record. The rain was gentle, steady, substantial, cooling. Thunder echoed from either side of the hermitage. We were quiet—no need to talk—as we listened, watched, and kept working. Often, I found myself pausing, wanting to stay still and in that spot for a long time. Sitting on the porch or at Merton's desk, the surroundings encouraged a solitude that was both utterly calm and full of activity. I noticed the smallest of details: light moving through the trees, shadows creeping along the walls, the coolness of the floor, the sharp-soft tops of the long swaying grass, the faint smell of damp, burnt wood in the fireplace. Each thing around me begged for more investigation and then asked me to wait, to feel the deep contentment of remaining silent and letting everything be, as it is.

Performing *Words and Silences*

When it came time to premiere *Words and Silences* in the fall of 2022, I was excited to perform it with others and to slough off the last remnants of the pandemic. Over the course of an extraordinary week, the ensemble and I rehearsed, performed, socialized, and returned to Kentucky once again.

Practice began on a Monday afternoon.[24] As soon as the ensemble started to play, I knew the piece was going to work. The performers—Phil Rodriguez, Jeremy Woodruff, Katie Porter, and William Lang—were so professional and generous that it was easy to trust and share with them. They responded to the project, too: I could hear how they cared about each note and about each other. From the beginning, it felt like a real band.

On Tuesday, we rehearsed most of the day. My then fourteen-year-old son, Henry, visited us in the morning. He quietly moved throughout the auditorium, sitting in each section, listening. I hope he remembers being there when he is older. In the evening, we all had dinner together at our house along with my wife Jen. She patiently helped behind the scenes, giving us time to work. She also helped keep us (me) grounded and not too serious. There were jokes and laughing and some musicians' shop talk as well (but not too much).

On Wednesday, we had a last rehearsal, then dinner, then waiting. The dressing rooms were nice, quiet, and cold. The entire building felt stuck in the 1950s. The moments before a show can wreak havoc with your mind. I focused on practicing careful breathing and on observing rather than thinking; surprisingly, these were not simple tasks. Some of the time I was alone, trying not to be nervous, but then I would wander into the green room to see the other musicians as a distraction. The trombone player, William, was keeping his instrument warm with virtuosic runs and scales; Katie could be heard playing long tones on her bass clarinet a few doors down; trumpeter Phil was wandering the hallways, improvising; and Jeremy occasionally joined me, moving between conversation and playing melodies on his alto saxophone.

Then, there was the call to go on stage. I avoided making eye contact with anyone in the audience; it might have been too much, emotionally. Fortunately, I had a new pair of glasses that allowed me to see the score and keyboard clearly but not much else. It was an advantage to have the audience be a blur. The performance—nearly an hour—felt like five minutes. Performing is like meditation: your mind wanders, and you have to gently bring it back to focus without getting nervous or mad at yourself. It was the best performance I could have asked for: everything worked, and to my ears, the performers sounded lovely.

After, a buzzing feeling—of relief and of love—for family and the musicians and the audience, of course, but also a feeling of deep connection to the world in that moment, standing on the stage. The feeling is this: there is a river below us, below our thoughts, below the stage, below the ground. For a moment, we can dip a toe in it and sense all the others there, too. Onstage, I said hello to people but do not remember much. Henry joined us, playing a few notes on the piano and snapping photos of the band. My mom was there, too.

The next morning, we left early for Kentucky to record at Thomas Merton's hermitage. Kevin Davison joined us again to film it. When we arrived, Brother Paul Quenon was already waiting for us. "This is beginning to look a bit like a cult," he said with dry humor, presumably about the fact that I kept bringing more and more people with me to the hermitage. Moments before we began to record, Paul stepped outside to listen. He said, "We should take down the windchimes! They might get in the way." He was right, of course, and his keen sense of listening helped us avoid having the windchimes take over the recording. We did the entire album in one take, and then we scrambled to pack everything up.

A few days earlier, Paul wrote to me with bad news: The abbot had reserved the hermitage for the week, and could we reschedule? Feeling the pressure of having the musicians with me only for that one day, I decided to push Paul, asking if we could be there for just a few hours. I received a short reply, that the abbot would "make himself absent" from 1:00 to 5:00 in the afternoon. Grateful, yet feeling as if I had pressed too hard, we went ahead with our plans.

At the hermitage, I told Paul that asking the abbot to leave his retreat for the afternoon had been weighing on my mind. He said it had been weighing on his mind, too. He spoke in an honest, authentic, and empathetic way— no judgment. Somehow, that acknowledgment made the tension of being there dissipate. I had a strong sense that Paul's spiritual training and mastery comes out in this way, in addition to being eager to work, light in his step, filled with humor and delight, sharp and serious, playful.

Paul shared his playful humor with us one more time that day. At 4:55, as we were loading up the cars to leave, Paul came tearing up the drive in a camouflage ATV. He hopped out (in his robes and sneakers) and said, "Now, I've brought my shotgun, and I'm gonna chase you off the property!" We laughed; it was truly unexpected and funny and made us feel comfortable with him. And then, quietly, he said, "No, seriously, you had better go before we see the abbot walking up the way." Meanwhile, Phil had brought his frisbee golf discs and was taking advantage of the large fields to get some throws in. I had visions in my mind of a stray disc hitting an unsuspecting abbot in the head. But that didn't happen! It all worked out. It was just fine.

We took our picture together on the porch and left. Paul invited us to vespers and to see the chapel. We went in and sat down, and a profound exhaustion came over me—fatigue, happiness, wonder. The interior of the chapel was sparse, with white brick walls. The late-afternoon light from the stained windows projected across the plain back wall, abstract streaks of color slowly moving and changing. We could only stay a few moments, and I felt restless, with an urge to get on the road before weariness completely overwhelmed me.

We stayed together that night in a big old house in Louisville. It had more beds than people. And here we let go and enjoyed each other's company, listening to hours of music and sharing conversation with one another deep into the night. And then, it was over. William and Phil both left from Louisville, and Katie and Jeremy left the following day from Columbus. Dropping them off at the airport, I became emotional. I felt a deep sadness to see them leave but grateful for our friendship and for this most extraordinary week. The funny thing is that there was so much uncertainty during these moments—Will someone get sick? Will the music even work? Will I forget everything?—that in retrospect seems distant or even silly. But the

The *Words and Silences* band poses with Brother Paul Quenon on the front porch of Thomas Merton's hermitage at the Abbey of Gethsemani in Trappist, Kentucky. From left to right: Jeremy Woodruff, Katie Porter, Brother Paul Quenon, William Lang, Phil Rodriguez, and Brian Harnetty. Photo courtesy of Kevin Davison.

uncertainty and anxiety are simply part of the process, part of the big wave one must ride to move through the experience.

Alone once more, I thought about our performances of *Words and Silences* as I drove home from the airport. When we played together, the music had an emotional quality I had not anticipated. One piece, named "One Plus One Equals One," stuck with me, because of both our shared experience and its words. It draws from a curious recording Merton made, in which he reads the text of another Sufi mystic, Sarmad Kashani (ca. 1590–1661 CE):

> When one manifests itself in a different form it is called two. But two is nothing other than one and one put together while one itself is not a number. It is to be remarked that the structure of this putting together of two ones is one. And the product of this putting together which is called two is also one number. So that the essential form here is one, the matter is one, and the two ones put together are also one, i.e., one, manifesting itself in the form of the many. Thus, one produces the number two by manifesting itself in two different forms. The same is true of three, for example, which is one and one and one. And the

nature and structure of its oneness is exactly the same as in the case of two.[25]

Merton reads Kashani's words in a clear, detached voice. They reflect, as Merton says, "the one and the many." I placed this passage at the center of the piece, and the music was cut out to make space for the words, the opposite of "A Feast of Liberation." The text—filled with repeating patterns between the numbers "one" and "two"—reminded me of the writing style and wordplay of the poet and writer Gertrude Stein. I also brought back earlier melodic motives, this time fleshed out with additional instruments. Harmonically, the music is static, remaining the interval of a fourth higher than at the beginning of the album: it is opening outward instead of closing in.

In this piece, I couldn't help but hear a culmination of *Words and Silences* and the multiyear process of shaping an archival performance out of the Merton tapes. I heard the "flatness" of Beckett; the dichotomy of pairs of opposites from Ibn al-'Arabî; an open, bewildered perplexity; the twinning of Merton and the tape recorder; and the exposed, vulnerable, uncertain "I" of Merton sitting alone in his hermitage. And in these moments, with all their contradictions—between past and present, inward and outward, living and dead, time and space, everything and nothing—I heard them together and moved between them; I heard both unity and multiplicity, and the opposites of the world melted into each other.

CHAPTER EIGHT

Home: *The Workbench*

Gifts from My Father

My father repaired mechanical things: watches, clocks, appliances, cars, mowers, typewriters, radios, and record players. It was his superpower, and his patience and curiosity with these modest and everyday items gave him a mythical status in our family. As a child, I loved to sit alongside my dad at his workbench. I would pretend I was repairing, tinkering, or inventing, just as he did. The workbench was both shabby and orderly, and everything he needed was within reach.

After my father died in 2021, I spent a lot of time in my parents' basement in Westerville, Ohio, sitting once again at the workbench. The house was quiet, and I strained to listen to the silent objects, trying to remember their sounds, holding them both in my hands and in my memory. I couldn't bear to move anything. Not yet. Everything remained frozen in place.

Instead, I thought about the house and our lives within it. My parents and sisters moved there in 1965 (I was not born yet). It was part of a new subdivision off Africa Road called Parkmoor, built on the fields and hills of the old Moss farm and just outside of town. The house was a humble ranch placed in the middle of a treeless lot of dirt and rocks. The unfinished road dead ended a few hundred feet beyond the edge of the property. My parents planted grass and shrubs, and slowly the place became a well-cared-for home. My father planted trees, too: saplings of pine, plum, buckeye, dogwood, redbud, and apple, as well as silver, red, and sugar maples, all from his father's land in Junction City.

As I grew up, the house and yard were where I first knew and understood my place in the world. I can remember the sounds of the screen doors squeaking open and closing with a bang and the blinking rhythms of the fluorescent light over the kitchen sink as it came to life. On warm summer nights, my parents would bring an old TV out onto the back porch, and we would pop popcorn and watch reruns of comedy shows among the din of cicadas, crickets, and grasshoppers. I also remember the creaking floorboards in the hallway; if you stood in the right spot, you could move back and forth and make the wood scrape and groan. Sometimes, my sisters would listen to music in the family room, dancing and singing along with the Bee Gees, John Denver, and Devo. And of course there was a piano, and I loved hearing its sounds throughout the house. In the basement, there was a porous line between my father's tools and my own toys. A half-repaired typewriter always sat on the workbench, with tiny springs and clamps scattered about. Each time my father finished repairing a typewriter, he would use his index fingers to punch out the phrase, "The quick brown fox jumps over the lazy dog." It efficiently tested all the letters of the alphabet to make sure they were in working order.

Some four decades later, I reluctantly began to clean out my parents' basement. Each day, I would spend several hours there, working. I was amazed to see how my father's collections of things were organized, even the junk. I found one box filled with nothing but empty orange plastic pill bottles with every label carefully removed; it was beautiful and luminous and seemed to project its own warm glow. Or there were metal boxes with dozens of pull-out drawers filled with spools of copper wire, rivets, spare Christmas tree lights, and clock keys. Sometimes, the objects were imbued with subtle humor, as when I found several used pizza boxes. Inside them were plastic candy trays filled with antique radio knobs. The knobs, in many shades of brown and in different shapes and sizes, looked like chocolates, and I had to laugh at the sly joke of storing them this way. As I slowly sifted through each item, I was confronted with the same questions: Should I keep it or throw it away? Is it valuable or sentimental? Should it be kept in the family? At the same time, I began to wonder if there were sonic traces of my father embedded in these collected, repaired, and loved objects. I thought, *Do they have their own agency? And, can we activate and listen to them?*

Many years before I was born, my dad made the workbench out of rough, sturdy wood. I imagine it is the kind of bench you might see all over the country in garages and basements of a certain generation of mechanics and tinkerers. On its surface, the workbench was splattered with paint, solder, and bits of colored tape. It was dented with pockmarks, and there were pencil drawings, too, of geometric shapes, a room diagram, and hastily worked out math calculations. In these marks, you could see my father's mind at work.

A fluorescent light hung over the workbench with a bright glare. In the center, my dad kept a carpet store remnant: a beige rectangle used to catch runaway screws and to focus his work. On the shelving above, there were hanging audio speakers and multicolored cables, unused batteries, and a neatly pinned cross made of palm leaf. Stacked tins of wood stains and

THE WORKBENCH
brian harnetty

The artist Samantha Rehark's hand-drawn album cover for *The Workbench*.

putties filled one shelf, alongside spray cans of paint, poison, voltmeters, rubber bands, tape measures, a yellowed *Far Side* comic clipped from a newspaper, light switches, stacked rolls of tape, and more vacuum tubes and resistors than could be counted. Lining the back wall were boxes of radio parts, antique wooden levels, and repurposed coffee and tuna cans now full of brushes and screws. A decade-old calendar hung above, as if suspended in time, and several IBM mechanical pencils were lined up and at the ready. My dad's tool case sat open on the far left of the workbench, and a heavy, red metal vice anchored the right. The tool case was filled with half-used rags, needle-nosed pliers, grease guns and oil droppers, homemade magnetized screwdrivers, an assortment of outlet plugs and cables, and a small American flag hanging from the side.

When I think about this workbench and its items, I see them as gifts. In each object, I note the way my father cared for it, and I observe his organizational mind. In the tools and parts and machines, I see a stand-in for how he cared for others, how he cared for me. I also know that he used this workbench until his last days; it was always changing, evolving. Many years ago, Lewis Hyde's book *The Gift* made a permanent mark on me. In it, he talks of gift economies and how the power of a gift lies not in property or ownership but in the gift's exchange. It is its circulation and movement that keep it alive. I carried this notion with me and felt how the workbench was affecting me, changing how I understood myself and the world around me.

After some time, my mother went to live with my sister Lisa, and we prepared our parents' house to be sold. My mother's memory was failing with the beginnings of dementia, and she reluctantly decided that it was best to give up her home. It was understandably difficult for her to let go of the house, as if its objects—furniture, antique dishes, paintings, a sewing machine, a marble-topped wash table—were not merely functional but carried with them the joys and struggles of six decades of marriage and generations of family history. It was hard to witness her hesitancy, this unwilling separation.

Once she left, I continued to visit the house. It was still full of things, as if my parents just stepped out and would be back shortly. But now that they were no longer there, the house felt empty. As my siblings and I packed up boxes of items, the house had become a temporary, vanishing archive, slowly disappearing room by room. At the same time, I had the notion that I was dismantling my mother's sense of place and disrupting her bearings, and perhaps my own, too.

Looking back, it is no coincidence that in those months before selling my parents' house, I became consumed with archiving our family photos. I bought a scanner and spent hours each evening sifting through and digitizing old slides and negatives, fastidiously creating tags and folders and desperately holding onto the last remaining traces of the home where I grew up. Most of the photos were taken before I was born, and I found myself thrown into a world of familiar people as I had never known them and who did not know that I would later exist. The process once again troubled my understanding of archives; they had now become intensely personal and almost too much to endure. Old lessons were relearned: no matter how hard I tried, the objects were not enough to bring loved ones back or restore my mother's mind, and the meanings embedded in each photo and document elusively slipped through my fingers. At the same time, I felt their burden; I was often seized with a yearning to run away, to let these objects go, to jettison their heavy weight.

Despite these impulses, I decided I would take the workbench and reassemble it at my home. When I finally got it moved into my garage, I realized that it had become a kind of shrine: a memento mori, yes, but also an attempt to make permanent the way I had always seen and understood this assemblage of tools and machinery. I made note of this feeling and how it unsettled me. I did not want the workbench to become fixed and unyielding. I resolved to continue to explore it with a light touch and to be open and curious about how it might change. In my mind, I was following a hunch I had about creating a new sound and video piece as a portrait of my father. Eventually, this would become *The Workbench*, which includes sampled recordings of my father combined with a chamber ensemble of bass clarinet, piano, violin, and cello.[1] However, I first needed to identify and gather what materials I might use.

Before the Rain Comes

I began to make sound recordings of the workbench's objects. I recorded a pair of pocket watches and was astonished that after carefully winding them up, they both came to life. I also recorded several of my father's radios, paying close attention to their static and buzz as I moved slowly in and out of stations on the dial. Then there were the electric hums, dings, and striking sounds of old typewriters, each with its own distinct sonic signature. A broken music box added to this collection of sounds; if I listened closely, I heard its fan whirring in fits and starts as the tines plucked a broken melody from the metal comb. These recordings were a starting point for me, a way to sonically understand the physical nature of the workbench.

I searched in vain for archival recordings that might represent my father's life. At first, I planned on using radio broadcasts from his childhood in the 1930s, sounds that I thought he may have heard on his family's radio. But this strategy did not work; the recordings' connections to my father were tenuous and vague. I then turned to my phone, where I had inadvertently kept a year's worth of family voice messages. It was extremely difficult to relisten to the recordings. They were too fresh. Each time I heard my father's voice, it immediately affected me. I was emotionally overwhelmed, and I had to turn the recordings off.

Slowly, I became used to the recordings. I listened to them again and again, memorizing each inflection, each "uh" and "um." I began to appreciate the grain of my father's voice and his use of words. This repeated listening allowed me to step back and become slightly detached—enough to keep working on the piece, enough to feel like it was worth sharing with others. I also noticed that it felt joyful, a gift that the creative process had provided to me without my fully realizing it.

Sometimes my dad's phrasing was archaic, as in the time he called me to cancel a planned trip we were going to take to his hometown, Junction City. Despite the sadness I felt, I loved how phrases like "right at the present time" sounded as if from a bygone moment. "Hi, Brian, this is your dad," he began. "Give me a call when you can. It has to do with what we talked about earlier. Maybe going down to J.C. [Junction City] tomorrow. I just canceled out on that right at the present time, but that's, that's the main concern, I guess. And we'll have to maybe schedule another day sometime."

On other calls, he would triumphantly share that he had completed a repair, often on an object that we had puzzled over together. In this case, it was an old surveyor's compass from the 1850s, which once belonged to our ancestor Thomas Spare: "Okay, hey! Uh, Brian, this is your dad. I just wanted to let you know that I got that surveying equipment, uh, repaired. And it's working fine. Give me a call if you can; uh, we'll see what else we can get into." And then when I listened back to the first recording that was saved on my phone, I was amazed at its poetic timing. I had an intuition that this message could set the tone for the piece: "Hi, Brian, this is your dad. I'm just returning your call and letting you know we just went out for a long walk. And uh, we finally got back, before the rain comes. So, thanks for calling, and we're fine, and I hope you're fine, too. Bye-bye."

Each time he called, my father would announce, "This is your dad." Of course, I knew who it was, but this was yet another way for him to insert his playful, subtle humor. I also liked how he spun the language to give emphasis to his story. When he said "long walk," for example, he stretched "long" out just enough to make me feel and see him moving slowly and persistently along the road, though I knew at that point he was unable to travel very far at all. And even now, each time I listen to the words "before the rain comes," I am deeply moved. It is the combination of their phrasing, how they foreshadow the transition from life to death that he would undergo, and the way that they are spoken—like a declaration and with certainty—that make me feel as if I am listening to the message for the first time.

There is one more recording of my father in *The Workbench*. In the silence of his last days in hospice, I instinctively took out my recorder and turned it on. I can't remember why I did so. I must have felt the need to do something, anything. I have never felt so unable to help. So, I resorted to the one thing I practice more than anything else: I listened. In the recording, my dad is calmly sleeping and breathing. The monitors and machinery and room lights have all been turned off, and occasionally we hear a nurse or an announcement off in the distance. I can't recall how long the recording was, nor do I remember turning the recorder off or for how long I sat there after.

It Is about My Father, Too

A year and a half later, I began to make *The Workbench*. Building from earlier projects, my process was rooted in gathering, transcribing, and collaging the materials. I went through my father's small collection of records, which consisted mostly of 1950s crooners and jazz recordings. I methodically listened to each one and made brief melodic transcriptions of parts that I found interesting. I played with these fragments, and they became new melodies, ones that were unrecognizable from their sources yet loosely tethered to them. I imagined my father listening to these old records, and I liked that the new melodies shared some qualities with them.

Then, after working for several months, the project once again became too much. I could not move forward with it. I was overwhelmed: not by the number of recordings, as before, but by the emotional weight of the few I had. I decided to stop working, to take a break. When I had saved enough money, I bought a plane ticket to visit one of my oldest friends (and frequent contributor on my previous albums), the musician and composer Jeremy Woodruff. He lived in Berlin, and I gratefully spent a week there with him, riding bikes throughout the city, drinking cheap wine in ragged, overgrown parks, and continuing our decades-long endless conversation. The biggest gift Jeremy offered, however, was to simply let me be sad, to follow the random and crooked path of grief. When Jeremy had to work, I wandered the streets and rode the U-Bahn alone. I visited museums and sat on park benches, unable and unwilling to say or do much. And yet, the physical distance from Ohio offered a needed rest and reevaluation of the project's purpose and my own. Just as I had done as a young man in London, I went far away from my home to see its value. I began to assemble the dozens of melodic fragments I had made earlier, ensuring that they worked together, like parts of a clock.

After I returned to Ohio, I then used the same process of working with musicians as earlier projects, a process that combined the symbolic language of notation and the nonsymbolic sounds of recordings. Each musician recorded short, looped fragments several times, adding new textural, rhythmic, or melodic elements. When I received these recordings, I listened to them with fresh ears, making note of their sonic qualities. Then, I collaged the recordings together with the samples from my father and the objects from his workbench. Finally, I transcribed this recording to make a performance score for the ensemble.

The detachment I felt after working with the recordings, and again in Berlin, buoyed me through the next weeks and months of composing, recording, rehearsals, and even interacting with the audience members at the project's premiere. This first performance took place in Ohio, and the venue was a darkened black box theater. The room was full beyond capacity. I was grateful that I did not have to perform and that the piece was safe in the competent hands of the Unheard-Of Ensemble, whose members were open and generous during each step of my unorthodox working process.[2]

When I finally got to my seat in the back row, sandwiched between my wife Jen and a stranger, everything changed. Many emotions flooded in at once. I was forced to let go, sitting in such a vulnerable spot, among all of those people. I didn't have a choice.

The music began. It is both elegiac and curious as it slowly builds momentum over the course of eleven minutes. A repeated chord progression first heard in the piano anchors the piece. Throughout, my father's voicemails punctuate the musical movement; his everyday questions and statements are poignant. At times, we hear the repaired objects, too, of the pocket watches or of distant radio static.

The video—filmed by Kevin Davison—methodically explores the workbench. We see tools, radios, speakers, a typewriter, and many small collections of things. At first, I was worried that filming a stationary workbench for such a long time might become boring. But in fact, the opposite happened: the textures, colors, and variety of the objects—a green mint can, a cigar box, a tangled rainbow of speaker wire, a rescued bird's nest sitting in a roll of blue painter's tape—seemed to encourage a slow, still contemplation. The objects are arranged just so; they reveal how my dad's personal workspace can become an archive of everyday objects charged with meaning and aesthetic pleasure.

At the end of the piece, the instruments and samples come together. The slowly turning music box's fragmented and broken melody is heard in coun-

A still from the video for *The Workbench*. Photo courtesy of Kevin Davison.

terpoint, offering an innocent, plaintive contrast to the music. Gradually, we hear the recording of my father in hospice. It is raw, intimate, and dignified and lends gravity and sorrow to the piece. The instruments drop away, one by one. And then, when the music box runs out, we are left alone with my father sleeping. And yet, I can't help but think that this shocking moment is perfectly ordinary, too. Despite being so personal, the recording of my dad becomes archetypal: the sounds we hear connect to everyone, for we all confront death. As we listen to him moving through the last stage of life, we are left alone with the fundamental issue of what it means to be human and mortal.

After the performance, the crowded room slowly emptied. I looked down and noticed that my watch had warned me that my heart was racing dangerously fast, even though I had been sitting still. When I checked to see at what time the alert had gone off, it was exactly during the eleven minutes of the piece.

An older man walked up to me. He seemed a little hesitant, as if his emotions were also right at the surface. He looked at me and simply said, "Your piece . . . It is about my father, too." Before I could respond or get his name, the man turned around and disappeared into the crowd. I think this might be the best compliment one can get. The exchange reminded me that we are all fallible and connected. We must come to terms with the fragility of our lives. The music, then, becomes a conduit to our humanity, a single link in a chain of gifts that feel like they have somehow landed in our laps.

Now that the project was completed, I wondered what might happen next: Would the workbench become fixed and unchanging? As I came back to my garage where the workbench was located, however, I saw that this was not possible or even desirable. I kept using things—a pocketknife to cut twine in the garden, a screwdriver to fix a door, a ruler to measure the length of a found feather—and I realized that I was continually altering the workbench. I was messing it up. And then, my son soon felt comfortable using it to repair his guitars; it was the perfect height for his lanky frame. And my wife was there, too, placing pots and cups and vases on its sturdy top as they were coming and going from the heat of her kiln.

So, this is what I mean when I talk about the workbench as a "gift" and as a gift in motion. Without human interaction, the workbench remains static, inert. But as soon as we use it, we are activating it. We are adding our own tiny stories to it, and it silently reflects and records these stories—a drip of paint, a nail hole, a chip out of its side—if we are only patient enough to pay attention to them. I learned this lesson many years ago with archives, when I realized they could contain every kind of thing in the world, except for human relationships. They depend on us to discover and activate their layers of meaning and feeling. The same is true here. And now, I am happy to just keep using this workbench as, well, a workbench.

Afterword

In my early twenties, I first read Italo Calvino's 1983 novel *Mr. Palomar*. I was attracted to both its structure and story, of a lone character trying and failing again and again to systematically understand and catalog the world around him. Palomar is not really a hero; in fact, he is more like a bumbling, misguided, anxious, earnest fool. According to Calvino, there are three themes Palomar grapples with: visual descriptions of the world around him, cultural and anthropological storytelling, and speculative meditations (the last part of the book, for example, is aptly called "The Silences of Palomar"). Throughout the book, Palomar attempts to carefully observe every aspect of a single wave in the ocean, count every blade of grass in his yard, and describe every star in the sky. Invariably, he fails.

In one story, Palomar visits a cheese shop. The seemingly limitless variety of cheeses excites him. He decides to try a bit of each so that he understands the entirety of the world of cheese and can know which one is the best. But just as soon as he devises a plan to do so, he becomes overwhelmed. Under pressure, it is impossible for him to grasp this collection of things. Defeated, he leaves with just a single sample, the "most obvious, most banal" cheese.

In each case, Palomar's downfall is his aim to possess knowledge as if it were fixed and to create a singular, rigid hierarchy of each collection's contents. He tries to comprehensively understand something that continues to change, grow, expand, and unfold even as it slips through his fingers. Palomar gets caught up in his own schemes and a desire to describe or analyze, rather than the simpler but messier acts of trying, tasting, experiencing, and making mistakes.

I am familiar with Palomar's predicament, and I see it as a cautionary tale. When I first read the book, I was attracted to its sense of wonder, and it fueled my own youthful desire to grasp things that can't be fully understood. I also remember feeling like Palomar all those years ago when I first arrived at Berea. It was as if I were a child standing on a diving board, frozen, unable to either jump in the water or go back. But with the encouragement of the archivists at Berea, I gave up and dove in. And then later, after meeting relatives of people on the recordings, I felt the deep connections of an unfolding circle of community, music, media, listening, performance, and return. During these moments, I learned how to both be and not be like Palomar: to explore with awe and wonder what this impossibly complex and beautiful world offers and yet to let go of the desire to capture, control, and possess everything. What is the point, really, of experiencing life — my teacher Michael Finnissy would often remind me — only to dust it off, remove its blemishes, and put it behind glass or on a shelf, taking it out of circulation?

The project of this book — and really of my life — has always been to witness and pay attention to the world and then to find ways to share these experiences with others. It is a process of continually cracking open my innermost self and then moving outward. For me, this means listening to recordings to marvel in their sounds and voices and to follow their stories to see where they lead me: each tape, record, or field recording is an adventure. It also means understanding communities and places through sound, where I meet everyday people and learn about their extraordinary lives. My core values—including a grounded curiosity, openness, and empathy—are embedded in this practice, and they course through each interaction I have with others and each listening experience. And finally, it means that I am always working to find ways to compose directly from my own life—to not make music *about* a subject but to be in that subject and to respond to it candidly and fully, to find sounds that I love, get as close to them as I can, make something new and raw and unrefined and imperfect and beautiful with them and then to pass them along.

Over the years, I saw that to perform an archive, one need not be comprehensive, authoritative, or professional; instead, this process is subjective, flawed, and personal. Likewise, one can lightly hold onto an archive without possessing it, and there is no single "correct" approach but many. When combined with an archival stewardship, the materials unfold and are brought to light in new ways: if you cannot count all the stars or touch each blade of grass, then these things can become both metaphors and pointers to the infinite, something bigger than we can possibly grasp. And then, finally, even our own actions are brought back into the fold of an archive (or, perhaps more accurately, into the fold of our shared lives, world, and universe), contributing to its continual movement and expansion, where it never finds its end.

Acknowledgments

I want to share my sincere thanks to the many family members, friends, colleagues, organizations, teachers, mentors, and role models who have helped over the past two decades to make this project possible, including A Blade of Grass, Ryan Agnew, the family of Reuben Allen, David Belcastro, Karen Belisle, Bellarmine University and the Thomas Merton Center, Cheryl and Roger Blosser, Mary Jo Bole, John Bondurant, Tyler J. Borden, Aaron Michael Butler, Todd Carter, Lucas Church, Contemporary Arts Center Cincinnati, Creative Capital, Lane Czaplinski, Kevin Davison, Jerry DeCicca, Paul De Jong, Dan Dennis, Lynneda Denny and the family of the Leonard Roberts Trust, Lisa Dent, Jo Dery, Joe Duddell, Duke Performances at Duke University, Adam Elliott, Experimental Sound Studio, James Farley, Michael Finnissy, Liz Fisher, Chris Forbes, Robert and Jane Muncy Fugate, Michael Gillespie, Janice Glowski, the Greater Columbus Arts Council, Aaron Greenwald, the Anne Grimes Family, Rachel Grimes, David Grubbs, Jocelyn Hach, Mack Hagood, Ann Hamilton, Keith Hanlon and Secret Studio, Tom Hansell, Marilyn and Paul Harnetty, Jennifer and Henry Harnetty, Chuck Helm, Jacqui Hoke, the family of Amanda Styers Hook, Rich Housh, Stuart Hyatt, Lewis Hyde, Alex Inglizian, Jonathan Johnson, Zoe and Jack Johnstone, Kurt Kellerson, Jeff Kimmel, Rich Kirby, Drew Klein, Jessica Knapp, Bela Koe-Krompecher, Jacob Kopcienski, William Lang, Lance and April Ledbetter, Robin Coste Lewis, Roger Lipsey, the Little Cities of Black Diamonds Council, Damon Locks, Loghaven Artist Residency, Fred Lonberg-Holm, Jason Macke, Lou Mallozzi, the MAP Fund, Marble House Project, Steve Martland, Michael Mercil, the Merton Legacy Trust, New Directions Publishing Corporation, Now You Know Media, the Ohio Arts Council, Will Oldham, Yuri Ono, Josh Ottum, Nathaniel Parsons, Dave Pascoe, Paul Pearson, Marina Peterson, Katie Porter, Brother Paul Quenon, the family of Neva Randolph, Lisa Rehark, Samantha Rehark, Harry Rice, Anna Roberts-Gevalt, Phil Rodriguez, Laura Sammons, Robert Saxton, Nat and Niki Segnit, Cory Seifker, Robert Sember, the family of Ina Simmons, Dick Sisto, Ryan Skinner, Cauleen Smith, Travis Stimeling, Dao Strom, Sunday Creek Associates, Ben Taylor, Michael Torres, the Unheard-Of Ensemble, Jane van Voorhis, Jasper Waugh-Quaesbarth, Wexner Center for the Arts at The Ohio State University, John Winnenberg, Jenna Wojdacz, Jeremy Woodruff, Jack Wright, and Justin Zimmerman.

Various recordings held by Thomas Merton Center by Thomas Merton, from New Directions Pub. acting as agent, copyright © 2020 by the Trustees of the Merton Legacy Trust. Reprinted by permission of New Directions Publishing Corp. Transcriptions and lyrics of various recordings from the Berea Sound Archives at Berea College are used with permission. Transcriptions and recordings from the Little Cities of Black Diamonds Archive are used with permission.

Notes

Abbreviations in Notes

AGColl   Anne Grimes Collection of American Folk Music, Library of Congress, Washington, DC
LCBDColl   Little Cities of Black Diamonds Tape Collection, Shawnee and New Straitsville, Ohio
SAColl   Southern Appalachian Collections, Berea Sound Archives, Hutchins Library, Berea College, Berea, Kentucky
SR/ESColl   Sun Ra/El Saturn Collection, Creative Audio Archive, Experimental Sound Studio, Chicago, Illinois
TMColl   Thomas Merton Collection, Thomas Merton Center, Bellarmine University, Louisville, Kentucky

Introduction

1. Ernst, *Digital Memory and the Archive*, 174.
2. "The Phonautograms of Édouard-Léon Scott de Martinville," folder Sounds, First Sounds website, www.firstsounds.org/sounds/scott.php.
3. I admire this quote from the composer Alvin Lucier (1931–2021): "Careful listening is more important than making sounds happen." Lucier, *Reflexions*, 430.
4. See Cook and Schwartz, "Archives, Records, and Power"; and Jackson, *Lines of Activity*.
5. Burkholder, "Borrowing."
6. Peterson and Brennan, "Sonic Ethnography," 374.

Chapter One

1. Lexie Baker and J. P. Fraley, interview by Barbara Edwards, October 26, 1973, tape BK-OR-003-003-A, Barbara Kunkle Collection Reel Audio Tapes, SAA 92, SAColl.
2. Prichard Quartet, 1958, tape SC-OR-786-002-A, John Miles Gospel Music Radio, SAColl.
3. Hiram Stamper, interview by Bruce Greene, tape BG-CT-132-22, Bruce Greene Collection Cassette Recordings #1, Bruce Greene Kentucky Fiddle Music Collection BCA 0090 SAA 090, SAColl.
4. Jackson, *Lines of Activity*, 35.
5. Bob and Jean Helton, interview by Bruce Greene, October 30, 1997, tape BG-CT-221-A-16, Bruce Greene Collection Cassette Recordings #1, Bruce Greene Kentucky Fiddle Music Collection, SAA 90, SAColl.

6. Addie Graham and Opsa Guthrie, interview by Barbara Edwards, February 28, 1975, tape BK-OR-013-002, Barbara Kunkle Collection Reel Audio Tapes, SAA 92, SAColl.

7. Addie Graham, unaccompanied singing, tape BK-OR-013-003-A, Barbara Kunkle Collection Reel Audio Tapes, SAA 92, SAColl.

8. Augoyard and Torgue, *Sonic Experience*, 21.

9. Benjamin, *Illuminations*, 236.

10. Grubbs, *Records Ruin the Landscape*, 140.

11. Ralph Maynard, interview, tape AM-OR-076-035-B, Appalachian Museum Oral History Collection RG 14.12 AM-OR-03, SAColl.

12. Walter McNew, interview by Bruce Greene, August 25, 1989, tape BG-CT-175-11, Bruce Greene Collection Cassette Recordings #1, Bruce Greene Kentucky Fiddle Music Collection, SAA 90, SAColl.

13. Ernst, *Digital Memory and the Archive*, 182–83.

14. Frankie and Lionel Duff, interview by William Tallmadge, June 1968, tape WT-OR-02-A-02, WT-Or Audio Masters, William Tallmadge Collection, SAA 33, SAColl.

15. Chalmer Howard and others, interview by William Tallmadge, June 21, 1968, tape WT-OR-017-A-01, William Tallmadge Collection, SAA 33, SAColl.

16. William Tallmadge, calendar/notebook, June 21, 1968, William H. Tallmadge Baptist Hymnody Collection, December 1967–January 1969, BCA 0035 SAA 033, SAColl.

17. Derrida, *Archive Fever*, 7.

18. Barthes, *Camera Lucida*, 20.

19. "Erin Marshall, Part Two," posted on October 10, 2015, folder Sound Archives Fellowship Presentations 4-19-06 PR-DV-503_H26, Berea College Collections, Berea Sound Archives, Hutchins Library, Berea College, Berea, Kentucky, https://berea.access.preservica.com.

20. Personal communication with Rich Kirby during an Appalshop workshop titled "Ballads, Biscuits, and Gravy," 2008.

Chapter Two

1. *American Winter* was released on Atavistic Records in 2007.

2. *Pretty Bird* was a self-released album in 2003.

3. Addie Graham and Opsa Guthrie, February 28, 1975, tape BK-OR-013-002, Barbara Kunkle Collection Reel Audio Tapes, SAA 92, SAColl.

4. Coon Creek Girls rehearsal 1950, Tom Wood's early 1950s Renfro Valley broadcast recordings, tape TWJ-OR-008, T. J. Wood Jr. Collection, SAA 139, SAColl.

5. Secular ballads and hymns by Frankie Duff, interviewed by William Tallmadge, June 20, 1968, tape WT-OR-015, WT-OR Audio Masters, William Tallmadge Collection, SAA 33, SAColl.

6. A. L. Phipps, interviewed by Harry Rice, May 11, 1993, tape AC-CT-373-001, SAColl.

7. *The Commandos* radio program, February 14, 1943, tape WS-ET-43034 / 035, WHAS Radio Historical Collection, HC 41, SAColl.

8. Berzilla Wallen, unaccompanied singing, April 19, 2006, tape AC-OR-005-095-05, SAA 106, SAColl.

9. Dellie Norton, unaccompanied singing, April 19, 2006, tape AC-OR-005-095-05, SAA 106, SAColl.

10. Dillard Chandler sang a similar version of the song on the album *Old Love Songs and Ballads*, Smithsonian Folkways Recordings, SFW CD 40159, 2005, https://folkways-media.si.edu/docs/folkways/artwork/SFW40159.pdf.

11. Addie Graham, unaccompanied singing, tape BK-OR-013-003-A, Barbara Kunkle Collection Reel Audio Tapes, SAA 92, SAColl; Mary Lozier, interviewed by Barbara Edwards, July 29, 1973, tape BK-OR-009-001, Barbara Kunkle Collection Reel Audio Tapes, SAA 92, SAColl.

12. *Rawhead and Bloodybones* was composed in 2011 and released on Dust-to-Digital Records in 2015.

13. Jane Muncy, recordings of tales, recorded by Leonard Roberts, 1955, tape LR-OR-050, Leonard Roberts Field Recordings, SAA 57, SAColl.

14. Hiram Stamper, interviewed by Bruce Greene, possibly 1980, tape BG-CT-132, Bruce Green Collection Cassette Recordings #1, SAA 90, SAColl.

15. Muncy, recordings of tales.

16. I. D. Stamper, Celebration of Traditional Music, 1977, tape AC-OR-005-055-04, SAA 106, SAColl.

17. The experimental artist and filmmaker Harry Smith released the *Anthology of American Folk Music* in 1952 on Smithsonian Folkways Records. The artwork, recordings, and Smith's approach to the music were an important influence on my work.

18. This process came out of a desire to let go of some of my training as a composer and to refocus on the act of listening. At the time, it meant that I gave up on the symbolic language of notated scores and composed directly with recorded sounds. Later, I would find ways to bring sounds and notation back together, but this was an important act of stripping away everything to see what was fundamental and important to me.

19. Estill South, interviewed by Leonard Roberts, October 1949, tape LR-OR-003-A-07, Leonard Roberts Collection Reel Audio Tapes, BCA 0057 SAA 057, SAColl.

20. Manon Campbell, interviewed by Bruce Greene, March 19, 1977, tape BG-CT-136-02, Bruce Green Collection Reel Audio Tapes, SAA 90, SAColl.

21. Titon, *Old-Time Kentucky Fiddle Tunes*, 1.

Chapter Three

1. *Silent City* was released on Atavistic Records in 2009.

2. Sinclair Gospel Serenade, WRVK, July 5, 1959, tape CQ-OR-002, from WRVK Radio, SAA 109, SAColl.

3. Bennett, *Vibrant Matter*, viii.

Chapter Four

1. Sun Ra and Arkestra, SR-C222-B, SR/ESColl.

2. Eshun, *More Brilliant than the Sun*; Kreiss, "Performing the Past"; Lock, *Blutopia*; Sites, "We Travel the Spaceways"; Szwed, *Space Is the Place*.

3. Dery, "Black to the Future," in *Flame Wars*.

4. Sun Ra and Arkestra, "Close Your Eyes," July 16, 1971, SR-R018, Reel 60, SR/ESColl.

5. Sun Ra, "Poems over Phone," December 20, 1972, SR-C211, SR/ESColl.

6. Sun Ra lecture, University of California, Reel 179, SR-R149, SR/ESColl.

7. Corbett, *Wisdom of Sun Ra*.

8. From the Fourth Annual Charles Olson Memorial Lecture, Cape Ann Museum, Gloucester, MA. October 19, 2013.

9. Harold Sherman, "Unknown Voice," Reel SR-R429-A, SR/ESColl.

10. Radio broadcast, KMPX, May 24, 1971, SR-R073, Reel 46, SR/ESColl.

11. Burkholder, "Borrowing."

12. Sekula, "Photography between Labour and Capital," 194.

13. Sekula, "Body and the Archive," 64.

14. Lessard, "Between Creation and Preservation."

15. Weheliye, *Phonographies*; Eshun, *More Brilliant than the Sun*.

16. Personal communication, 2013.

17. Personal communication, 2013.

18. Sun Ra and Arkestra, January 1, 1981, SR-C256-B, SR/ESColl.

19. Sun Ra and Arkestra, "Cosmic Tones," Cosmic Tones for Mental Therapy, March 28, 1974, SR-R003, SR/ESColl.

20. "19721102 Chicago," Astro Black, November 2, 1972, R423-A, SR/ESColl.

21. Sun Ra and Arkestra, "Ronnie/Love Me Love Me," May 2, 1973, SR-R172, SR/ESColl.

22. NBC News analysis, January 12, 1974, SR-C200, SR/ESColl.

23. Sun Ra, solo performance, "Take the A Train," SR-R056, Reel 16, SR/ESColl.

24. Sun Ra, "Mixing—1616 Butler," November 8, 1972, SR-C201-A, SR/ESColl.

25. "768-1390 Answering Machine Outgoing," 1976, SR-C230, SR/ESColl.

26. See Bloxam, "Cantus Firmus."

27. Sun Ra, "Hustlin' and Bustlin' for Baby," SR-R438, Reel 163, SR/ESColl.

28. Sun Ra, "Alan Burke Interview," SR-R156, Reel 189, SR/ESColl.

29. Sun Ra, "Lee Cultural Center," March 1, 1970, SR-189-A, Reel 176, SR/ESColl.

30. Sun Ra, solo performance, 1980s?, SR-C-213, SR/ESColl.

31. Sun Ra, "5 Spot," June 14, 1975, SR-C203-A, SR/ESColl.

32. Sun Ra, "Sunrise, Sunset, Too," Sun Ra singing to himself, SR-C223-B, SR/ESColl.

Chapter Five

1. Hildegard Westerkamp broadly defines a soundwalk as "any excursion whose main purpose is listening to the environment" ("Soundwalking," *Autumn Leaves*, 49).

2. Courbin, *Village Bells*.

3. Before European immigrant settlement (often referred to as "settler colonialism"), this region had a diverse Indigenous population. The early mound builders, including the Adena and Hopewell peoples, lived throughout southeastern Ohio. Many centuries later, the Shawnee, Moxahala, Wyandot, and Delaware tribes also occupied and

hunted in the hills and forest lands there, including those in what is now called the town of Shawnee and the surrounding Little Cities. By 1817—and after the defeat of Tecumseh's Confederacy and the larger defeat of the Shawnee tribe—the Shawnee were forced to northern Ohio. But this did not last long. When the Indian Removal Act was passed in 1830, the Shawnee were once again forced to move, this time west of the Mississippi River, to Kansas. By the time the town of Shawnee was established in 1872—and the time my ancestors arrived—there were few to no Native peoples left, their erasure cruel and complete.

4. Tribe, *Little Cities of Black Diamonds*.

5. This class, titled Ethnography of Performance, at Ohio University, was taught by Dr. Marina Peterson.

6. The first performances of *Shawnee, Ohio* took place in 2016. It was commissioned by the Wexner Center for the Arts, Duke Performances, and the Contemporary Arts Center Cincinnati. It was also supported through a Creative Capital Award. Chuck Helm, who at the time was the performance curator at the Wexner Center, was instrumental in supporting the project. The album version of the project was released on Karl Records in 2019, and a revised and fully completed version was premiered at the Wexner Center for the Arts and with Creative Capital in 2021.

7. hooks, *Belonging*, 4–5.

8. Dishon and Winnenberg, *Shawnee*, 6.

9. Dishon and Winnenberg, *Shawnee*, 42.

10. The fully digitized sound archive now resides both at The Ohio State University's Center for Folklore Studies Archive in Columbus, Ohio, and the Little Cities of Black Diamonds Archive in New Straitsville, Ohio.

11. Ina Simmons, interview and singing, "Pearl Bryan," recorded by Anne Grimes, Box 1, Tape 3, Side 2, AGColl; and Amanda Styrers Hook, interview and singing, "Terrill," recorded by Anne Grimes, Box 2, Tape 31, Side 2, AGColl.

12. Reuben Allen, interview and singing, "Homestead Strike," recorded by Anne Grimes, Box 1, Tape 24, Side 2, AGColl.

13. Green, *Wobblies, Pile Butts, and Other Heroes*, 249–50.

14. Toop, *Sinister Resonance*.

15. Photo, "McCuneville Ann Davis Ricketts funeral 1909," LC-PH-32, LCBDColl.

16. Photo, "Grandma-and-Grandpa-Ashby," DO-PH-819, LCBDColl.

17. Photo, "Corning Theater—Valley Street," LCBDColl.

18. Photo, "Brick plant at Kachelmacher, Ohio," DO-PH-1239, LCBDColl.

19. Photo, "Corning Band Trio," LC-PH-183, LCBDColl.

20. Photo, "Hungarian Band Congo," DO-PH-670, LCBDColl.

21. Photo, "Band beside Garrison's Hardware," LC-PH-542, LCBDColl.

22. Photo, "Shawnee Cemetery Memorial Day Parade," DO-PH-998, LCBDColl.

23. "Soundscape" refers to the environmental and human sounds of a given place or immersive environment—in short, the "sonic environment" (Schafer, *Soundscape*).

24. Photo, "Oil Well Supply," DO-PH-832, LCBDColl.

25. Photo, "New Straitsville," DO-PH-1083, LCBDColl.

26. Photo, "Picture from Mine," DO-NC-392, LCBDColl.

27. Photo, "Frying eggs on the mine fire," LC-PH-287, LCBDColl.

28. Photo, "The World's Greatest Mine Fire," DO-PH-742, LCBDColl.

29. Neva Randolph, interview and singing, "My Station's Gonna Change," recorded by Anne Grimes, Box 1, Tape 3, Side 2, AGColl.

Chapter Six

1. Another interesting example is the composer Cornelius Cardew's (1936–81) late music, which focused on an audience of everyday people. Its neoromantic style was radically different from Cardew's younger avant-garde works, and he tried to tailor the music to fit this audience with only mixed success. For my own project, my hope was to maintain a sense of personal musical style while fostering a more direct and meaningful exchange with a community. Long-term friendships slowly built a sense of trust, and a back and forth sharing of ideas helped inform the music as I was composing it.

2. Barthes, *Camera Lucida*, 27.

3. Here, I am deeply indebted to many people, but especially to my friend the composer and conductor Joe Duddell. With every project, his critical listening led to better music and better recordings. This form of sharing and exchange is crucial to the creative process.

4. Jim Bath, interview, recorded by Dot Dishon, Tape 01, LCBDColl.

5. Anonymous boy, interview, Tape 29, LCBDColl.

6. Joshua "Judd" Matheney, interview, Tape 32, LCBDColl.

7. Schwartz, *Making Noise*.

8. "Miner Saved by Wife's Apron, Tied over His Face," *Dayton Daily News*, November 6, 1930.

9. "Miner Saved by Wife's Apron."

10. "Toll in Mine Blast Will Be Greatly Increased," *Dayton Daily News*, November 6, 1930.

11. Justin Zimmerman, dir., *Meeting Again: Remembering the Millfield Mine Disaster* (Bricker-Down Productions, 2001).

12. *Athens News*, December 4, 1995, 7; *Ohio Geology Newsletter*, Ohio Department of Natural Resources, Winter 1996, 7.

13. AthensMessenger, "Residents Urge Review of Fracking," YouTube, May 24, 2012, www.youtube.com/watch?v=KkHLAFoSyZo.

14. Grimes, *Stories from the Anne Grimes Collection*, 118–19.

15. Neva Randolph, interview and singing, "My Station's Gonna Change," recorded by Anne Grimes, Box 1, Tape 3, Side 2, AGColl.

Chapter Seven

1. Thomas Merton, "Merton reads his own poetry," self-recorded, April 22, 1967, CD-213 Tr-01, Merton Archive, TMColl.

2. Merton, *Learning to Love*, 222.

3. Thomas Merton, "Merton on birds," self-recorded, April 24, 1967, CD-213 Tr-08, Merton Archive, TMColl.

4. For examples, see Lipsey, *Angelic Mistakes*; and Pearson, *Beholding Paradise*.

5. Thomas Merton, "Poems for hospital," self-recorded, June 3, 1967, CD-214 Tr-03, Merton Archive, TMColl.

6. Thomas Merton, "Experimental reading—Samuel Beckett," self-recorded, April 24, 1967, CD-213 Tr-08, Merton Archive, TMColl.

7. Merton, *Learning to Love*, 224.

8. Thomas Merton, "Experimental jazz meditation," self-recorded, 1967/04/22, CD-213 Tr-03, Merton Archive, TMColl.

9. Thomas Merton, "Ideas on use of audio tape," self-recorded, tape 213-17, Merton Archive, TMColl.

10. Thomas Merton, "Madness and Civilization by Michel Foucault," self-recorded, May 19, 1967, CD-214 Tr-08, Merton Archive, TMColl.

11. Feldman, *Give My Regards to Eighth Street*, 143.

12. James, *Varieties of Religious Experience*.

13. Baldwin, "The Creative Process," in *Collected Essays*, 669–72.

14. Thomas Merton, "Notes on Sufi Ibn Al Arabi," self-recorded, April 23, 1967, CD-213 Tr-05, Merton Archive, TMColl.

15. Merton, *Learning to Love*, 223.

16. Schroeder et al., "Humanizing Voice."

17. Thomas Merton, "New Year's Eve," self-recorded, tape 12-31-1967, Merton Archive, TMColl.

18. Augoyard and Torgue, *Sonic Experience*, 21.

19. Merton, *Learning to Love*, 177.

20. Rilke, "Widening Circles," in *Book of Hours*, 48.

21. Klee, *Pedagogical Sketchbook*, 53.

22. *Words and Silences* was released in 2022 on Winesap Records. It was commissioned by the Wexner Center for the Arts and was supported with a MAP Fund grant.

23. Thomas Merton, "Relation of God to nature," self-recorded, April 30, 1967, CD-213 Tr-09, Merton Archive, TMColl.

24. The premiere took place at Mershon Auditorium in Columbus, Ohio.

25. Thomas Merton, "Notes on Sufi Ibn Al Arabi," self-recorded, April 23, 1967, CD-213 Tr-05, Merton Archive, TMColl.

Chapter Eight

1. *The Workbench* was released on Winesap Records in 2024.

2. The Unheard-Of Ensemble commissioned *The Workbench*, in coordination with the Johnstone Fund for New Music.

Discography and Filmography

Discography

The following albums may be found—along with a compilation album to complement the book—on Brian Harnetty's Bandcamp page (https://brianharnetty.bandcamp.com) and on all streaming services. A media companion with additional clips and related videos can be found at https://www.brianharnetty.com/noisy-memory.

Harnetty, Brian. *American Winter*. Atavistic Records (US). Released October 9, 2007.
Harnetty, Brian. *Rawhead and Bloodybones*. Dust-to-Digital Records (US). Released November 20, 2015.
Harnetty, Brian. *Shawnee, Ohio*. Karl Records (Germany). Released April 26, 2019.
Harnetty, Brian. *Silent City*. Atavistic Records (US); Ruminance Records (France). Released August 11, 2009.
Harnetty, Brian. *The Sociophonic Key*. Scioto Records (US). Released June 19, 2012.
Harnetty, Brian. *The Star-Faced One*. Atavistic Records (US). Released May 7, 2013.
Harnetty, Brian. *Words and Silences*. Winesap Records (US). Released October 7, 2022.
Harnetty, Brian. *The Workbench*. Winesap Records (US). Released January 19, 2024.

Filmography

Harnetty, Brian. *Shawnee, Ohio*. Winesap Music, 2021. 60 min.
Zimmerman, Justin, dir. *Meeting Again: Remembering the Millfield Mine Disaster*. Bricker-Down Productions, 2001. 10 min.

Bibliography

Primary Sources

Archives

Anne Grimes Collection of American Folk Music, Library of Congress, Washington, DC
Little Cities of Black Diamonds Tape Collection, Shawnee and New Straitsville, Ohio
Southern Appalachian Collections, Berea Sound Archives, Hutchins Library, Berea College, Berea, Kentucky
Sun Ra/El Saturn Collection, Creative Audio Archive, Experimental Sound Studio, Chicago, Illinois
Thomas Merton Collection, Thomas Merton Center, Bellarmine University, Louisville, Kentucky

Periodicals

Athens (OH) News
Dayton (OH) Daily News

Secondary Sources

Books

Augoyard, Jean-François, and Henry Torgue, eds. *Sonic Experience: A Guide to Everyday Sounds*. Montreal: McGill-Queen's University Press, 2005.
Baldwin, James. *James Baldwin: Collected Essays*. New York: The Library of America, 1998.
Barthes, Roland. *Camera Lucida: Reflections on Photography*. New York: Macmillan, 1981.
Benjamin, Walter. *Illuminations*. New York: Schocken Books, 1968.
Bennett, Jane. *Vibrant Matter: A Political Ecology of Things*. Durham, NC: Duke University Press, 2010.
Calvino, Italo. *Mr. Palomar*. Boston: Houghton Mifflin Harcourt, 1983.
Carlyle, Angus, ed. *Autumn Leaves: Sound and the Environment in Artistic Practice*. Paris: Double Entendre, 2007.
Corbett, John. *The Wisdom of Sun Ra: Sun Ra's Polemical Broadsheets and Streetcorner Leaflets*. Chicago: Whitewalls, 2006.
Courbin, Alain. *Village Bells: Sound and Meaning in the 19th-Century French Countryside*. New York: Columbia University Press, 1998.

Cox, Christoph, and Daniel Warner, eds. *Audio Culture: Readings in Modern Music*. New York: Continuum, 2004.

Derrida, Jaques. *Archive Fever: A Freudian Impression*. Chicago: University of Chicago Press, 1995.

Dery, Mark. *Flame Wars: The Discourse of Cyberculture*. Durham, NC: Duke University Press, 1994.

Dishon, Rob, and John Winnenberg. *Shawnee: Reflections upon the First 125 Years 1873-1998*. Nelsonville, OH: Sunday Creek Associates, 1998.

Ernst, Wolfgang. *Digital Memory and the Archive*. Vol. 39. Minneapolis: University of Minnesota Press, 2013.

Eshun, Kodwo. *More Brilliant than the Sun: Adventures in Sonic Fiction*. London: Quartet Books, 1998.

Feldman, Morton. *Give My Regards to Eighth Street: Collected Writings of Morton Feldman*. Edited by Bernard Harper Friedman. Cambridge, MA: Exact Change, 2004.

Green, Archie. *Wobblies, Pile Butts, and Other Heroes: Laborlore Explorations*. Urbana: University of Illinois Press, 1993.

Grimes, Anne. *Stories from the Anne Grimes Collection of American Folk Music*. Athens: Ohio University Press, 2010.

Grubbs, David. *Records Ruin the Landscape: John Cage, the Sixties, and Sound Recording*. Durham, NC: Duke University Press, 2014.

hooks, bell. *Belonging: A Culture of Place*. New York: Routledge, 2008.

Hyde, Lewis. *The Gift: Creativity and the Artist in the Modern World*. New York: Vintage, 2007.

Jackson, Shannon. *Lines of Activity: Performance, Historiography, Hull-House Domesticity*. Ann Arbor: University of Michigan Press, 2000.

James, William. *The Varieties of Religious Experience: A Study in Human Nature*. London: Routledge, 2003.

Klee, Paul. *Pedagogical Sketchbook*. London: Faber and Faber, 1953.

Lipsey, Roger. *Angelic Mistakes: The Art of Thomas Merton*. Brattleboro, VT: Echo Point Books and Media, 2018.

Lock, Graham. *Blutopia: Visions of the Future and Revisions of the Past in the Work of Sun Ra, Duke Ellington, and Anthony Braxton*. Durham, NC: Duke University Press, 1999.

Lucier, Alvin. *Reflexions: Interviews, Scores, Writings*. Köln: Edition MusikTexte, 1995.

Merton, Thomas. *Learning to Love: The Journals of Thomas Merton*. Vol. 6, 1966-1967. Edited by Christine M. Bochen. San Francisco: Harper, 1998.

Pearson, Paul M. *Beholding Paradise: The Photographs of Thomas Merton*. Mahwah, NJ: Paulist, 2020.

Rilke, Rainer Maria. *Rilke's Book of Hours: Love Poems to God*. New York: Penguin, 1997.

Schafer, R. Murray. *The Soundscape: Our Sonic Environment and the Tuning of the World*. Vermont: Destiny Books, 1994.

Schwartz, Hillel. *Making Noise: From Babel to the Big Bang and Beyond*. Cambridge, MA: MIT Press, 2011.

Szwed, John F. *Space Is the Place: The Lives and Times of Sun Ra*. New York: Da Capo, 1998.
Titon, Jeff Todd. *Old-Time Kentucky Fiddle Tunes*. Lexington: University of Kentucky Press, 2001.
Toop, David. *Sinister Resonance: The Mediumship of the Listener*. New York: Continuum, 2010.
Tribe, Ivan M. *Little Cities of Black Diamonds: Urban Development in the Hocking Coal Region*. Athens, OH: Athens County Historical Society and Museum, 1988.
Weheliye, Alexander G. *Phonographies: Grooves in Sonic Afro-Modernity*. Durham, NC: Duke University Press, 2005.

Journal Articles and Essays in Edited Collections

Baraka, Amiri. "Jazzmen: Diz & Sun Ra." *African American Review* 29, no. 2 (1995): 249–55.
Bloxam, M. Jennifer. "Cantus Firmus." In *Grove Music Online*. Oxford: Oxford University Press, 2001. www.oxfordmusiconline.com.proxy.lib.ohio-state.edu/grovemusic/view/10.1093/gmo/9781561592630.001.0001/omo-9781561592630-e-0000004795.
Burkholder, J. Peter. "Borrowing." In *Grove Music Online*. Oxford: Oxford University Press, 2001. www.oxfordmusiconline.com/subscriber/article/grove/music/52918pg1.
Cook, Terry, and Joan M. Schwartz. "Archives, Records, and Power: The Making of Modern Memory." *Archival Science* 2 (2002): 171–85.
Kreiss, Daniel. "Performing the Past to Claim the Future: Sun Ra and the Afro Future Underground, 1954–1968." *African American Review* 45, no. 1 (2012): 197–203.
Lessard, Bruno. "Between Creation and Preservation: The ANARCHIVE Project." *Convergence: The International Journal of Research into New Media Technologies* 15 (August 2009): 315–31.
Peterson, Marina, and Vicki L. Brennan. "A Sonic Ethnography: Listening to and with Climate Change." *Resonance* 1, no. 4 (2020): 371–75.
Schroeder, Juliana, Michael Kardas, and Nicholas Epley. "The Humanizing Voice: Speech Reveals, and Text Conceals, a More Thoughtful Mind in the Midst of Disagreement." *Psychological Science* 28, no. 12 (2017): 1745–62.
Sekula, Allan. "The Body and the Archive." *October* 39 (1986): 3–64.
Sekula, Allan. "Photography between Labour and Capital." In *Mining Photographs and Other Pictures, 1948–1968: A Selection from the Negative Archives of Shedden Studio, Glace Bay, Cape Breton*, vol. 13, by Leslie Shedden, Don Macgillivray, Allan Sekula, B. H. D. Buchloh, and Robert Wilkie. Halifax, NS: Press of the Nova Scotia College of Art and Design and the University College of Cape Breton Press, 1983.
Sites, William. "We Travel the Spaceways: Urban Utopianism and the Imagined Spaces of Black Experimental Music." *Urban Geography* 33, no. 4 (2012): 566–92.
Westerkamp, Hildegard. "Soundwalking." *Sound Heritage* 3, no. 4 (1974). Rev. 2001.

Index

Page numbers in italics refer to illustrations.

Abbey of Gethsemani, 136, 150–51, *155*
Afrofuturism, 70
"After Death Judgment Will Find Your Soul" (Randolph), 131
"After the Sound of the Tone" (combine), 83–84. See also *The Star-Faced One* (album)
Allen, Marshall, 68
Allen, Reuben, 103; "Homestead Strike," 103–4
All My Life (Baillie), 133
American Winter (album), 5, 30–38, 42, 69, 81; "I'll Cross the Briny Ocean, I'll Cross the Deep Blue Sea," 34; "I Was Interested in the Story You Just Told Me about the Funeral," 38; "The Night Is Quite Advancing," 28; "The Soldier Pulled Off His Uniform of Blue," 38–42
Ammons, Albert, 149; "Boogie Woogie Prayer," 149
Anderson, Sherwood, 114–15; *Winesburg, Ohio*, 114–15
"Another Way" (CF), 84–85. See also *The Star-Faced One* (album)
Appalshop (arts center), 27
archival performance, 3–5, 70, 129, 137, 156
archival stewardship, 3, 5, 9, 29, 78, 168
Armstrong, Louis, 146
Ascension (Coltrane), 149
Ashby, Grandma, 105
Ashby, Grandpa, 105
Ashley, Robert, 32
"Au Clair de la Lune" (song), 2
Augoyard, Jean-François, 18

Baillie, Bruce, 132–33; *All My Life*, 133
Baker, Lexie, 10
Barthes, Roland, 27, 65, 114
Bath, Jim, 117–19
Beckett, Samuel, 137, 138–39, 151, 156; *Krapp's Last Tape*, 139, 146
Beiderbecke, Bix, 146
Belonging (hooks), 92
Benjamin, Walter, 19–20
Bennett, Jane, 64
Berea Appalachian Sound Archives, 8–22, 24, 26
Berea College, 9
Berry, Wendell, 51, 151
Blosser, Cheryl, 93, 113
Bondurant, John, 42, 53
"Boogie Woogie Prayer" (song), 149
"Boy" (song), 120–22, *134*. See also *Shawnee, Ohio* (album)
"Breath, Water, Silence" (song), 148–49. See also *Words and Silences* (album)
Bryan, William Jennings, 102
Burke, Alan, 84–86
Butler, Aaron, 68
Byatt, A. S., 151; *Possession*, 151

Cage, John, 54
Calvino, Italo, 167; *Mr. Palomar*, 167
"Campaign Song" (song), 102
Campbell, Manon, 46–47
cantus firmi (CFs), 84
Cardew, Cornelius, 176n1
Carpenter, Nora, 9
Carter, Todd, 70
Celebration of Traditional Music festival, 9

185

CFs (cantus firmi), 84–85
Chandler, Dillard, 173n10
"Chicago: 1972" (interlude), 82. See also *The Star-Faced One* (album)
Coin, Sam, 119
collage, 2, 3
Coltrane, John, 146, 149; *Ascension*, 149
"Come Join the Knights of Labor" (song), 114
The Commandos (radio program), 38–39
Corbett, John, 70
"Cosmic Tones" (interlude), 82
counterpoint, 3
"Country Gardens" (Grainger), 98
Courbin, Alain, 90
Creative Audio Archive (CAA), 70

"Darlin' Corey" (folk song), 41
Davis, Chip, 38
Davison, Kevin, 150, 153, 164
Derrida, Jacques, 26
Dishon, Dot, 117–18
Doctorow, E. L., 51
"Down by the Riverside" (folk song), 24
"Drunkard's Dream" (folk song), 33–34. See also *American Winter* (album)
Duchamp, Marcel, 74
Duddell, Joe, 176n3
Duff, Frankie, 23–24, 34–36
Duff, Lionel, 23, 34–36
Dylan, Bob, 146

"Eight Hours" (labor song), 114
Ellington, Duke, 83
"The End of a Perfect Day" (song), 114
Ernst, Wolfgang, 1, 23
Experimental Sound Studio (ESS), 69–70

Fair Rosmarin (Kreisler), 98
Faulkner, William, 51
"A Feast of Liberation" (song), 149, 156. See also *Words and Silences* (album)
Feldman, Morton, 143
field recordings, 20, 32, 33, 45–46
Finnissy, Michael, 2, 32, 113, 167

Fitzgerald, Ella, 133
"5/2/1973" (interlude), 82. See also *The Star-Faced One* (album)
Floyd, George, 149
Folk Songs of North America (Lomax), 32
Forest Listening Rooms project, 135
Foster, Ted, 53
Foucault, Michel, 137, 143, 146, 151; *Madness and Civilization*, 143
fracking, 128–30
Fraley, J. P., 10
From Hazard to California (photograph), 13, 14

The Gift (Hyde), 160
"The Girl I Left Behind Me" (folk song), 21
Graham, Addie, 16–18, 28–29, 33–34, 38–41; "Young People Who Delight in Sin," 17–18; "Drunkard's Dream," 33–34
Graham, Opsa, 17, 33
Grainger, Percy, 98; "Country Gardens," 98
"Greedy Fat Bear" (folktale), 46–47. See also *Rawhead and Bloodybones* (album)
Grimes, Anne, 100–101, 131–32
Grubbs, David, 20

Harnetty, Brian, 134, *155*
Harnetty, Florence, 61, 62, 63
Harnetty, Gus, 49, 58, 61
Harnetty, Henry, 51–52, 72, 148, 152
Harnetty, Jane, 58, 61, 62, 63–65
Harnetty, Jen, 31, 51–52, 56, 72, 152
Harnetty, John, 49
Harnetty, Karen, 58
Harnetty, Lisa, 61, 62, 63, 160
Harnetty, Marilyn, 56, 61, 62, 63
Harnetty, Paul, 48–49, 56–59, 60, 61, 162
Harrod, John, 9
Hartson, Yank, 117, 118
"He Is Knocking" (hymn), 11
Helton, Jackie, 15–16; "I Know It Was the Blood," 15
Henton, Sean, 120

heterophony, 25
Hill, Doc, 117, 119
hip-hop, 3, 72
"Hold the Fort" (labor song), 122
"Homestead Strike" (song), 103–4
homophones, 75–76
Hook, Amanda, 102
hooks, bell, 92; *Belonging*, 92
Hound, R. H., 53
Howard, Chalmer, 24–26
Howell, Jane (née Williams), 96, 106
"Humming" (interlude), 82. See also *The Star-Faced One* (album)
Hyde, Lewis, 160; *The Gift*, 160

Ibn al-'Arabî, 144, 148, 149, 151
"I Know It Was the Blood" (hymn), 15
"I'll Cross the Briny Ocean, I'll Cross the Deep Blue Sea" (song), 34. See also *American Winter* (album)
interpretation, 3
"It's Your Date, Simple as That" (combine), 83. See also *The Star-Faced One* (album)
Ives, Charles, 3
"I Was Interested in the Story You Just Told Me about the Funeral" (song), 38. See also *American Winter* (album)
"I Would" (interlude), 82. See also *The Star-Faced One* (album)

"Jack" (song), 128–31. See also *Shawnee, Ohio* (album)
"Jack Munro" (hymn; aka "Lay the Lily Low"), 129–30
Jackson, Shannon, 12
Jacobs, Ken, 124
J Dilla (DJ), 54
Jenkins, Thomas, Jr., 70
"Jim" (song), 116–20, 121. See also *Shawnee, Ohio*
Johnson, Jonathan, 119
Jones, Loyal, 27, 28, 41
Jones, Norma, 53
Joyce, James, 42

Kapsalis, Terri, 70
Kashani, Sarmad, 156–57
Kasich, John, 130
Kimmel, Jeff, 68
King, Cathy, 83
King Tubby (sound engineer), 54
Kirby, Rich, 28, 29
Klee, Paul, 147; *Pedagogical Sketchbook*, 147
Kozma, Sigmund, 125–28
Krapp's Last Tape (Beckett), 139, 146
Kreisler, Fritz, 98; *Fair Rosmarin*, 98
Kunkle, Barbara, 9, 10, 16, 17, 18, 33, 41

Lang, William, 152–54, 155
"Lay the Lily Low" (hymn; aka "Jack Munro"), 129–30
Les Noces (Stravinsky), 42
Levertov, Denise, 151
Lewis, Meade "Lux," 149; "Boogie Woogie Prayer," 149
Little Cities of Black Diamonds Archive, 93, 104–7
Locks, Damon, 70, 79, 80
Lomax, Alan, 32; *Folk Songs of North America*, 32
Lonberg-Holm, Fred, 68
"Lonesome Road" (folk song), 43–44
"Lonesome Scenes of Winter" (folk song), 34–35. See also *The Star-Faced One* (album)
Lozier, Mary, 38, 40
Lumière brothers, 124

Madlib (DJ), 54
Madness and Civilization (Foucault), 143
Maggard Mines, 20
Mallozzi, Lou, 69
Martland, Steve, 32
Matheney, Joshua "Judd," 122–25
Matthews, Hazel, 117, 119
Maynard, Ralph, 20
McKinley, William, 102
McNew, Walter, 21–22; "The Girl I Left Behind Me," 21

Meatyard, Ralph Eugene, 151
Meeting Again (film), 126
"Memory's Garden" (song), 114
"Merrywise" (song), 43. See also *Rawhead and Bloodybones* (album)
Merton, Thomas, 136–52, 155–56
Millfield Mine disaster, 125–26
Montgomery, Wes, 146
Mr. Palomar (Calvino), 167
M Train (Smith), 151
Muncy, Jane, 42–45
"My Station's Gonna Change" (Randolph), 111, 131

New Straitsville mine fire, 103–4, 108–9
"The Night Is Quite Advancing" (song), 28. See also *American Winter* (album)
"1971: Close Your Eyes" (interlude), 82. See also *The Star-Faced One* (album)
"1974: Not Ordinary Things" (interlude), 83. See also *The Star-Faced One* (album)
Norton, Dellie, 38–41
nostalgia, 4, 92

Oldham, Will, 54–56, 65
Old Time Kentucky Fiddle Tunes (Titon), 47
Oliveros, Pauline, 32, 54
"One Morning in May" (folk song), 40
"One Plus One Equals One" (song), 155. See also *Words and Silences* (album)
Owens, Buck, 146

Partch, Harry, 32
Paxton, Sam, 57
"Pearl Bryan" (song), 102
Pedagogical Sketchbook (Klee), 147
performance (term), 3
Perry, Lee "Scratch," 54
Peterson, Marina, 4, 92
Phipps, A. L., 36–38
polyphony, 84
Porter, Katie, 132, 152–54, *155*
Porter, Walter, 125
Possession (Byatt), 151

postmodernism, 79
Pretty Bird (album), 31
Prichard Quartet, 11

Quenon, Paul, 150, 151, 153–54, *155*

Randolph, Neva, 102, 110, 131–33; "After Death Judgment Will Find Your Soul," 131; "My Station's Gonna Change," 111, 131
Rauschenberg, Robert, 83
Rawhead and Bloodybones (album), 5, 42–47, 81; "Merrywise," 43
"Rawhead and Bloodybones" (folktale), 44–45
readymades, 74
"Redwing" (folk song), 44–45
Reece, Florence, 128–30
Reed, Mike, 70
Rehark, Samantha, *159*
"Rehearsal Side 1" (interlude), 82. See also *The Star-Faced One* (album)
Reich, Steve, 3
The Renfro Valley Barn Dance (radio program), 34
Rice, Harry, 10, 36–38
Ricketts, Ann Davis, 104–5
Ricketts, Skip, 113, 135
Rilke, Rainer Maria, 147
"Ring around the Rosie," 121
Roberts, Leonard W., 9, 42–43, 46; *South from Hell-fer-Sartin*, 42
Roberts-Gevalt, Anna, 120
"Rock of Ages" (hymn), 37
Roden, Steve, 32, 113–14
Rodriguez, Phil, 152–54, *155*
"Rose in the Bud" (song), 114, 127

sampling, 3, 29
Schubert, Franz, 32; *Winterreise*, 32
Schwartz, Hillel, 125
Schwitters, Kurt, 3
Scott de Martinville, Édouard-Léon, 2
Sebald, W. G., 51
Sekula, Allan, 78

"Seven Beers with the Wrong Woman" (song), 102
Shaw, Rob, 70
Shawnee, Ohio (album), 6, 92, 111–35; "Boy," 120–22, *134*; "Jack," 128–31; "Jim," 116–20, *121*
"Shine on Me" (song), 131
Shuttleworth, Jack, 109–11, 113, 131
Shuttleworth, Mildred, 109–11, 131
Silent City (album), 5, 49–61, 65–66, 811, 115; "Sleeping in the Driveway," 55–56, 58; "Some Glad Day," 65–66; "Well, There Are a Lot of Stories," 56
Simmons, Ina, 102
Simon, Jack, 109
"Sleeping in the Driveway" (song), 55–56, 58. See also *Silent City* (album)
Smith, Cauleen, 70, 79
Smith, Harry, 32, 173n17
Smith, Jimmy, 140, 146
Smith, Patti, 51, 151; *M Train*, 151
"The Soldier Pulled Off His Uniform of Blue" (song), 38–42. See also *American Winter* (album)
"Some Glad Day" (song), 65–66. See also *Silent City* (album)
South, Estill, 46–47; "Greedy Fat Bear," 46–47
South from Hell-fer-Sartin (Roberts), 42
Spare, Thomas, 162
Stamper, Hiram, 11, 43–44
Stamper, I. D., 44–45; "Redwing," 44–45
The Star-Faced One (album), 5, 68, 76, 79–85
Stein, Gertrude, 156
Still, James, 8
St. Patrick's Church, 50, 59, 60
Stravinsky, Igor, 42; *Les Noces*, 42
Sun Ra, 5, 54, 68–88
"Sunset in the East, Sunrise in the West" (CF), 86–87. See also *The Star-Faced One* (album)

"Take the A Train" (song), 83
Tallmadge, William, 23, 24–26, 33, 34–35
"Tarry with Me O My Savior" (hymn), 24–26
Taylor, Breonna, 149
Tecumseh Theater, 94–97, 99
"Terrill" (song), 102
Thomas Merton Center, 136
Titon, Jeff Todd, 47; *Old Time Kentucky Fiddle Tunes*, 47
"Together Again" (song), 147
Toop, David, 104
Torgue, Henry, 18
Tribe, Ivan, 113
"The Trooper and the Maid" (folk song), 40

Unheard-of Ensemble, 164

Vietnam War, 83
"Vote for the Local Option" (song), 102

Wallen, Berzilla, 38–41
Watergate scandal, 83
Wayne National Forest, 91
Welch, Charles, 118
Welch, Eddie, 118
"Well, There Are a Lot of Stories" (song), 56. See also *Silent City* (album)
Westerkamp, Hildegard, 174n1
Wheeler, Billy Edd, 129
"Which Side Are You On?" (song), 128–29
Williams, Jane (née Howell), 96, 106
Williams, John E., 96, 106
Williams, Mary Lou, 146
Williams, Mordecai, 93–94, 96, 98–99, 114, *115*, 133
Williams, William, 96, *115*
Winesburg, Ohio (Anderson), 114–15
Winnenberg, John, 99–100, 113, 121, 133
Winterreise (Schubert), 32
Wojdacz, Jenna, 52
Wolff, Christian, 54
Woodruff, Jeremy, 68, 119–20, 152–54, *155*, 163

Words and Silences (album), 6, 148–49, 152–56; "Breath, Water, Silence," 148–49; "A Feast of Liberation," 149, 156; "One Plus One Equals One" (song), 155

The Workbench (album), 6, 159, 161, 163–66

Wright, Jack, 128–31

"You'll Go and I'll Go with You" (song), 131

"Young People Who Delight in Sin" (folk song), 17–18

Zimmerman, Justin, 126; *Meeting Again*, 126

www.ingramcontent.com/pod-product-compliance
Lightning Source LLC
Chambersburg PA
CBHW021857230426
43671CB00006B/425